D1555297

ONE UNITED
PEOPLE

ONE UNITED
PEOPLE

The Federalist
Papers and the
National Idea

EDWARD MILLICAN

THE UNIVERSITY PRESS OF KENTUCKY

Copyright © 1990 by The University Press of Kentucky

Scholarly publisher for the Commonwealth,
serving Bellarmine College, Berea College, Centre
College of Kentucky, Eastern Kentucky University,
The Filson Club, Georgetown College, Kentucky
Historical Society, Kentucky State University,
Morehead State University, Murray State University,
Northern Kentucky University, Transylvania University,
University of Kentucky, University of Louisville,
and Western Kentucky University.

Editorial and Sales Offices: Lexington, Kentucky 40506-0336

Library of Congress Cataloging-in-Publication Data

Millican, Edward.
  One united people : the Federalist papers and the national idea /
  Edward Millican.
      p.   cm.
  Includes bibliographical references.
  ISBN 0-8131-1678-3 (alk. paper)
  1. Federalist.   2. Nationalism—United States—History.
3. Political science—United States—History.   I. Title.
JK155.M55   1990
320.5′4′0973—dc20   89-48254
                                                                CIP

This book is printed on acid-free paper meeting
the requirements of the American National Standard
for Permanence of Paper for Printed Library Materials.
                            ∞

To my grandmother,
Katie Martha Devore Hellbrueck
(1895-1989)
She remembered the "good old days"
and typified what was good about them.

Contents

Acknowledgments

This book owes its existence to many people, of whom the author is only one. I would like briefly to indicate some of the others who made this work possible.

My parents, Francis and Nedralind Millican, and my grandmother, Katherine Hellbrueck, provided material and emotional support that kept me going in the toughest times. Michael Cargal gave essential logistical assistance and brought a novelist's sensitivity to his critique of the manuscript. Yvette Sarrazin helped turn my academic prose into readable English. My son, Joshua Millican, showed admirable patience with a father permanently chained to a computer terminal.

Samuel H. Beer, Professor Emeritus at Harvard University, offered generous encouragement and advice to one who was certainly in need of it. Professor Richard B. Morris also read the manuscript and set me right on several points. Professors Henry L. Janssen, Tore Tjersland, and E. Victor Wolfenstein provided many helpful comments and served as models of scholarly integrity and perceptiveness.

I have been cheered by the friendship and love of many people, including my brother Rick Millican, Marcie MacLeod, Neon Seville, Ann Shanahan-Walsh, Howard Wayne, and Rick Wood. My family in Georgia— my father, Dr. Ed S. Cook, Jr., Helen, brother Ed, sister Leslie, Margie Berman-Cook, Ben, Sam, and my grandmother, Mrs. Ed S. Cook, Sr. ("Babe")—also bolstered my morale with their affection. I am glad that we can share this moment.

The University Press of Kentucky, in the persons of editor Jerry Crouch and managing editor Evalin Douglas, has been uniformly patient, courteous, and helpful. The anonymous readers who evaluated this manuscript have, particularly in one case, aided my book significantly with their criticisms.

I am greatly indebted to previous students of *The Federalist*—especially Gottfried Dietze, Garry Wills, and David F. Epstein, who have written full-length studies of the work. I have not always agreed with them, but I have freely appropriated the fruits of their labors. The nationalist point of view I espouse owes much to the scholarly contributions of Douglas Adair, Samuel

H. Beer, Irving Brant, Jacob E. Cooke, Martin Diamond, Hans Kohn, Richard B. Morris, Peter S. Onuf, Jack Rakove, and Anthony D. Smith.

I thank Sheri DeWolf for the loan of her computer and Andree Stern for her translation of a work by Rousseau.

Last, but certainly not least, I would like to pay tribute to the three great men without whom all this definitely would not have been possible—Alexander Hamilton, James Madison, and John Jay. The pleasure of their distinguished company has been the main fringe benefit of writing this book.

1
Will the Real Publius
Please Stand Up?

Critics agree that *The Federalist* is a great work of political theory, but they do not agree on what it says. It is venerated as a guide to the mysteries of American government and as a fount of political wisdom in general, but the content of that wisdom is a subject of considerable debate. This celebrated tract is variously regarded as favoring a powerful central government, a weak central government, states' rights, the total eclipse of the states, the rule of special-interest groups, the submersion of special-interest groups, and numerous other mutually contradictory ideas. The work has been quoted on both sides of a great number of heated political controversies, and many diverse factions claim to take inspiration from it. We Americans might find ourselves somewhat at a loss, were we to try to heed the injunction of Machiavelli that for "a religion or a republic . . . to live long, it must be often brought back to its beginnings."[1] *The Federalist* is probably the single best source of information we have on the intentions of our Founders, but there seem to be about as many different readings of that volume as there are political sects now jockeying for power.

To definitively decide between these various competing opinions is not a simple task. The present study attempts to clarify the issue by examining the argument of *The Federalist* in a comprehensive and thorough manner. The full-length consideration given to the work here enables us to distinguish the main theme of the treatise from lesser motifs that have frequently confused matters in previous studies. We will conclude that *The Federalist* expresses an essentially nationalistic viewpoint. The authors of the great tract presuppose the existence of a tangible, and paramount, American national interest, and they maintain that this interest can be upheld only by an energetic and truly sovereign central regime. This conception of *The Federalist* is not exactly a novel one. Indeed, it has been endorsed by some very reputable commentators in the past. But it has also been challenged by many others, just as reputable, who have advanced entirely contradictory interpretations of the work.

Before plunging ahead into this controversy, it might be well to specify why the inquiry is important. Why should the modern reader attempt to understand this document of a bygone era?

As every student of American history is aware, *The Federalist* comprises a series of essays written by Alexander Hamilton, James Madison, and John Jay under the pseudonym "Publius." These eighty-five pieces were first published in certain New York newspapers in 1787 and 1788 as an argument on behalf of the proposed United States Constitution, which was then being considered by state ratifying conventions. The widely admired essays were soon collected and reissued between hard covers, and the resulting volume has become without doubt America's most acclaimed work of political philosophy. George Washington accurately predicted that it would "merit the notice of posterity," and Thomas Jefferson called it "the best commentary on the principles of government ever written." Nor has the applause for this work been confined to our shores. Alexis de Tocqueville, for example, deemed it "an excellent book, which ought to be familiar to the statesmen of all countries," and John Stuart Mill said it was "even now the most instructive treatise we possess on federal government."[2] Twentieth-century scholars have almost universally shared these sentiments.[3]

The Federalist is important for three reasons: its authorship, its subject matter, and its impressive argument. Any one of these would have gained it at least some renown. Together, they comprise an intellectual critical mass of enormous dimensions.

The authors, especially Hamilton and Madison, are among the most significant political leaders of our history. Alexander Hamilton, secretary of the treasury and virtual prime minister during the Washington administration, bore chief responsibility for guiding our country onto the path of commercial expansion and capitalistic development that we have basically followed ever since his day. James Madison, the "Father of the Constitution," was the man who played the largest role in arranging the Philadelphia Convention, setting its agenda, and molding its final product. Had either of these two men not lived, the birth of the American nation would have been affected in a major way, and probably not for the better. John Jay, less well known to the modern world than his colleagues, was a brilliant diplomat and jurist who performed many essential services for the fledgling United States. If we wish to understand the public motives of the most eminent founders of the American republic, we certainly will find it useful to consult the pages of Publius.

The subject of the treatise also commands our attention. The three Publii do not discuss some transient topic of little relevance to the present day, but the venerable instrument of government that still holds our country together. As prominent chieftains of the movement that gave us our constitution, these men are unimpeachable witnesses concerning the original meaning of that document. In *The Federalist*, they attempt an exhaustive examination of the various provisions of their novel scheme, and their account has come to be regarded as virtually the official exposition of our government. No treatment of any disputed issue of American constitutional practice can be considered complete without some reference to the words of Publius. Thus a federal court judge in 1975 dismissed a challenge to then president Ford's pardon of former president Nixon partly on the basis of a certain passage in *The Federalist*[4]—just one example among many of how the work continues to influence our affairs by virtue of its role as a constitutional oracle. Even a concept as fundamental to our system as judicial review finds its principal justification, not in the text of the constitution, which is silent on the point, but in the comments of Publius.

Finally, *The Federalist* is notable for the high quality of its argument, a unique blend of pragmatic experience and general theory. The authors had studied much history and political science, but book knowledge was by no means the only, or even the principal, source of their insights. As active politicians who contested elections, held office, and tried to direct policy, they had learned at first hand about such things as the selfishness of special interests, the need for strong leadership, and the ubiquity of folly. They had seen enough of life to know that the truth is not always pleasant and that conclusions which seem logical on paper sometimes do not follow when put to a real-world test. But, if they little resembled those pure thinkers who generate splendid concepts while lodged in ivory towers, neither were they mere empirics. They were able to lift their gaze from the pressing crises of the day to ponder the larger meaning of their activities. Most critics agree that behind Publius's shrewd commentary on eighteenth-century American affairs is a rational, coherent, fairly complete perspective on politics as such—a perspective that deserves inclusion in the human race's permanent repertoire of political ideas.

Of the three reasons for attending to *The Federalist*, it is this last, the tract's underlying viewpoint on government per se, that is the focus of the present inquiry. Previous analyses of the argment of Publius have tended to emphasize its significance as an arbiter of constitutional questions, but that aspect is not the central concern of the following pages. It is here presumed that the general political outlook of the great treatise constitutes the work's best claim to the attention of posterity. Constitutional disputes in the United States will arise only occasionally, and then not necessarily in relation to the most critical issues. But, because Hamilton, Madison, and Jay based their case largely on what they plausibly asserted to be enduring elements of political behavior, their fundamental notions of government can frequently be applied to the problems of the modern world. Indeed, if *The Federalist* is really to be ranked as one of the political classics of Western civilization, this clearly cannot be merely on the basis of its role as an adjunct to the particular charter of a single community, but must result from the light it throws on the essential nature of politics everywhere.

Before we can follow the advice of Publius, however, we must know what it is. And, as noted, there exists a remarkable lack of consensus on this point.

A dispute among later readers concerning the meaning of a hallowed text is not exactly an unprecedented phenomenon. But rarely has it been carried so far as in the instance of *The Federalist*. The various interpretations of this work do not differ on mere points of detail, but with regard to the most important tendencies of the argument. The plan of the present study does not permit an exhaustive synopsis of the debate on this subject, but we may usefully review a representative sample of the sundry views expressed over the years. Opposing interpretations may be grouped broadly into three categories:

First, Publius is regarded by some as a firm nationalist. This interpretation is the oldest of the three and seems most sensitive to historical circumstances. It maintains that Hamilton, Madison, and Jay were energetic leaders who were concerned with promoting the welfare of the United States as a whole. Having served in the national government during the Revolution or under the weak Articles of Confederation, they had all felt the frustration of trying to impose a consistent line of conduct on a gaggle of thirteen fully sovereign entities. They wanted a potent general authority, able to take positive action on a continent-wide basis. They favored the Constitution because they felt it would strengthen their hands as national officials. Hamilton, particularly, was already formulating his far-reaching plans for restructuring the American economy through forceful governmental measures. Indeed, he and his colleagues would have preferred an even stronger central regime than the one recommended by the Philadelphia conclave. These attitudes, it is claimed, are reflected in *The Federalist*, the main motif of which is said to be the need for centralized direction of the country's affairs.

This conception of the work has a distinguished pedigree. It can be traced back to our country's greatest jurist, John Marshall, whose magisterial rulings during his lengthy tenure as chief justice of the United States, from 1801 to 1835, definitely established the U.S. Supreme Court as the final arbiter of the Constitution and reinforced the supremacy of the federal government over the states. Marshall enunciated the nationalist interpretation of *The Federalist* in his opinion in the case of *Cohens v. Virginia*, in

1821, wherein he maintained that, because the essays were "written in answer to objections founded . . . on . . . diminution of State sovereignty," they are therefore entitled to most "consideration" when they "frankly" acknowledge increases in the power of the central government.[5] In other words, according to Marshall, the work is to be implicitly believed when it endorses the concept of national supremacy, but taken with a grain of salt otherwise. This reading of Publius, stamped with the great chief justice's formidable imprimatur, helped unite America in the early nineteenth century.

An eminent scholar of the present century who embraced this view was Irving Brant, a writer of liberal inclinations who tended to perceive the American Founders as the New Dealers of their day. In his six-volume Pulitzer Prize–winning biography of Madison, Brant contended that his eminent subject had "flowered in a more fertile soil of national feeling than has been recognized in later periods of negation," and that "Madison's words and actions," including his writings in *The Federalist*, "reveal him as a vigorous exponent of national sovereignty." Marshall's "classic justification for an expanding Federal authority" was, said Brant, but a "paraphrase" of Madison's Publius.[6] More recently, Jacob E. Cooke, whose editorial labors have provided us with what is now regarded as the definitive text of *The Federalist*, has contended in his biography of Hamilton that the argument of Publius contains a "political creed" featuring a "constant trust in the curative power of national supremacy" and an equally "abiding distrust of state sovereignty."[7] Primarily, the nationalist interpretation of *The Federalist* seems to appeal to certain liberals and to those scholars, whatever their personal political affiliations, whose principal orientation is the study of American history, and who are therefore led to consider the great work chiefly in relation to its own period.

Markedly different from the version just discussed is the anticonsolidationist reading of Publius. This interpretation begins with the premise that the key feature of our system is not that the national government has been accorded certain specific prerogatives, but that these prerogatives have been most carefully restricted. The Founders, in this view, did not give us a pure nation-state when they adopted the U.S. Constitution. They did buttress the power of the federal authorities, to be sure, but they deliberately left many governmental functions in the hands of the states, which remained integral parts of a rather complex political structure. The anticonsolidationists assert that *The Federalist* chiefly expresses a distrust of political power in general, a fear of governmental concentration, and a perception of the states as guardians of the rights of the people. Those who favor this view also quote Publius to show that the partition of the governmental powers at the federal level—the creation of separate legislative, executive, and judicial branches, and the further splitting of the legislature into two bodies—was meant to foster divisions within the central government, making it slower to act and therefore less dangerous. Needless to say, this does not look like the plan of a vigorous national regime.

The first significant anticonsolidationist commentary on *The Federalist* was probably that of Henry B. Dawson, a quarrelsome and acerbic scholar and a self-styled "states-rights Democrat," who published in 1863 an excellent edition of the work based solely on the original newspaper sources. To this edition, which soon became a standard, Dawson affixed a long introduction, which became something of a scandal, wherein he held that the argument of Publius tended to support the doctrine of "state sovereignty."[8] At the time, this view was thought to be heretical and shocking—especially coming, as it did, from a Northerner during the Civil War. But Dawson's opinion eventually became acceptable in polite company. A later observer sharing this notion was Felix Morley, a Pulitzer Prize–winning former editor of the right-wing journal *Human Events*. In his book *Freedom and Federalism*, Morley declares that the "objective" of the Founders "was not nationalism." Rather, he contends, the "rights of the several states" have been preserved "inviolate" to protect their "widely differing political and social customs" from "centralized governmental oppression." And Morley observes that "the *Federalist Papers* . . . argued almost two centuries ago that the connection between Freedom and Federalism is neither accidental nor capricious."[9]

Incidentally, President Ronald Reagan once invoked this interpretation of *The Federalist*. He did so in a 1981 address previewing his efforts to shift social responsibilities away from the national government to state and local levels.

> My Administration is committed—heart and soul—to the principles of American Federalism, which are outlined in the original Federalist Papers of Hamilton, Madison, and Jay.
>
> The designers of the Constitution realized that in federalism there is diversity.
>
> The Founding Fathers saw the federalist system as constructed something like a masonry wall. The states are the bricks, the national government is the mortar. . . . Unfortunately, over the years, many people have increasingly come to believe that Washington is the whole wall. . . .
>
> Let us restore Constitutional Government, let us renew and enrich the power and purpose of states and local communities.[10]

Thus President Reagan finds justification in *The Federalist* for policies diametrically opposed to the nationalistic tendencies of Chief Justice Marshall. This anticonsolidationist version appeals at present, naturally, mostly to publicists and politicians of a conservative stripe.

Improbable as it may seem, the third reading of the work differs as much from the first two as they do from each other. This view regards Hamilton, Madison, and Jay as spokesmen for the wealthy classes of America and sees their main objective as the frustration of majority rule. According to this interpretation, the Founders did not favor state sovereignty, because they saw the states as too open to democratic pressures. Their nationalism, however, was less a positive ideal than a mere negative resultant of their desire to clip the wings of these troublesome provincial entities. The Founders intended to create a dominant but passive federal regime that would leave the rich safely in possession of their property. The central authorities established by the proposed Constitution would, they hoped, be rendered relatively immobile, and therefore harmless, by the separation of governmental powers, and also by the push and pull of the numerous competing special-interest groups to be found in the country as a whole. National policies would be moderate compromises that would not threaten the position of the social elite. Here, it is claimed, can be found the germ of the distinctively pluralist American political system, and it is all explained in Madison's renowned *Federalist* No. 10.

The original formulation of this variation of the argument of Publius is to be found in Charles Beard's *Economic Interpretation of the Constitution of the United States*, first published in 1913. This study appeared at a time when progressive-minded Americans were becoming increasingly concerned about the problems associated with industrial monopolies, and also about the unresponsive legislators and reactionary jurists who seemed to be shielding these economic concentrations from the righteous wrath of the public. Beard's analysis purports to show that the Constitution of the United States has been specifically designed to lead to this outcome. The book was heartily applauded by some and roundly condemned by others, and has remained extremely controversial—and influential—to this day. Beard does praise *The Federalist* as a "wonderful piece of argumentation," but he makes plain his conviction that the authors of the work were the advocates for a narrow, self-interested group, and that they principally desired to hamper and restrain government, not to invigorate it.[11]

A later critic concurring with Beard is James MacGregor Burns, pillar of the East Coast liberal establishment and, like Brant and Morley, a winner of the Pulitzer Prize. Burns observes that the Constitution was "intended more to thwart popular majorities in the states . . . than to empower national majorities," and that it has consequently given us a regime of "sharply limited powers" and "a balance of checks" that is usually prone to "inaction." Burns cites *The Federalist*, especially No. 10 and No. 51, to prove that Madison, who conceived this purposely weak arrangement, saw government as "a necessary evil to be curbed, not an instrument for the realization of . . . a nation's broader interests."[12] A more upbeat statement of this conception of Publius is provided by Albert Balitzer, in a little study—financed by the American Medical Political Action Committee— which maintains that our modern PACs embody the finest traditions of American democracy. "The authors of *The Federalist*," says Balitzer, wished to foster "the spirit of compromise in private and public measures," and No. 10 shows that they sought to "permit the entry of private interest into public counsels, reminding government of the existence of opposite and rival powers."[13] In general, the pluralist interpretation seems to appeal to those scholars, whether liberal or conservative, who perceive in *The Federalist* intimations of the American political system as it is today.

So, depending on whom we believe, Publius is either a positive nationalist who aims to submerge the states and enable the federal government to take vigorous action against partial interests on behalf of the whole people; or he is an antinationalist who wants to restrain the central government and to preserve the states as expressions of the popular will; or he is a negative nationalist who wants to submerge the states because they are expressions of the popular will and to establish a weak federal government that will not permit the whole people to take action against minority interest groups. Anyone seeking to follow in the footsteps of the Publii will find a trail that seems to lead in several directions at once. Why is this the case?

This confusion over the meaning of *The Federalist* derives from certain problems intrinsic to the tract itself, and also from the biases of later critics. The work was not wholly straightforwardly written, and it therefore requires much commentary in order to be understood properly. Yet what commentary there has been, alas, has often been the reverse of helpful.

The inherent ambiguity of *The Federalist* stems from several sources. One often mentioned by later critics is that the work was composed in haste by very busy men who were not in agreement on all issues. The writing proceeded, as Professor Douglas Adair points out, at the fairly rapid clip of about a thousand words a day, and each of the authors was heavily engaged, besides, in political and governmental affairs.[14] Thus the words of Publius, for all their importance, could not be weighed at leisure. The essays often went literally straight from the writer's pen to a waiting press, with no time for a careful review of the contents. It would not be surprising were this the source of great confusion. Yet few of the inconsistencies of *The Federalist* really appear to be due to this factor. Hamilton, Madison, and Jay were intimately familiar with the ground they were covering, and we do not find them to have made any major errors through carelessness Nor do we find much evidence of a "split personality." These men differed on many things, but not on the subject of this treatise.

Of far more significance is the fact that the Publii did not always want to be perfectly clear. Their aim was not to discuss an idea logically, but to prevail in a political contest, and they were fully prepared to do a bit of fudging in order to achieve that objective. They skirted difficult issues and molded their phrases to suit their audience, in the manner of our modern public relations experts. Some critics have accused them of outright dissembling,[15] but this is going too far. By the standards of political debate, they are honest enough. They carefully avoid any statements that could later be used to call into question the essential powers of the new government. Nor do they shrink from expressing unpopular sentiments on occasion—as in their forthright assertion of the need for a political check on the wayward masses. But they use their rhetorical skills to make unpleasant truths seem as palatable as possible, and they stress considerations important to the electorate even when their own priorities are entirely different. Attentive analysis is necessary to decipher their real position; superficial reading may well leave a wrong impression.

Another prolific cause of misunderstanding can be found in the disjunction between the underlying perspective of *The Federalist* and certain of the specific provisions of the plan produced by the Philadelphia Convention. That such a disjunction could exist may appear surprising. The very purpose of the treatise was, after all, as Garry Wills puts it, to defend "the Constitution with a theory of government," so it will be natural to presume that Constitution and theory must be congruent. Yet, as Wills himself notes, this is not entirely the case.[16] The proposed instrument of government contained features that were not really desired by the authors of *The Federalist*, but that served to make the novel charter more acceptable to the public. Hamilton, Madison, and Jay naturally called attention to these popular aspects of the design, even though they themselves did not especially care for them. Therefore, the statements of Publius that are descriptive of the Constitution do not always accord with what seems to be his overall point of view on politics. Publius often affirms the federal nature of the new regime, for example, but—as Martin Diamond showed in a famous article—he gives little indication of truly believing that federalism is a good thing in principle.[17]

This last point warrants some emphasis, for it is critical to an understanding of the present study. We find that Publius views the American people as a coherent society with a common interest and that he believes this community should be ruled in a centralized fashion by a wise, though popularly responsive, elite. This is a nationalistic attitude, unquestionably. Also, the institutions of the suggested central regime are justified and explained in terms that frequently reflect nationalistic values. But it is clear that the Constitution will not set up a wholly unified nation-state, and Publius never claims that it will. He acknowledges, in fact he insists, that the states retain considerable power under the scheme of the Convention. If anything, he is inclined to exaggerate the federal aspects of the new plan. This combination of a strongly nationalist outlook with a partly federal proposal certainly leaves a disharmonious impression.

And, finally, the argument of Publius on occasion appears to lead in more than one direction because it is, unavoidably, rather complex. Hamilton, Madison, and Jay were not superficial thinkers. They were well aware that important political questions, such as the one they were discussing, frequently involve multifarious, even seemingly contradictory, considerations. Simple-minded formulas were not their style. They sought a government able to act on behalf of necessary national purposes, but restrained from actions likely to be detrimental to society as a whole. They wanted a regime that would control the impulses of the multitude, yet be founded on popular consent. They called for a slowly moving legislative process and for the swift execution of the laws. They wished to concentrate national power, yet divide it to make it safe. Different passages from *The Federalist*, taken out of context and placed side by side, may well seem incongruous. Care is needed to unravel these ostensible inconsistencies.

So serious are the problems with this text that a recent critic has maintained they are insuperable. Albert Furtwangler praises the "civility" of *The Federalist*, but nonetheless contends that the vagaries of its composition render its value entirely problematical. This tract is not, he says, a true account of the views of Hamilton, Madison, and Jay; nor is it the expression of a complete political philosophy.[18] It is only an inspired piece of journalism, produced for a specific, transient occasion. Judging from what we have just seen, this claim has some plausibility. Furtwangler overstates the case, however. It is true that these essays, being polemical in nature, may lack the deductive rigor of a work of pure theory. And the Publii may have exaggerated their love for a few features of the Constitution. But it does not follow from this that they concealed their general principles of politics. The fundamental outlook of the authors is in fact clear and consistent and can be discerned by thoughtful reading. Furtwangler's skepticism is excessive— although his book does usefully serve to remind us of the many barriers to an understanding of *The Federalist*.

Clearly, whatever its merits, Publius's treatise requires a large amount of attention and annotation to be entirely comprehended. Unfortunately, attempts made along these lines have not always been truly enlightening. The message of *The Federalist*, difficult enough in itself, has been further obscured, not clarified, by the efforts of later writers. This adverse evaluation does not, of course, apply to all critics—not even to all of those who have been quoted in this chapter—but, unfortunately, rank partisanship and a certain narrowness of vision have predominated in the scholarly literature on the subject.

This regrettable circumstance, ironically, stems mostly from the fact that the work is so highly regarded in America. *The Federalist* occupies such an eminent place in our political thinking that our pundits usually attempt, whenever possible, to trace their pet prescriptions back to it. So, instead of taking pains to weigh and compare the many diverse apects of Publius's viewpoint, critics and admirers have tended to concentrate exclusively on isolated segments that they have found personally congenial. They have treated this work as a quarry, from which they have extracted a few choice nuggets of quotation, leaving the rest behind. It is a sort of tribute to Hamilton, Madison, and Jay that their sentiments have been thus treated, but it is a kind of homage they would no doubt wish to have been spared.

This excessive partisanship is probably the main reason for the scarcity of book-length studies of *The Federalist*. When the object of the writer is merely to present a few isolated passages in a simplistic way, great length is wholly superfluous, even possibly dangerous. It is a somewhat amazing fact that the first large-scale treatment of the great tract did not appear until 1960, 173 years after Publius wrote.[19] And even that work, by Professor Gottfried Dietze, focuses disproportionately on the issue of individual rights and is consequently rather simplistic.[20] Any serious attempt to come to grips with the argument of Publius must accept the fact that there is at least a semblance of textual warrant for each of the principal interpretations of *The Federalist* and that, even if they are not all equally valid, some care is required to decide between them. A preview of the conclusions of the present inquiry is not out of place at this point.

In this study I contend that John Marshall was on the right track. The crafty old chief justice may not have been less biased than other critics, but his ulterior motives happened to coincide with those of Hamilton, Madison, and Jay, and so his partisan opinion accurately reflected their genuine position. The argument of Publius is in fact a blueprint for the creation of a centralized national government, to which a more or less superfluous federal structure has been attached.

The major premise of *The Federalist*, the pivotal concept that gives coherence and meaning to the whole work, is the notion that the American people comprise a national community with a distinct interest. Jay sounds this theme at the very commencement of the discussion, in *Federalist* No. 2, when he declares his compatriots to be united by the ties of their common homeland, ancestry, language, manners, political values, religion, and practical concerns.[21] It was, to be sure, the last of these that clearly seems to have been uppermost in the minds of the authors: Publius constantly sounds the refrain that the material welfare of each segment of America is intimately tied up with the welfare of the remainder. Also, he contends that any divisions on our part will provide openings for the sinister machinations of foreigners—the sort of thing that would today be called neocolonialism. The bedrock conviction of Publius is that Americans will flourish together or not at all. If *The Federalist* can be credited, this is the true rationale for the United States Constitution.

The need for unity explains Publius's evident preference for a strong central regime. Indeed, the advantages of centralization are a principal motif of *The Federalist*. The authors insist that the important problems of America can only be solved on the national level. Only the federal authorities can fairly consider the wants of all our citizens, act uniformly over the entire country, or bring all the resources of the nation to bear on a single point. President Regan's contrary impression notwithstanding, Publius evinces little regard for the states. These are depicted as havens for second-rate politicians and as agencies through which partial viewpoints may be expressed to the detriment of the general good. According to Publius, the main defect of the Confederation is the inordinate power of the states, and the proposed Constitution is designed to mend that flaw.

But is not a strong central government difficult for the people to control? Publius thinks not. *The Federalist* contends that the gap between the national regime and the citizenry is bridged by the representative system. Federal officials are freely chosen by the people, either directly or indirectly, and so are led to act in accord with the wishes and the feelings of their constituents. Periodic elections ensure the fidelity of our rulers. Constant public supervision of government, possible in a localized democracy, is not necessary, nor even particularly desirable. Our national chiefs will surely be characterized by that superior wisdom and virtue to be expected in those who have been singled out by the suffrage of their fellow citizens. It is to the advantage of the nation that they regulate our private and local affairs from the perspective of the whole, and this requires that they be somewhat insulated from extraneous pressures. This system is, in Publius's view, purely republican, because it remains within the power of the people to remove the national officials, if in the end their measures prove mistaken.

Clearly, Publius is prescribing a nationalistic cure for the ills of America. Indeed, when the situation of Hamilton, Madison, and Jay is thoroughly understood, it becomes plain that, with the establishment of the Constitution, they were consummating a national revolution similar to the others that have swept the world in the last two centuries. And their plan of government was not very different from the sort of regimes that have usually been set up in the wake of these later upheavals. A modern term would be *guided democracy*. The argument of Publius suggests that our Founders were precursors of the likes of Bismarck, Atatürk, and Ho Chi Minh. The authors of *The Federalist* differed from most of these other leaders, of course, in the sincerity of their commitment to the system of free popular elections. But they were nationalists through and through, without serious qualification.

As already noted, *The Federalist* makes a rather weak case for federalism. The states are assigned certain positive functions—as local administrative entities and centers for rebellions against national tyranny—but Publius does not really appear to take these matters very seriously. The drawbacks of the federal system are presented as forcefully as the advantages. True, Publius seems more genuinely favorable toward the separation of powers and checks and balances within the new central government, but support for these provisions is not truly inconsistent with a nationalist attitude. Indeed, separation of powers is in some ways designed to render the national regime more swift and decisive, rather than otherwise, by concentrating certain authorities in the hands of the president and the Senate. And, finally, the notion that Publius, particularly Madison, is an advocate of political pluralism, is quite incorrect. Madison did not believe, nor did he contend in *Federalist* No. 10, that public policy should arise out of the interplay of special-interest groups. He did not like special-interest groups, which he called "factions," and he wanted them removed from the governmental process, not made part and parcel of it. Thus a careful analysis of the text of *The Federalist* diminishes the supposed importance of these competing themes, thereby confirming the key significance of the nationalist aspect of the argument.

This conclusion is reinforced when the work is considered in relation to the political thought of its era. The prevailing view in the Western world in 1787-88 was that a republican government was only possible in a small state, on the model of the *polis* of the ancient Greeks. Yet, in spite of this conventional wisdom, Publius proposed to take away from the American states a substantial degree of their power and to transfer that power to a far larger political entity, the nation, while preserving the popular character of the American regime as a whole. The shift of authority upwards is the real story, not the retention by the states of a portion of their former potency. In justifying this virtually unprecedented course, the authors broke new theoretical ground: they became the first self-conscious architects of a modern nation-state. Textual and contextual considerations alike conspire to emphasize the importance of Publius's nationalism.

Interestingly enough, a strongly nationalistic *Federalist* provides little comfort for either modern conservatives or liberals. Thus conservatives must face the fact that the great work displays no special regard for the ideology of the free market. Publius is a neo-mercantilist—that is, an adherent of "economic nationalism"—not an advocate of undiluted laissez-faire.[22] Nor are Publius's true views on the states palatable to the present-day Right. Yet neither is Publius a liberal, at least not by current standards. Liberals tend to be idealists and humanitarians. But Publius is a cool-headed realist who accepts the crucial role of force in human affairs, who bluntly observes that strict adherence to the law is less important than national survival, and who calls for virtually an executive monopoly on the conduct of our foreign policy. Right and Left alike may have some uncomfortable moments as they peruse the pages of Publius.

Indeed, in general, *The Federalist* appears quite a bit less respectful of our favorite American political pieties than we might have expected. It may be true that the American people have always on the whole been heterogeneous, privatistic, individualistic, and distrustful of public authority, and that these characteristics have helped to shape our governmental style. But far from praising these typically American political traits, Publius criticizes them, while lauding the quite opposite virtues of positive, vigorous, and uniform national government. It is somewhat remarkable that our country's greatest work of political thought is not a celebration of our usual prejudices, but a warning, given by three of our greatest leaders, that our characteristic biases have serious shortcomings.

Just two additional topics of a preliminary nature remain to be considered in this first chapter: the tendencies of the latest scholarship relevant to *The Federalist*, and the aim and structure of the present critique.

The controversy over the true meaning of *The Federalist* has raged for many years along the lines already indicated. But some current developments pertaining to this debate deserve our special attention. Much recent research and commentary on the intentions of the Founders tends to support, either directly or indirectly, the nationalist reading of the argument of Publius. In this connection, we may note the continuing vitality of the school of thought that considers staunch nationalism to be the best description of the attitude of America's first leaders. And we may also observe how another scholarly view, seemingly far removed from the nationalistic conception, actually appears to lead back to it.

A vigorous argument for the nationalist interpretation is voiced by

Samuel H. Beer in a 1965 article on the derivation of modern liberalism, and in his 1977 presidential address to the American Political Science Association. Beer explores the implications of "the national theory of American federalism," which asserts that "a single sovereign power, the people of the United States, created both the federal and state governments, delegating to each a certain limited authority."[23] This concept, he says, has unfortunately been contested by the rival "states sovereignty theory," but the national idea is "the better account of the state of mind and will of the American people at the time of the foundation of the Republic."[24] In a subsequent essay critical of the Reagan administration's New Federalism, Beer condemns the notion that the states created, or in any sense have priority over, the federal union, and he defends the "theory that ultimate authority lies" with "the whole people of the nation." Surveying the course of American national development, he stresses Hamilton's firm "belief that this American people must make vigorous use of its central government for the task of nation building." On present-day issues, Beer deprecates not only the federal-level cutbacks of the Reagan administration, but also the "destructive pluralism—sectional, economic, and ethnic" that has lately been popular on the liberal side.[25]

Another eminent scholar who has given support to the nationalist conception of the American founding is Richard B. Morris, who is currently engaged in the important project of editing the papers of John Jay.[26] In a 1967 book, *The American Revolution Reconsidered*, Morris points out that our country's bid for political independence was "the first example in modern history of a successful revolt against the Established Order," and "provided the first lessons in how to achieve decolonization and how to move forward from colonial subordination to equality among states." Morris sees an essential continuity between the events of 1776 and the Federalist movement of 1787: "The War of the Revolution heralded the end of parochial colonialism and the fulfillment of nationhood; the Constitution, which underwrote national survival, must be considered an integral step in that revolutionary process." Throughout this period, says Morris, the American people willingly followed "the aristocratic politicians who had proved themselves so adept at manipulating votes and opinion."[27] Morris repeats these views in a later study with more emphasis on the twentieth century, *The Emerging Nations and the American Revolution*,[28] and in a recent entertaining short treatment of the authors of *The Federalist*. Hamilton, Madison, and Jay were "all three Nationalists," he concludes.[29]

A substantial historical account that embodies this opinion is Jack Rakove's account of the Continental Congress, *The Beginnings of National Politics*, published in 1979. Rakove quotes Beer with approval, rejects the

Beardean thesis of the motivations of the Founders, and endorses "the 'nationalist' interpretation of the origins of American union." The earliest American leaders, he says, "intended to vest certain sovereign powers in Congress and to subordinate the states to its decisions."[30] This conception of the Revolutionary era would certainly encourage us to see *The Federalist* as an argument for national supremacy.

Besides these overtly nationalist critics, another contemporary set of scholars has articulated a perspective on the founding period which, when correctly understood, seems to lend plausibility to the nationalist interpretation. This is the "ideological" school, whose adherents have pretty well dominated scholarly discussions of the founding period during the 1970s and 1980s. These writers by no means possess a wholly uniform attitude; they disagree freely among themselves on numerous points. What they share is a common interest in a certain historical topic. Following Bernard Bailyn and Gordon Wood, they explore the contention that the Revolutionary era saw a basic shift in republican thinking, away from a classically derived devotion to public virtue and the welfare of the community, toward a more modern concern for the private rights of individuals—notably including property rights.[31] Commentators of the ideological school have analyzed *The Federalist* in light of this paradigm and have reached some surprisingly diverse conclusions.

Thus Wood maintains that the Federalist movement discarded antique ideals. He notes that whereas the Revolutionary leaders of 1776 had called in classical style for "the sacrifice of individual interests to the greater good of the whole," the disillusioning decade that followed had induced many Americans to adopt a more realistic view of human nature. They conceived that their country "would remain free not because of any quality in the citizens of spartan self-sacrifice to some nebulous public good, but . . . because of the concern each individual would have in his own self-interest and personal freedom." The Federalists replaced the concept of a cohesive, homogeneous community with that of society as a collection of clashing groups. They continued to seek "the public good," but they perceived it now as a harmonizing and protection of private interests, rather than as something standing above those interests. Wood acknowledges the nationalism of the Publii, but he plainly regards this facet of their ideology as a secondary feature. Like Beard, he believes that the backers of the Constitution principally wished to use national authority to safeguard property rights from state legislative encroachments.[32]

One particularly modern feature of the Federalist argument, says Wood, is the lip service paid to the democratic ideal. He thinks, however, that the supporters of the Constitution adopted this stance only for reasons of

expediency. They were obliged to counteract the classical republican preference for small-scale government, and they did so "by appealing over the
heads of the states directly to the people." By accepting the absolute political
sovereignty of the populace, Wood observes, the Federalists were able to
give their new centralized regime a democratic aspect and to justify their
disregard of Confederation procedures. He somewhat curtly dismisses this
tactic as "disingenuous"—indeed, he appears disappointed that the Federalists did not express an openly oligarchic attitude. On the whole, he feels
that they combined real elitism and bogus populism with marked neglect of
the kind of civic virtue that considers the common welfare before private
advantage.[33]

Many commentators of the ideological persuasion concur with Wood in
this evaluation. Yet some do not, and it is notable that two of these are critics
who have produced full-scale examinations of *The Federalist*. Garry Wills
and David F. Epstein may be bracketed with the ideological school because
of their concern with the question of Publius's civic virtue. As it happens,
they find him to have a great deal more of it than Wood will allow.

Wills's study has unquestionable literary merit and clearly has been
written with a popular audience in mind. It is also cogently argued, and quite
a change from Wood. Wills finds a "classical zeal for republican virtue . . .
at the very heart of *The Federalist*." The Publii appreciated the "dark side" of
human nature, to be sure, but they also maintained, "with Montesquieu, that
public virtue is an absolute necessity for the existence of a republic." They
certainly anticipated that there would be sufficient "republican virtue . . . in
the citizens" to "lead to a choice of wise and virtuous leaders." They wished,
not a weak and strictly limited national government, impotent for bad; but a
strong one, resting on implied powers, which could be used for good. They
were far more influenced by Humean notions of sociability than by Lockean
concerns for property rights, and they did not intend to set faction against
faction but rather wanted to wholly bar private interest groups from the
policy-making arena. They modeled themselves on ancient Roman statesmen and chiefly sought to bring about the election of an Olympian elite to
public office—political methods very different from those of the present
day. America has "changed, and then changed again," since Publius's era,
Wills observes.[34]

This analysis is actually rather compelling, as far as it goes. Yet one
troubling question remains. If Publius's message is really so remote from our
current notions of politics, why should we attend to it now? Wills gets
around to considering this fairly important point only in the very last
paragraph of his book, and his less than satisfactory answer is simply that
The Federalist informs us of what Madison and the other Founders believed.

Thus the great treatise explains America "historically,"[35] but apparently in no other way. Its principles evidently cannot be applied to our current problems. Ironically, if Wills's conclusion on this subject were widely accepted, probably few of us would feel inclined to consult either his book or that of Hamilton, Madison, and Jay. Wills regards the Publii as nationalists and rejects the anticonsolidationist and pluralist readings of their argument. Yet, like Wood, he seems to consider the nationalist theme less than crucially important, since he devotes but little space to it.

Unlike Wills's commentary, Epstein's book on *The Federalist* is relentlessly professional and scholarly and makes no concessions to the general reader. This critic tries to straddle the gap between Wills and Wood. Epstein discovers more concern for property rights in Publius than Wills sees, yet he nevertheless denies that the essays entirely "rejected a classical republican tradition in favor of Lockean liberalism." He notes that Publius is concerned with the securing of both "the public good" and "private rights," which "are central concerns of, respectively, republican and liberal thought." He believes the argument of *The Federalist* is based on a unique "psychology" that sees human beings as both "political"—that is, impelled by their nature to participate in community affairs—and "selfish"—that is, self-indulgently motivated by "passion" and "ambition."[36] Thus, according to Epstein, Publius combines classical values with a modern view of human beings as intrinsically self-regarding. This critique shows notable analytic powers and on points of detail frequently sets new standards of accuracy in the interpretive history of *The Federalist*; its overall conception appears incomplete, however.

Epstein makes scant reference to the concrete political goals of the Publii, and he never systematically attempts to place their thoughts in any kind of theoretical context or to explain from whence they derived the singular outlook on politics that he sees as the foundation of their case. His general thesis seems a bit artificial and too precisely tailored to the subsequent windings of scholarly fashion on *The Federalist* to be entirely correct. Epstein reveals little regard for the non-nationalistic versions of Publius's argument: he notes the authors' commitment to a powerful central government, casts doubt on their devotion to federalism, and gives short shrift to the pluralist reading of the essays.[37] Yet no more than Wood and Wills does he find this nationalist tendency to be worthy of extended remark.

Thus these commentators on the ideological question disagree conspicuously on whether Publius's views are archaic, modern, or an odd amalgam of both. It is interesting that the three critics all consider Publius a nationalist, although none of them takes much notice of the fact. Yet it is precisely the national theme that, when brought to the fore, is able to harmonize their superficially discordant interpretations of *The Federalist*.

Nationalism, it should be noted, is a wholly modern conception. Wood is quite correct to observe that Federalist objectives—"to establish a strong and respectable nation in the world" and "to create a flourishing commercial economy"—required a centralized, elite government very different from that enjoined by old republican principles.[38] Wills, in emphasizing the supposedly obsolete cast of Federalist thought, has been somewhat misled by surface appearances. The Founders may have worn knee britches and enjoyed the perusal of the classics, but their situation was not essentially different from that of certain twentieth-century leaders who wear jungle fatigues and read Marx. Regimes and peoples in all parts of the globe today are confronting the problems of creating viable nation-states. The issues of national self-determination, economic development, neocolonialism, centralized government, and guided democracy are even now of tremendous pertinence to many countries in the Third World. These matters were also of vital concern to Hamilton, Madison, and Jay and are explored in depth by Publius. *The Federalist* looks forward, not backward, in time.

Yet the classical affinities of the work also seem real enough, as Wills and Epstein show. We appear to have a paradox—a basically modern political theory presented to us in language reminiscent of Plutarch. The paradox is resolved, however, when we observe that nationalism is not the polar opposite of classical republicanism, but a closely allied viewpoint—a modern mutation of it, in fact. Although by no means identical, the two doctrines share a number of important characteristics, including the conviction that the welfare of the individual is inseparable from that of the community as a whole. The notions of civic virtue that originated in the archaic *polis* are therefore meaningful in the world of nation-states, and it is not out of place for nationalists, especially eighteenth-century nationalists, to speak in such terms.

Moreover, an appreciation for the nationalism of the Publii enables us to make sense of the incongruity Wood thinks he has found in the Federalist case: the mixture of centralization and elitism with acceptance of popular sovereignty. As we will see, the combination of a strong central government with populism is a defining trait of the nation-state, and it is quite common for a national impulse to be carried by an elite, especially in the early days of a country's existence. As sincere nationalists, the authors of *The Federalist* are not disingenuous when they avow their regard for the rule of the people and assert that it is compatible with a vigorous, territorially extensive, regime.

The positive importance of the Framers' nationalism is perceived by some critics of the ideological school. Cathy Matson and Peter Onuf assert that "the most important ideological challenge" facing the Founders "was to reconcile individual rights with the common good," and that they solved this problem "by conceiving of their new nation as . . . bound together by compatible private interests." The agreement of "patriotism and self-interest . . . became a staple in nationalist rhetoric," Matson and Onuf point out.[39] In another article, Onuf notes how the "proponents of commerce and economic development pressed the need to harmonize interests and create a true national community founded on free exchange and interaction." The "dream of development," he contends, "represented an authentic impulse toward national integration, while giving a new legitimacy to the boundless ambitions of countless Americans."[40] Thus these scholars see nationalism as arising out of a Federalist reshaping of classical values to fit the modern, bourgeois world.

In summary, current treatments of Publius and the founding era appear to show a convergence of the nationalist and ideological interpretations, while the two most recent full-scale analyses of the text of *The Federalist* notably reject the anticonsolidationist and pluralist readings. Yet there never has been a comprehensive examination of the great treatise based on the premise that the nationalistic concept ties together its whole argument. The present investigation aims to fill that gap.

This study is a work of textual analysis. It includes a review of the statements made in *The Federalist* to determine whether they fit together to make a coherent general thesis and, if so, what that thesis is. "There are two rules of construction dictated by plain reason," says Madison in *Federalist* No. 40. They are: "that every part . . . ought, if possible, to be allowed some meaning, and be made to conspire to some common end;" and "that where the several parts cannot be made to coincide, the less important should give way to the most important part" (259-60). This book basically follows the procedure recommended by Publius. As previously noted, the intention is to illuminate the general outlook of the famous tract, not particularly to resolve conundrums of constitutional law.

The method is to consider the *Federalist* papers one at a time, more or less in the sequence they came out. This course may seem too simple to be suitable, but there are valid reasons for employing it here. First, it presents the argument of Publius as it was conceived by Hamilton, Madison, and Jay. Second, it assists in avoiding what has hitherto been the besetting sin of much scholarship on this topic: the tendency to select material that favors a particular interpretation while neglecting the rest. All the papers are reviewed, and awkward passages are therefore difficult to ignore. Third, and perhaps most important, a large-scale, paper-by-paper examination of the entire *Federalist* appears never to have been done. After two hundred years, the project seems to be worth undertaking. The essays are grouped according to authorship, to facilitate a search for the "split personality" that many critics have claimed to find in the psyche of Publius. The few deviations from strict chronological sequence that appear in the present inquiry have been motivated by the desire to consider each author's contributions as a unit. It is, incidentally, a merit of Epstein's study that it does "roughly" follow Publius's order—though it does not attempt to do so as systematically as is done here.[41]

The principal purpose of this inquiry is to interpret the text of *The Federalist*, but the words of Publius are not examined in isolation from the circumstances surrounding their composition. Such contextual factors as the private opinions of the authors, the politics of early America, and the ideological currents of that era are all obviously relevant to this investigation. I will not claim that nationalism is the only idea in *The Federalist*, or that the work's other concepts are not worthy of notice in their own right. The argument of Publius is many-faceted and profound and can be validly approached in a number of ways. This study demonstrates, however, that many of the alternative themes of the great treatise—separation of powers, representation, elitism, and popular sovereignty, for example—can be understood as aspects of a larger nationalist perspective, and that the general outlook of nationalism permeates the essays as a whole. Taking into account the political and ideological context of the papers, the preeminence of the national theme appears clear.

In order to peruse the message of Publius with full comprehension, the reader must have a firm grasp of the intentions of the authors. This subject is covered in the next chapter. We first consider the problem that faced Hamilton, Madison, and Jay in October 1787, when they commenced the composition of *The Federalist*.

2
The Political Objectives of Publius

In a word, the situation in October 1787 was critical. America was on a cusp. The Philadelphia Convention, which had conferred in closed session throughout the summer for "the sole and express purpose of revising the Articles of Confederation," had adjourned on September 17, conveying its conclusions to Congress.[1] The Convention proposed to "revise" the Articles by junking them completely and replacing them with a wholly new constitution providing for a much stronger national regime. Congress, then meeting in New York City, promptly approved the Philadelphia conclave's suggestion that the recommended government be submitted to the states and, if ratified by at least nine of them, take effect between those agreeing. The question was not, however, referred to the state legislatures, which stood to lose much power from adoption of the new plan, but to special state conventions, chosen directly by the people to determine the issue. Thus the battle for the U.S. Constitution would have to be won at the grass roots, and nowhere was the outcome less certain than in New York, the home of Hamilton and Jay.

The main problem in New York was the impost—a duty levied by the state on imported merchandise. It was the state's chief source of revenue and was particularly prized by New Yorkers because it fell largely on outsiders. As was observed in 1788, "half the goods consumed in Connecticut, or rather three-fourths of them, all the goods consumed in Vermont, and no small part of those consumed in . . . Massachusetts, are bought in New York and pay an impost of five percent for the use of this State."[2] The proposed Constitution, however, would assign such duties exclusively to the sphere of the federal government, denying them to the states. New York's impost was, in fact, a perfect example of the sort of abuse the Constitution was designed to correct, although the inhabitants of the state naturally did not see things that way. The main political faction in the state, the followers of Gov. George Chilton, were flatly opposed to the Convention's scheme.

The war of words began immediately in New York. Earliest in the field was "Cato," who published his first article on September 27, one day before Congress formally sent the Constitution to the states. While this writer's initial offering was vague, his later missives expressed definite hostility to the work of the Convention. Cato was possibly Clinton, although historians are not certain.[3] Verbal facility was not, however, the governor's strong suit, and Cato was soon joined in his opposition by two rather more formidable reasoners: "Brutus," whose essays began appearing in the newspapers on October 18, and the "Federal Farmer," whose first five letters came out as a pamphlet in early November. Brutus is usually thought to have been Robert Yates, a delegate from New York to the Philadelphia Convention, who had withdrawn from that gathering in disapproval. The Federal Farmer is supposed to have been Richard Henry Lee of Virginia, then a member of Congress and a longstanding foe of a strong national government. There actually appears to be little evidence to support either attribution.[4] But whoever the writers were, their arguments were effective.

This is not to say that the Federalists, as the Constitution's backers called themselves, were exactly silent. They gave as good as they got. One of the most active publicists on the Federalist side was Alexander Hamilton—indeed, he may have been a bit *too* active at first. Cato's first letter was answered three days later by a writer using the name of "Caesar," who called his antagonist a "demagogue," questioned his "virtue" and "patriotism," and hinted that, were the Constitution to be rejected, a strong regime might be established by force.[5] This ill-tempered response was apparently not well received, and Caesar quickly dropped from sight. Modern authorities deny that Hamilton wrote the Caesar letters, which do, however, sound like something he might have said in an unguarded moment.[6] Whether or not he actually penned these unhelpful remarks, he seems to have concluded that a more detached and philosophical approach was in order.

Hamilton's plan was ambitious. He envisioned a comprehensive treatment of the subject, which would run to twenty essays or so.[7] For assistance, he turned first to his good friend Jay, who promptly penned four papers. Unfortunately, Jay then fell seriously ill and was forced to abandon the project, although he did later contribute a single additional paper. Hamilton also solicited the help of Gouverneur Morris, who turned him down, and William Duer, who proved inadequate. Hamilton then approached yet another of his long-time associates, James Madison, member of Congress from Virginia, and this time he found a worthy collaborator.

It was well that Hamilton had secured the aid of a colleague, because, as he said in a preface to the first hardcover edition of *The Federalist*, "a desire to throw full light upon so interesting a subject has led, in a great measure unavoidably, to a more copious discussion than was at first intended."[8] Instead of some twenty essays, the final count was eighty-five. Initial publication was in the newspapers of New York. *Federalist* No. 1 appeared on October 27, in the *Independent Journal*. The next six numbers followed at the rate of twice a week. Publius then increased his pace and brought out the rest of the articles four times weekly, although on occasion he failed to hold to this grueling schedule. Hamilton wrote the bulk of the first thirty-six essays, which were printed through the first week of January 1788. Madison then assumed the lion's share of the literary labors and produced almost all of the next twenty-seven articles, the last of which came out on March 1. He then left for Virginia in order to lead the ratification struggle there, so Hamilton carried the enterprise through to completion. Publius abruptly ceased publication after April 2. The state courts were in session by then, and Hamilton, an attorney, had to make a living. The last eight essays originally appeared in the second volume of the first bound edition, published by J. and A. M'Lean, dated May 28.

A notable literary dispute arose in later years concerning the authorship of several of the essays. Modern critics, however, have pretty well decided that Madison's claim, given in an 1818 edition of *The Federalist*, is accurate, and the present study proceeds on that basis.[9] By this count, Hamilton wrote fifty-one essays, Madison twenty-nine and Jay five. It has been asserted that Hamilton and Madison had "remarkably similar prose styles,"[10] yet while this may be true with regard to such features as word choice and sentence structure, their modes of argumentation are in fact very different. Hamilton debates like a lawyer: he immediately takes up the ground most favorable to his cause, uses every argument he can think of, good or bad, and concedes nothing to the opposition. Madison analyzes like a theorist: he examines all aspects of a question from a seemingly objective standpoint, views its many complex ramifications, and concludes that, on the whole, the answer he prefers is correct. Whether Madison was really more objective than Hamilton is doubtful, but the effect is certainly different. Jay is a nice medium: more pragmatically oriented than Madison, but more philosophical than Hamilton. All three are about equally effective, their differences of approach notwithstanding.

In terms of both quality and quantity, *The Federalist* simply overwhelmed all other writings on the constitutional ratification question. It was immediately recognized and acclaimed as a work of genius. And its bulk was accentuated for the citizens of New York City by the practice of the local newspaper editors of reprinting the numbers that first came out in other journals. Some readers complained. "Twenty-seven Subscribers" protested that "we take M'Lean to read Publius in the best edition, and he gives us two at a time; and Childs for the daily news and advertisements, but they are curtailed, and we are disappointed for the purpose of serving up the same Publius at our expense; Loudon we take for his morality and evangelic sentiments; but here we again are imposed upon, by being made to pay for the . . . same Publius, who has become nauseous, by having been served up to us no less than in two other papers on the same day."[11] Repetition, however, is an effective persuader, as our modern advertising experts are well aware.

Yet all this brilliance and all this industry seemingly was to no avail; the election for the New York State ratifying convention was held in late April, and the Constitution was decisively beaten. The figures are not entirely certain, but the best modern estimate is that the Anti-Federalists received 56 percent of the statewide vote.[12] The distribution of this vote, moreover, was such that the opponents of the Constitution elected more than two-thirds of the delegates to the convention. As in other states, the urbanized regions were favorable to the Constitution, whereas the rural areas were against it. The Federalists were successful in New York City and the immediately adjacent counties, but nowhere else. "In this state," Hamilton ruefully reported to Gouverneur Morris, "as far as we can judge, the elections have gone wrong."[13] It seemed that the Constitution was doomed in the state of New York.

In view of this result, doubts have been expressed concerning the actual effectiveness of *The Federalist* as a piece of political propaganda. Even at the time, it was said that Publius was perhaps a little too elevated in tone to catch the ear of the public. An Anti-Federalist critic ridiculed "the dry trash of Publius in 150 numbers," while a North Carolina Federalist noted that Publius was "certainly a judicious writer, though not well calculated for the common people."[14] Yet a careful examination of the New York returns does not entirely sustain this unfavorable verdict. The *Federalist* papers obtained extensive circulation only in the vicinity of New York City, and the Federalists carried that area by a huge margin. On the other hand, the essays were rarely reprinted upstate, many rural voters being illiterate in any case, and it was there that the Constitution lost. Many other factors no doubt contributed to this result, but the omnipresence of Publius in the urban media seems to have done the Federalist cause no harm.

The New York State convention met in Poughkeepsie on June 17 and proceeded to leisurely debate the new Constitution clause by clause. As the oratory droned on, week after week, word arrived at Poughkeepsie that New Hampshire, and then Virginia, had ratified, being the ninth and tenth states to do so. Thus it was certain that the proposed Constitution would go into effect, and that it would include all the important states besides New York. The more responsible Anti-Federalists at Poughkeepsie knew that their state could not, under these circumstances, stay unattached. A face-saving formula was devised, and on July 26 New York, by a convention vote of 30 to

27, became the "eleventh pillar" of the union. The laurels of victory went, as is so often the case, not to the party that fought the best fight, for the opposition to the Constitution had clearly prevailed in the New York election, but to the side that was favored by contingent events.

Yet if the Federalists in New York were less than completely successful in terms of practical politics, their efforts were not therefore fruitless. As a rule, there is nothing more obsolete than the propaganda of a past election, but the comments of Publius have far outlasted the particular occasion for which they were written. It is time to take a closer look at the three statesmen who composed the most philosophically profound campaign document in United States history.

Alexander Hamilton, who conceived *The Federalist* and wrote the bulk of it, was perhaps the most creative and farsighted political leader in American history. He was our Richelieu. Yet he also undoubtedly had the most convoluted psyche of any of the Founders, the origin of which may be found in the circumstances of his birth in the Virgin Islands. He was illegitimate—as John Adams put it, "the bastard brat of a Scotch pedlar."[15] Yet his shiftless father, James Hamilton, was something more than an itinerant trader: he was a younger son of a Scottish lord, and Alexander was related, through him, to quite a few of the titled personages of Scotland, including the premier peer of that nation, the Duke of Hamilton. Indeed, he was a distant cousin of King George III. So Hamilton's birth was to him a source of both great shame and immense pride. He was the offspring of an illicit connection, but the blood of the crowned heads of Europe flowed in his veins. His mother, who cared for him, was a tramp in the eyes of the world, whereas his father, who abandoned him, was of patrician lineage. It is no wonder that he bore psychological scars all his life.

This uncommon nativity explains much about Hamilton. We can see why this totally self-made man, who rose to eminence from a low condition, was such an unabashed admirer of aristocratic values and how he adapted so naturally to moving in the highest social circles. We can understand his almost compulsive adherence to the most rigid standards of honorable behavior—at least in the public sphere—and also his cynicism concerning the motivations of the human race in general. He was determined to act in a manner worthy of his noble ancestors, yet he expected very little in the way of nobility from others. Most people had feet of clay, in his experience; everything good was mixed with something base. His old foe Jefferson astutely noted that Hamilton was an "honest . . . man" who believed "in the necessity of either force or corruption to govern men."[16] Thus while he himself never stooped to pocket illicit gains, his financial program as secretary of the treasury included a direct appeal to the self-interest of financial manipulators. And, finally, we can comprehend Hamilton's sporadic lapses into erratic and self-destructive behavior. Because no matter how admired he was or how unblemished his public record, his personal demons were able to get the better of him at times.

On most occasions, of course, Hamilton was perfectly rational. He was a shrewd political operator with a coherent vision of the future. He believed that America should build an industrial base, and that the promotion of capitalistic investment was required for this purpose. He was a staunch nationalist. His wartime service as an aide to General Washington had convinced him of the incompetence of the existing Congress, with its shifting committees and its subservience to the states, and he felt that only a strong national government could achieve the kind of restructuring of the American economy that he wished to see. His economic views owed little to Adam Smith. He derided as "one of those wild speculative paradoxes" the idea that "trade will regulate itself" without the "encouragements or restraints of government." The nation might "oppose effectual impediments" to "the avarice of individuals," he believed.[17] He had been a delegate to the Constitutional Convention from New York, but he was regularly outvoted by the two Clintonians who made up the rest of his state's contingent, and he therefore took little part in the deliberations at Philadelphia. His main contribution was an ill-advised, if brilliant, speech in favor of a regime including a president and a senate appointed for life. The proposed Constitution, he felt, was rather weak, but he accepted it as better than nothing.

Alexander Hamilton was thirty years old in 1787, the youngest of the three Publii. He was below middle height, no more than five feet, seven inches tall, and slender, but he carried himself erect, with a military bearing. His eyes were a deep blue. He was highly energetic and exuded an obvious sexual vitality that attracted women and either attracted or repelled men. John Adams, who was obviously in the latter category, once sniffed that Hamilton had "a superabundance of secretions which he could not find whores enough to draw off."[18] He dressed according to the latest styles. His conversation was lively and gay, yet profound. Depending on his opinion of the person he was with, he could be charming or almost openly contemptuous. A fellow delegate to the Philadelphia Convention praised his "talents" and his "eloquence" and observed that "there is no skimming over the surface of a subject with him," but added that his "manners" displayed "a degree of vanity that is highly disagreeable."[19] He had married into a very rich and prominent New York family, the Schylers, and was a member of Congress and the guiding spirit of New York's Federalist party.

John Jay, Hamilton's initial choice for collaborator on *The Federalist*, was more widely known in 1787 than either of the other two authors. He had previously been president of the Continental Congress, minister to Spain, and a key member of the team that negotiated the treaty of peace with Great Britain. He was currently the Confederation's secretary for foreign affairs. The American Revolution thus gave him the opportunity to play an important role on the world stage—yet, ironically, his entry into politics had come as part of an effort to stall the rebellion that made his career possible. In May of 1774, the conservative merchants of New York had moved to wrest control of the resistance movement from the radical Sons of Liberty, and they named Jay, a mild-mannered young attorney of good family, to a committee that represented their views. Jay proved to be a natural politician and was soon busily engaged in writing stirring resolutions and presiding at meetings of patriots. Within a year, he had been chosen to represent his colony in Congress. His emergence as a leader of the American people did not please all of his initial sponsors, however.

Jay may have assisted in displacing the vulgar mechanics from positions of prominence in the struggle against Parliament, but this was only so that he might lead the cause more cautiously to the same general conclusion. True, he opposed independence. He went so far as to avoid being present in Philadelphia when the Declaration of Independence was signed. But once the decision for a rupture with Britain was made, he committed himself unswervingly to the new American nation. His Loyalist friends were most indignant at his seeming defection. "Popularity must be the Object at which Jay is aiming," wrote one.[20] This was not the case; Jay was, and remained, a forthright elitist. He believed that "those who own the country ought to govern it."[21] But he instinctively knew that popular opinion must be indulged, if a free people is to be successfully led.

Jay was, in his own placid way, fully as complex a person as his close friend Hamilton. Unlike most of the Founders, he was sincerely and devoutly religious. A visitor recalled "the scene in the family parlor, the . . . Patriarch and his children . . . uniting in thanksgiving, confession and prayer." Furthermore, Jay adhered to a standard of honorable behavior remarkable even for that age. He once curtly dismissed a scheme of Hamilton's as "a measure for party purposes, which I think it would not become me to adopt." Yet his experience in public life, aided by his cool, penetrating intellect, led him to conclude that kindness and simplicity are misplaced in politics. "Punishments must . . . become certain & Mercy dormant—a harsh System repugnant to my Feelings," he wrote during the Revolutionary War. "Lenity would be cruelty, & Severity is found on the Side of Humanity," he added. He once told a British negotiator that he "would not give a farthing for any parchment security whatever." "They had never signified any thing since the world began, when any prince or state, of either side, found it convenient to break through them," he said.[22] Even the honorable Jay did not hesitate to violate his instructions from home and negotiate with the British behind the back of our French ally, when he saw a chance to benefit his country.

Jay's "militant nationalism" stemmed partly from his concern for the weakness of the Confederate government. "A continental, national spirit should . . . pervade our country," he said. And it also stemmed in large part from his period of residence in Europe—most particularly his exposure to the monumental rudeness of the Spanish court. He saw little to attract him in the Old World. The countryside of Spain was "delightful," he wrote to Robert Morris, "but still, my friend, it is not America." "My affections are deeply rooted in America," he admitted to another correspondent; "I can never become so far a citizen of the world as to view every part of it with equal regard." At nearly six feet, Jay was the tallest, and at forty-two the oldest, of the authors of *The Federalist*. He was hooknosed, slightly stoop-shouldered, and balding. He had a gift for the pungent phrase. He once declared that Congress had "as much intrigue . . . as in the Vatican, but as little secrecy as in a boarding-school."[23] His chief character flaw was his inordinate vanity. A Spanish diplomat called him "a very self-centered man."[24] His religion did not blind him to the pleasures of life. "I am no friend to austerity," he said.[25] His essays in *The Federalist* are only five in number, but they contain many important passages and are of the same high quality as the rest.

James Madison, whose contributions to *The Federalist* show the most originality of thought and breadth of conception, will always be the academic's favorite Founder. His career and achievements convincingly prove that book learning can, after all, be directly relevant to the pragmatic problems of government—that political theory and political practice can be unified, to the clear benefit of both. Madison's personality was in some ways quite uncongenial to public life. He was very shy. He had a weak voice and often could not be heard when he spoke in public. He was not impressive looking: at five feet, four inches tall, he was the shortest man ever to become president of the United States. He had a tendency to be dominated by stronger personalities such as Hamilton or Jefferson—or Dolley. Madison did, however, possess two outstanding qualifications for political leadership—a truly awesome intellect and an extensive knowledge of the literature of political science—and these made up for all the rest. There may have been greater politicians than James Madison, and greater thinkers, yet as a combination of the two he is hard to beat. It is not uncommon for philosophers to dabble in the real world or for rulers to put their reflections on paper. But seldom do we find, as here, a major political figure who is also a creative theorist and whose pragmatic success can be largely ascribed to his grasp of ideas.

Madison was more responsible than anyone else for the document that emerged from the Constitutional Convention. He had readied himself for that meeting with the meticulous care of a graduate student preparing for a comprehensive exam. He perused some two hundred works on history and political science sent from Paris, at his request, by Jefferson. He then produced a lengthy memorandum, "Of Ancient and Modern Confederacies," which featured hundreds of citations of authorities from Polybius to the French *Encyclopédie*. He maintained that the invariable reason for the failure of these earlier unions was lack of sufficient power at the center. He was first on the scene at Philadelphia. He authored the Virginia Plan, which called for establishment of a national legislature, executive, and judiciary. This proposal, introduced at the very outset of the convention's deliberations, served as the basis for all subsequent discussions. Its general outline, if not all of its specific features, can be discerned in the Constitution. Madison spoke often at the Philadelphia Convention. In the words of a colleague, "in the management of every great question he evidently took the lead."[26] And, like a conscientious student at a seminar, he sat in the front row and took excellent notes, which are today the historian's best evidence for what actually happened at that historic assembly.

So Madison came honestly by the sobriquet of "Father of the Constitution." Moreover, although his views in later years shifted a bit, he was in 1787 almost as nationalistic as Hamilton and Jay.[27] Unlike virtually every other prominent Virginian of his day, he had been educated out of his state. At Princeton he experienced the first stirrings of the American Revolution in the company of his classmates, who were from all parts of the union. Also, as a member of Congress, he had had his fill of the divisive behavior of the states under the Confederation. He had long favored the grant of additional powers to the central government. His social philosophy is not easy to characterize, except in negative terms: he was not a staunch elitist like the other Publii, nor an enthusiastic democrat like his friend Jefferson. He tended slightly to the democratic side, although he felt that "there can be no doubt that there are subjects to which the capacities of the bulk of mankind are unequal, and on which they must and will be governed by those with whom they happen to have acquaintance and confidence." Yet he explicitly repudiated the idea of a ruling aristocracy. If anything, he wished to promote equality. He was an advocate of laws to "reduce extreme wealth towards a state of mediocrity, and raise extreme indigence towards a state of comfort."[28]

Madison may have had scholarly inclinations, but he was not unsociable nor particularly solemn. The Philadelphia colleague who noted his influence and his "greatness" mentioned as well that he possessed a "sweet temper" and was "easy and unreserved among his acquaintance," with "a most agreable style of conversation."[29] His humor ran, in fact, to the off-color. Some of the poetry he wrote as a college student was deemed unprintable by a later editor.[30] He loved to gossip. He walked with an energetic, bouncy step. He dressed simply, in black, and he enjoyed horseback riding. He was thirty-six years old in 1787. He never became a blazing orator, but he did learn how to speak convincingly in a small group. In the Virginia ratifying convention, he defeated the flashy eloquence of Patrick Henry with his logic, even though he sometimes "spoke so low that he could not be heard."[31] Madison was the only one of the authors of *The Federalist* who was of English ancestry. His forebears were, as he said, "planters" who were "among the respectable though not the most opulent class."[32] He grew up in the shadow of the Blue Ridge Mountains, an area which was then definitely rustic. His father was the wealthiest planter in his county, but the Madisons had little pretention to hereditary gentility.

The three Publii obviously had quite distinctive personalities. Indeed, we can easily detect Hamilton's hardheaded pragmatism, Jay's suave high-mindedness, and Madison's somewhat theoretical rationalism in their respective contributions to *The Federalist*. The two main authors, Hamilton and Madison, present an especially vivid contrast politically as well as personally. They exemplify the two great opposing tendencies in the American polity of their era. Hamilton was a man of the city; a spokesman for the business and commercial interests; of aristocratic, though tarnished, antecedents; rather contemptuous of the commonality; fashionable and natty in dress; and pro-British. Madison, for all his intellectual tendencies, was an agriculturalist and a frontiersman; an advocate for social equality and political democracy, if a rather moderate one; of unpretentious life-style; and pro-French. The later antagonism of these two men is far easier to understand than the fact that, in 1787, they were on the same side.

Yet allies they were. In spite of their numerous personal and ideological differences, the three Publii were compatible enough to join in support of the proposed Constitution. What were they trying to accomplish by promoting this new regime?

One thing is clear. They were *not* motivated by any particular liking for the states as institutions of government, or by a wish to retain those bodies as integral parts of the American political system. Quite the contrary: they held the states responsible for most of America's problems, and they sought to wholly remove these troublesome entities from the national decision-making process. Their public and private correspondence from the 1780s regularly deplores the selfishness and short-sightedness of the states and repeatedly stresses the need to bring them under the firm control of the national authorities. It would be unnecessary to belabor this point, were it not that certain later commentators have labeled *The Federalist* a states' rights document. This interpretation lacks any historical warrant; it absurdly implies that Hamilton, Madison, and Jay invented and disseminated a political theory that was directly contrary to their actual sentiments.

Hamilton explained his beliefs concerning the states in his famous, or infamous, speech at the Constitutional Convention, in which he outlined his model of a sufficiently energetic national government. According to Madison's notes, Hamilton declared that "the general power . . . must swallow up the States powers. Otherwise it will be swallowed up by them." Moreover, he added, were the states to be "extinguished, he was persuaded that great œconomy might be obtained." Hamilton hastened to reassure his listeners that "he did not . . . mean to shock the public opinion by proposing such a measure. On the other hand he saw no other necessity for declining it." The states "are not necessary for any of the great purposes of commerce, revenue, or agriculture," he maintained. He recommended that the "Governour . . . of each State . . . be appointed by the General Government and . . . have a negative upon the laws about to be passed in the State of which he is Governour." This, he noted, would prevent the states from enacting any "laws . . . contrary to the Constitution or laws of the United States."[33]

Madison's conception of the proper role of the states in the American system can be found in the Virginia Plan, which proposed that "the National Legislature . . . be impowered to . . . negative all laws passed by the several States, contravening in the opinion of the National Legislature the articles of Union." This provision was denounced in the Convention as "terrible to the states," "improper & inadmissable," and "unnecessary." The idea was voted down by the delegates, partly on the grounds that, as Elbridge Gerry pointed out, "this will never be acceded to. It has never been suggested or conceived among the people." But Madison "considered the negative on the laws of the States as essential to the efficacy & security of the Genl. Govt." He was never reconciled to its absence from the Constitution's final version. Toward the end of the Convention, he declared himself still "a friend to the principle."[34]

Jay's feelings toward the states are revealed in two letters. He wrote James Lowell in 1785 that "it is my first Wish to see the United States assume and merit the Character of One Great Nation, whose Territory is divided into different States merely for more convenient Government and the more easy and prompt Administration of Justice—just as our several States are divided into Counties and Townships for like purposes."[35] Counties, of course, then as now, were always mere subordinate creatures of the states wherein they were located, with no independent authority or sovereignty. So far as the powers of the national government were concerned, wrote Jay to George Washington in 1787, "the more the better." He hoped that the separate states would retain "only so much" power "as may be necessary for domestic purposes." He recommended "their principal officers, civil and military, being commissioned and removable by the national government."[36]

In short, neither Hamilton, Madison, nor Jay had the slightest interest in preserving the autonomy of the states. Plainly, the political arrangements they regarded as best would wholly subordinate those entities to the national rulers. The Publii were for a federal government, not because they regarded the division of sovereignty between state and nation as a good thing in itself, but only because public opinion seemed unwilling to accept a stronger plan. Offhand, these men appear to be unlikely champions of states' rights, and a careful reading of *The Federalist* shows that they were no such thing. Yet if safeguarding the states was not their aim, what was?

The purposes of Hamilton, Madison, and Jay have frequently been discussed in the context of a rather larger question: What were the intentions of the Framers—the group that met in Philadelphia in 1787 and created and promoted the new Constitution? Actually, it is perhaps debatable whether this identification of the Publii with the Framers generally is valid. Furtwangler, for one, denies it.[37] Certainly not all of the Constitution's backers showed the disdain for the states exhibited by these three authors, as the fate of Madison's congressional veto proposal indicates. Yet Hamilton, Madison, and Jay were accepted as leaders by the Federalist party, and this suggests that their opinions were at least tolerable to most of their associates. It is probably on the whole permissible to regard the Publii as archetypal Framers, although we obviously should not assume that the entire group would necessarily have stood behind every sentiment to be found in *The Federalist*.

In their own day, and for many years thereafter, the Framers were usually regarded simply as upright statesmen devoted to popular government. Jefferson, although he did not wholly approve of their methods or of their final product, nevertheless called the Philadelphia Convention an "assembly of demigods," vouched for "the innocence of their intentions," and predicted before the result was known that "their . . . measures will be good and wise."[38] This exalted notion of the Framers became part of what Forrest McDonald has called the political "mythology" of our country, a tradition "preserved" by patriotic "nineteenth century" historians, each of whom, "in his turn recited the myths anew," while "embellishing them only enough to adjust them to changing times."[39] Yet even in the eighteenth century there was dissent: "Centinel," a Pennsylvania pamphleteer, charged during the ratification fight that the proposed Constitution was devised by "the wealthy and ambitious, who in every community think they have to lord it over their fellow creatures."[40] And Beard's famous study gave this negative view of the Framers an impressive intellectual justification.

Beard certainly acknowledged the Framer's dislike of the states. They wished, he said, to curtail the provincial legislatures because those bodies had shown a willingness to adopt measures—such as stay laws and paper money—advantageous to debt-ridden small farmers and equally damaging to their rich creditors. Also, Beard asserted, many of the Farmers were holders of public securities, speculators in western lands, or heavy investors in commercial and manufacturing ventures. These groups all expected the proposed government to be profitable for themselves. "At least five-sixths" of the convention delegates, Beard claimed, "were immediately, directly and personally interested in the outcome of their labors at Philadelphia, and were . . . economic beneficiaries from the adoption of the Constitution." Beard's reading of Publius, particularly *Federalist* No. 10, led him to conclude that the Framers, besides seeking to bridle the states, mainly desired a central regime so checked and hampered as to be unable to act. Beard admitted that the new national government was given major authorities, including full control over interstate and foreign commerce, but this was done simply to take these matters out of the jurisdiction of the states, he felt. "None of the powers conferred by the Constitution on Congress permits a direct attack on property," he observed.[41]

But this "revisionist" thesis has been controverted in recent years. A severe critic is Robert E. Brown, who gives us a complete chapter-by-chapter refutation of the *Economic Interpretation of the Constitution*. Brown contends that, in order for Beard to present a plausible case, he "had to violate the concepts of the historical method in many ways. These ran the gamut from omission to outright misrepresentation of evidence." Brown argues, for example, that only six of the fifty-five delegates to the convention actually had major holdings of the sort Beard described, although Beard presented his data so as to obscure the fact. Support for the new government was by no means confined to a narrow group, notes Brown: "We have many statements to the effect that the people in general expected substantial benefits from the labors of the Convention."[42] Other historians have skewered Beard in similar fashion. McDonald's magisterial tome *We the People: The Economic Origins of the Constitution* exhaustively reviews the holdings of the delegates to Philadelphia and to the various state ratifying conventions and finds that "on all counts . . . Beard's thesis is entirely incompatible with the facts." By the mid-1950s, recounts McDonald, "Beard's book was all-but-unanimously pronounced defunct."[43]

Indeed, Beard's own study raises questions as to the adequacy of his conception of the Founders, for the historian is careful to exonerate the greatest of America's first leaders from any partial motivations. Of Hamilton, Beard observes that he owned few if any securities; that the "augmentation of his personal fortune was no consideration with him"; that he "died a poor man"; and that "he was swayed throughout the period of the formation of the Constitution by large policies of government—not by any of the personal interests so often ascribed to him." Madison devoted himself "to political pursuits rather than commercial or economic interests of any kind"; he "was constantly in public life, and seems to have relied on the emoluments of office and his father's generosity as a source of income"; and he was able later to take a . . . disinterested view of the funding system proposed by Hamilton."[44] Beard did not discuss Jay, since he did not attend the Philadelphia Convention, but that statesman was certainly an upright individual. None of the three Publii, then, had a special axe to grind. Beard never explains why the honorable authors of *The Federalist* desired to boost the incomes of greedy capitalists, and he says not a word concerning those "large policies of government" that, apparently, were the real basis of the new regime.

Thus even if Beard is correct about the Constitution's backers in general—which is extremely doubtful—his analysis can tell us nothing about the Publii or their motives in writing *The Federalist*. Hamilton, Madison, and Jay may have believed in special–interest government, although they themselves did not intend to profit from it, but the suggestion is at least odd. These men do not seem the type to have held the views Beard ascribes to them. Thus once again we must ask: What were the Federalists up to?

The demise of the Beard thesis has led many modern historians to return to a concept resembling the traditional idea of the Framers as wise and honorable statesmen—but with a difference. Whereas the old view was simply that the early leaders of the United States were unstudied paragons of goodness, the new perception is that they were consciously playing a role. Their virtuous reputation was not gained by accident: this was an image they were trying very hard to project and also frequently to live up to. It is true that the Framers, being human, were far from perfect. As McDonald puts it, they were "a cantankerous lot who fought one another, in unseemly fashion, for power and wealth."[45] Yet the prime motivation of the most prominent among them was certainly something very different from personal material advantage.

Douglas Adair, in his oft-quoted essay *Fame and the Founding Fathers,* observes that the makers of the American union primarily desired glory and renown. The fame they sought, however, was not the transient notoriety of the moment. Their ambition was "to make history" and to gain "immortality" for their names. "Fame," notes Adair, "is the action or behavior of a 'great man,' who stands out, who towers above his fellows in some spectacular way." It is a somewhat ambiguous passion: "A man may stand out in his time and after because he is a brilliant and forceful scoundrel." It is a pagan, rather than a Judeo-Christian, motive. Yet on the whole, the desire for enduring fame "is neither ethically blind nor morally neutral," Adair declares. "The audience that men who desire Fame are incited to act before is the audience of the wise and good of the future—that part of posterity that can discriminate between virtue and vice." Therefore, says Adair, the "love of fame is a noble passion because it can transform ambition and self-interest into dedicated effort for the community."[46]

Hamilton, Madison, and Jay had read Plutarch, and they clearly identified with his heroes. That classical author was a lover of popular self-government, yet one of his main themes is that of the sagacious and disinterested leader who is not always understood by his own followers. Plutarch tells of such notable men as Aristides the Just, who was unfairly ostracized by the Athenians; and of Phocion, who when his speech was generally applauded turned to a friend and asked: "Have I inadvertently said something foolish?" Most relevant to the present discussion, we may read in Plutarch of Publius Valerius Poplicola, founder of the Roman republic, whose name was appropriated by the authors of *The Federalist.* Publius was wealthy, "a chief man in the community." He played a principal role in the overthrow of the last of the Roman kings. He was initially defeated as a candidate for the consulship; but when his loyalty to the republic was doubted, he was the first to swear his allegiance at the altar of the gods. When the people envied his big house, he had it pulled down. His vigorous actions when he finally became consul aroused public suspicion, as inclining toward monarchy. But when he reformed the Roman government, he imported many laws of democratic tendency from Athens. While he was alive, the Romans never sufficiently appreciated him. After he died, they gave him a public funeral.[47] This was Hamilton's role model.

Beard was correct on one point: the Framers were elitists, both in theory and in practice, at least by the standards of the present era. Like the other members of the upper classes of early America, the authors of *The Feder-*

alist could easily be distinguished from the common herd by their patrician manners and values. Even Madison, who was definitely less aristocratic in his attitudes than Hamilton or Jay, was a gentleman, not a plebian. The Publii felt that society would drift, or even possibly disintegrate, without the guidance of its most intelligent, knowledgeable, and responsible elements—that is, cultivated men like themselves. Such sentiments prevailed in the circles in which they moved, and they naturally tended to share the assumptions common to persons of their status. Robert Wiebe points out that "every member of the gentry presupposed both the existence and the necessity of a scheme that layered Americans according to their talents and society's needs."[48] This attitude may denote a certain lack of humility. But if the Framers were an elite, they were not a selfish one.

A dramatic example of the responsibilities, risks, and rewards of social leadership in eighteenth-century America, involving one of the three Publii, occurred at about the time of the writing of *The Federalist*. In mid-April 1788, a wild rumor swept New York City that the medical profession had been robbing graves to obtain bodies for dissection, and this triggered the so-called Doctors' Riot. A mob chased a group of physicians, who took refuge in the city jail. Several prominent citizens were summoned by the authorities to help control the disturbance. Among these was John Jay. As he hastened to the scene, he was felled by a thrown stone. The wound on his head was so gaping that it was at first thought to be mortal. In the end he fully recovered, although not without a lengthy period of convalescence. While on his sickbed, he was elected to the New York ratifying convention by a huge majority, failing to receive only 98 votes out of 2,833 cast.[49] Many of the rioters must have voted for him. As he lay recovering, he wrote an *Address to the People of the State of New York,* a very effective short piece on behalf of the Constitution. The semi-aristocratic attitudes of the Founders may seem objectionable today, but it is only fair to observe that their social position entailed duties and dangers that largely justified the deference they expected and sometimes received.

Usually, of course, the relationship between leaders and people was not so tempestuous. Yet this incident may serve as a paradigm for what the elite conceived to be their function within the American polity. It was their office to moderate, control, and direct the passions of the multitude. Even when actual violence was not threatened, the short-sighted and headlong resolutions of the commonalty were often dangerous to the overall social good, in the opinion of the gentry. And, as they were well aware, the democratic institutions of America did not make their appointed task of social leadership any easier. It is true that the holders of public office in early America came primarily from the wealthier classes, but the process of choosing these officials was by no means an exclusive one. Land ownership was so prevalent that, in spite of various state property qualifications, roughly 50-70 percent of all adult white males possessed the franchise.[50] The Publii thus were both community notables and politicians; they were above the people, yet also had to court them. This latter role was especially necessary for them, because there was no lack of plebeian upstarts ready, á la Centinel, to indict the well-born and powerful. Populist challenges did not usually succeed in the 1780s, because the public generally accepted elite leadership, but the perceived threat from below was always of concern to the gentry.

Yet the attitude of the three Publii toward popular government, although inevitably complex, was not on the whole unfavorable. They were well acquainted with the vagaries of the masses, but they were nonetheless staunch republicans who had been raised on Locke and Sidney and who saw the consent of the people as the only legitimate source of political authority. They had begun their political lives as leaders of a national rebellion, and they had no wish to sully their laurels; they intended to go down in history as great chiefs of a free community, not as tyrants or oligarchs. Indeed, their grumblings about democracy notwithstanding, popular politics really suited them very well. Collectively and individually, they won many more elections than they lost. Even Hamilton, who in his melancholy moments enjoyed bemoaning his lack of empathy with his compatriots, achieved most of his goals and received many tokens of the public's esteem. It is true that the Publii saw no reason why the people should be intimately involved with the daily functioning of the government, or why every vulgar whim should be instantly translated into imprudent action. Leaders selected directly or indirectly by the people ought to be accorded some leeway, they considered. But they never questioned the majority's ultimate right to choose and judge the rulers of the nation.

It is in this last-mentioned capacity, as national rulers, that the authors of *The Federalist* ought principally to be regarded. They undoubtedly approached political life with certain aristocratic biases. They are remarkable, however, not for these preconceptions, which they had in common with the rest of their class, but for the extent to which they managed to transmute their social elitism into nationalism. What other, less prominent, members of the American gentry were to their localities, the Publii were to the whole United States. Most merchants and country squires undertook no more than to guide the civic affairs and calm the riots of their immediate neighbors; the Framers aspired to conduct the business of an entire continent. In the argument of Publius, the image of the community notable is assimilated with and developed into the concept of the national statesman, fitted by ability and a central vantage point to manage the concerns of all America.

As officials of the federal government, responsible for finding solutions to the public problems of the United States, the Publii had long lamented their lack of sufficient powers. The list of hitherto intractable difficulties they faced in 1787 was impressive. The enormous national debt left over from the Revolutionary War remained undischarged, owing to the inadequate provision for a national revenue under the Articles of Confederation. The British remained in occupation of a part of our territory, in violation of the treaty of peace, and there was no American army to drive them out. His Majesty's government justified their high-handed behavior by referring to American delinquencies: state courts generally had refused to honor the treaty clause calling for restitution of the property of the Tories, and there was no national judiciary to bring the provincial jurists into line. Foreign nations, mainly the British, raised barriers to our exports, yet because the Confederation government lacked the authority to impose such impediments on our side, foreign commerce had free entry to our ports. The Spanish, ensconced in New Orleans, closed the Mississippi to our shipping.[51] Behind these issues of the day loomed the disquieting prospect of a national breakup. Along with Hamilton's economic designs, these were the considerations that most affected the Publii and caused them to desire a strong central regime.

Thus the Publii were nationalists. And their nationalism was a positive commitment, not a mere wish to hobble the provinces on behalf of the rich. Their classical readings had inclined them toward public life as the surest road to lasting fame. Therefore, they identified with their polity, the United States. They viewed the American people as forming a single great political community, and they regarded the dissolution of this society as a disastrous possibility, to be avoided at all costs. The Framers designed the Constitution, not to weaken popular government, but rather to give popularly chosen national officials like themselves the power to overcome discordant and refractory elements. Beard sees the Framers simply as affluent individuals and presumes that, as such, they must have desired to be insulated from the government. He overlooks the fact that they were practicing politicians. Far from wishing to avoid the authorities, they were the authorities. They were not tools of a faction, but leaders of a people.

True, the authors of *The Federalist*, like all Americans of their day, greatly respected what Hamilton called "the sacred rights of private property." But they did not believe that property should be exempt from public supervision. Even Hamilton admitted that under "extraordinary" conditions involving the "existence, or . . . permanent welfare" of the nation, these rights might be "infringed for the general good."[52] Beard is quite wrong when he says that the Framers granted their proposed government no power to conduct "a direct attack on property";[53] the authority to levy taxes, to coin money, and to impose tariffs seems amply sufficient for that purpose. The aim of the Publii was not to hedge property rights with invulnerable defenses, but to create a vigorous central regime that could, in fact, be used to regulate the capitalistic interests of the nation. The Publii were no doubt unhappy about various state actions that could be seen as derogatory to property—Rhode Island's inflationary money policy, for example. Also, Shays' Rebellion, with its vague hints of a levelling impulse, had disturbed the American elite. Yet it is wrong to perceive such factors as the only, or even the main, motive behind the movement for a new charter. Hamilton, Madison, and Jay had been advocates of a strong national government long before Capt. Daniel Shays began his seditious career, and for reasons far transcending a narrow concern for property rights.

To call the authors of *The Federalist* nationalists is to say that they adhered to a certain political theory. We must understand the exact content of that theory before we attempt to evaluate the argument of Publius. The next chapter discusses the origins and meaning of the national idea.

3
The Idea
of the Nation-State

Adair has pointed out that the "American Revolutionaries found in Plutarch not merely a generalized image of glory, but one very specific and concrete type of fame . . . the great lawgiver and the founder of a commonwealth."[1] There was Theseus, the heroic king of Athens, who "gathered together all the inhabitants of Attica into one town, and made them one people of one city, whereas before they lived dispersed, and were not easy to assemble upon any affair for the common interest." There was Romulus, who similarly populated his city with a miscellaneous concourse, many of whom had previously lived scattered "in small, unfortified villages." And there was Lycurgus, "the lawgiver of Sparta," who found his city distracted by "anarchy and confusion," whose own father was killed "endeavouring to quell a riot," yet who left his compatriots united and at peace with one another.[2] There also were Numa, Solon, and, of course, Publius Valerius, who accomplished similar projects. The authors of *The Federalists* desired to be numbered in this company.

More specifically, they sought to construct an American nation-state—which is a significant datum. The concept of a founding legislator was an old one, but the choice of a nation as the basis for the commonwealth being constructed was a new note. Consistent, self-conscious nationalism is only characteristic of the modern world. Authorities differ somewhat as to the exact moment when nationalism may be said to have come into existence—whether at the time of the partition of Poland in the 1770s, or during the French Revolution in 1789,[3] or merely "at the beginning of the nineteenth century."[4] But all agree in placing the origins of nationalism in the years around, or just before, 1800—that is, at more or less the date when *The Federalist* was written. Simple chronological fact indicates that, if Publius was indeed a nationalist, he must have been one of the very first.

This chapter defines the political theory of nationalism, discusses its relationship to the notion of a ruling elite, and shows its comparatively undeveloped status in 1787. We must have a firm grasp of these points in order to comprehend the nationalistic aspects of the argument of Publius.

Nationalism can be approached in a number of ways. It may be treated as a psychological condition,[5] a cultural pose,[6] or an adjunct to an economic system,[7] among other things. In the present context we view nationalism as a general political theory—a system of ideas that purports to explain the foundation of government. As a general theory, nationalism takes its place alongside such other ideologies as classical liberalism, fascism, Marxism, and the divine right of kings. The exact content of the nationalistic conception is perhaps arguable, because there is no single source whose statement can be considered entirely definitive. For the purpose of this study, however, the theory of nationalism is said to consist of four interrelated propositions, as follows.[8]

First, nationalists contend the human race can be divided into separate communities of sentiment and interest, called nations. These are populations the members of which are connected with each other and set apart from all outsiders by certain characteristics. They occupy a distinct territory that can be precisely marked off from the homelands of other nations. They speak a single language common to themselves alone. They have their own traditions and customs. They share similar notions of politics. They possess a common history and possibly a common ancestry. They have unique mannerisms and their own typical outlook on life. Their material interests are in harmony. Most important of all, perhaps, they feel themselves to be a nation: they consider their compatriots to be brethren, and they have a spontaneous desire to be associated with them. Collectively, they possess a general will that is the true source of all legitimate political power, and of all wise policy. Nations can either be large or small. As a rule, however, they extend far beyond the purview of a single city or neighborhood. Nationalists do not necessarily wholly reject humanitarian claims that transcend the nation or claims of individual right that may limit its jurisdiction. But on balance they feel that the national tie outweighs other political considerations.

This emphasis on the national bond has both a descriptive and a prescriptive aspect. Thus nations are considered to be entities in fact: they are believed to have objective existences and tangible interests, which they will always tend to express and which therefore must be factored into political calculations. Also, the existence of many different nations is held to be a good thing, because each has its own raison d'être and perspective on life and adds a thread to the tapestry of human experience.

Second, the nationalist theory contends that every discrete people is entitled to be free from foreign domination. Generally, such domination takes the form of an imperial structure, militarily imposed from the outside, although alien control may also be exercised indirectly through economic or diplomatic means. The imperial realm claims to govern on behalf of some universal value: peace, order, God's will, commerce, civilization, or another noble purpose far transcending the petty concerns of any separate national group. But nationalists believe that a regime imposed from outside, even if well-meaning, will never suit a nation's unique needs. Distinct peoples, nationalists observe, "would rather be governed like hell by themselves than well by their imperial rulers."[9]

The recognition that other peoples besides one's own possess the right to be free from foreign rule is a key insight, which above all else raises the nationalist impulse from an atavistic feeling to the status of a rational political theory. Thus Anthony D. Smith has drawn a distinction between two contrasting species of nationalism: "ethnocentric" and "polycentric."[10] The first of these regards the native ways as absolutely correct and generally perceives other peoples as fair game for conquest and enslavement. This view was characteristic of earlier, presumably less reflective, eras than the present—although, to be sure, the outlook of the Nazi regime in this century was also of this kind. Polycentric nationalists, however, regard their own peculiar usages as only locally correct, and they believe that self-determination applies to all peoples, not just to themselves. Nationalists of this sort might be assertive of the rights and interests of their own country, but they admit that other nations have legitimate rights and interests as well. This more tolerant nationalism is the main principle that, in theory, underlies the world's state system today.

Third, nationalists further maintain that each nation should be ruled by a single, sovereign, centralized state. Today, indeed, we often employ the terms *nation* and *government* interchangeably, but this inexact usage merely demonstrates the extent to which we have come to take the nationalist scheme of things for granted. Analytically, nations and governments are very distinct creatures. Nations are social entities, reflecting profound human attachments, which may or may not have their own independent governments, whereas governments are instruments of political rule that may or may not extend over just a single nation. There is no guarantee that these two entities will in fact coincide, although it is the nationalist presumption that they ought to: every nation should govern itself by means of one regime.

Centralization is indicated by the concept of the nation as a corporate entity with a single interest; to divide this naturally unified body politically only creates a basis for conflict where none should exist. Nationalists believe that the subordinate parts of the nations should be regulated from the standpoint of the whole. If a portion of the people concludes that its concerns cannot be fairly handled by the central rulers, then, from the nationalist point of view, this portion should secede from the rest and form its own, smaller but more coherent, nation-state. Nationalists believe that it is the height of inconsistency to remain within a country while seeking to hinder the overall governance of that country. National priorities, politically speaking, by definition take precedence over any others. Next to the ejection of the foreign oppressor, the greatest deed that a national hero can perform is the political unification of the people.

Finally, nationalists insist that the government of a people be framed in accordance with the customs and political values of the population concerned, that it be freely and genuinely consented to by them, and that it actually rule in their interest. The concepts of nationalism and democracy are quite closely related. It seems clear that nationalism, a view which finds the origin of political legitimacy in certain characteristics of the populace in general, could never have flourished until the democratic way of looking at things had become familiar—that is, until around the time of the French Revolution. In the nineteenth century, nationalist movements tended to have a strong affinity for the republican idea. Free popular elections and representative institutions were regarded as the obvious ways to ensure the fidelity of the rulers to the nation. The democratic overtones of the nationalistic concept have become less apparent in the twentieth century because of the spread of the national idea to places where democracy historically has not been practiced. Smith observes that, even so, nationalism generally retains a marked "populistic" orientation. Populism, he notes, "is a logical extension of one element in nationalist doctrine, the supremacy of the nation."[11] Even nondemocratic nationalisms must find some means of linking the regime to the masses—such as the mystical intuition of the charismatic leader.

Some nationalists have argued that a culturally uniform polity is a necessary condition for the existence of a democratic regime. A classic statement of this thesis is by John Stuart Mill, who says that "free institutions are next to impossible in a country made up of different nationalities." This is so because "among a people without fellow-feeling, especially if they read and speak different languages, the united public opinion, necessary to the working of representative government, cannot exist."[12] Ramsay Muir noted many years ago that "the only communities in Europe or in the world in which self-government"—he means democracy—"has been successfully applied are those in which the national spirit is dominant,"[13] and that judgment still generally holds true today.

These, then, are the four elements of the nationalist theory: national differentiation, self-determination, centralization, and popular government. Because *The Federalist* upholds a concept of the state based on these principles, we conclude the work to be essentially nationalistic in outlook. We should briefly note two aspects of Publius's treatment of the idea.

First, it is obvious that there is a certain tension between the various components of the national conception. Nationalism cannot simply be identified with pure democracy, nor even with populism. A nation is more than just the lowest common denominator of a certain population. It is a corporate body—a historical, cultural, and political assemblage that is greater than the sum of its parts, and that needs a certain amount of overall guidance and direction to hold together. To reconcile this need for centralized regulation with the equally important need for popular control is not an easy task, to be sure. The mode recommended by the Publii was that which Hamilton dubbed "representative democracy."[14] Yet the concept of representation is itself somewhat ambiguous, as we will see, and is capable of being interpreted in either an elitist fashion—"virtual" representation—or as pure majoritarianism.[15] The tension between the corporate and populist aspects of nationalism may be noted in *The Federalist*, particularly in that work's analysis of the two legislative branches of the new government.

Second, while Publius is clearly a nationalist, it seems equally plain that he is a Lockean liberal. This is interesting, because classical liberalism, which stresses the rights of the individual against the state, does not entirely comport with nationalism, which tends to emphasize the primacy of society. Publius harmonizes his nationalistic impulses with his liberalism by asserting that the citizens of America can become individually prosperous only if they recognize their membership in a great national community and agree to the overall management of a strong central government. Moreover, he declares that natural rights, to be effectual, must be consistent with the spirit of the people. Publius assumes that nationalism and liberalism are wholly compatible, so he cannot be said to favor one over the other. But he devotes far more attention to nationalistic topics than to assertions of abstract right.

The foregoing discussion has provided us with the archetypal concept of a nation-state. According to this idea, nations—natural groupings of human beings—are primary, and the state system should be subordinated to these preexisting communal realities. National likenesses are held to permeate entire populations and to mandate a populistic political style. Yet when we examine the origins of historical nation-states, we discover that this ideal pattern often does not obtain. Thus the national divisions of the human race are, in fact, far from clear-cut. We frequently find that a regime comes into being first, and its inhabitants begin to think of themselves as a nation only after their state has been in existence for some time. And nationalism, the ideology with a supposedly populistic tinge, is commonly introduced into a country by a sociopolitical elite. These seemingly paradoxical observations are all highly relevant to our consideration of *The Federalist*.

The issue of what is, or is not, a nation has been vigorously debated. Nations are usually defined on the basis of certain more or less objective characteristics: culture, geography, language, economic interest, and so forth. Yet none of these seems to be absolutely essential. Belgium and Switzerland have more than one official language, for example, and the Jewish people survived without a territorial base for two thousand years. Moreover, an individual may be subject to the tug of more than one national identity. Thus, many residents of sub-Saharan Africa in the late twentieth century can choose between three conceivable nationalities: one based on a tribal bond, limited in size but expressing an authentic native tradition; another focused on an existing state with present power, but with artificial boundaries drawn by the Western imperialists; and a third, pan-Africanism, grounded on a continent-wide cultural and racial likeness, but perhaps too grandiose to be practical. Which of these is the African's "real" nation is hard to say.

The attempt to define nations objectively has proven so futile that most modern authorities have given up the effort. The true essence of nationality, these critics assert, is not geography or ethnicity or language as such, but rather the subjective desire of a population to be associated together in a body politic. Hans Kohn puts it as follows: "Nationalism is first and foremost a state of mind." And Hugh Seton-Watson in like manner says that "a nation exists when a significant number of people . . . consider themselves one."[16] Nationalists do contend, of course, that the will to create a collective entity is most likely to arise and to persist when people living in a well-defined territory are united by social customs and material circumstances. But no set of human beings are ever alike in all things, and the assumption of a particular national identity always implies a communal decision to stress some characteristics instead of others.

The task of a nation-builder is to perceive, in the welter of possible political loyalties, the social connections that are most consistent with the deeply held values and conducive to the material interests of a given population, and to create a political entity organized around those connections. To say that a person's national identity is not necessarily foreordained is not, after all, to say that it is wholly arbitrary. Probably, in general, the nationalist appeals that succeed are those which are actually most reflective of the popular culture and are consistent with the popular advantage. Yet national sentiments seldom are of wholly spontaneous growth. It is oftentimes the hardest task of the nation-builder to convince the members of the target group that they belong together.

The orthodox nationalist assumption is that nations exist first and that governments are afterward founded on them. Sometimes this does happen, as in the case of Germany and Italy. Yet the sequence of events is frequently the reverse of this. In many cases, a regime is formed out of somewhat disparate popular materials, and only after the passage of some time and under the prodding of the state do the subjects of this government come to consider themselves a nation. Thus the region today occupied by the French nation is merely the territory annexed piecemeal over several centuries by the monarchs of the Capetian family. Bretons, Basques, Provençals, Alsatians, and Corsicans spoke tongues quite different from the dialect of the Île-de-France. Their laws and usages were not the same. They felt no real bond of kinship. Today's France was the creation—admittedly a largely inadvertent creation—of the Capetian regime. It was the monarchy's policy to smooth over the divisions of the domain in the interests of administrative convenience and to instill in the residents of the kingdom a pride in their common allegiance. The energetic measures of Cardinal Richelieu were a benchmark in this unifying process, although Richelieu was but one of a long line of vigorous royalist centralizers. The final result was a French national consciousness that was not at first a spontaneous popular feeling, but that ultimately became one.

The example of the French monarchy has been followed by many other governments that have sought to transform their subjects into nationals. Many of the so-called nation-states of the Third World today are still in the process of attempting to prevail upon their populations to shed their age-old tribal identities and to accept a wider definition of community. The spirit of Richelieu is alive and well in the twentieth century. The scholarly literature on nationalism distinguishes, as Meinecke notes, between "cultural nations and political nations," that is, between "nations that are primarily based on some jointly experienced cultural heritage and nations that are primarily based on the unifying force of a common political history and constitution."[17] The latter, it seems, are at least as numerous as the former.

These considerations enable us to understand why nationalism, an ideology with a populist tendency, is frequently introduced into a country by a sociopolitical elite. Nationalist feelings, although they may correspond to the objective interests and circumstances of a population, do not always permeate the masses. Along with the state, an educated minority can initially serve as the bearer of the national idea. Indeed, this elite often includes precisely those persons who have greatest access to the government—intellectuals, technical experts, administrators, professionals, politicians, and the upper classes in general. The nationalistic viewpoint usually takes root in the cities at first, among the more articulate groups, and spreads to the countryside and the peasantry only gradually. Innovations in politics, as in other fields of human endeavor, are often resisted by the inertia of the multitude, even when seemingly calculated for their benefit.

The anticolonial struggles of twentieth-century Asia and Africa particularly show the pivotal role of the well-educated, nationally conscious segments of native society. "In India and Indonesia, in Tunisia and Ghana," reports Rupert Emerson, "it is this thin layer of a new, highly Westernized elite, for the most part concentrated in the urban centers, which has supplied the leadership for the nationalist movements and manned the governments which took over with the coming of independence." The rural populations of these new countries are "poverty-stricken, illiterate, and effectively conscious of little beyond their immediate neighborhoods"; it is the "Westernized elite" that serves "as the crystallizing center for the inchoate disaffections of the mass." Yet the exigencies of the anticolonial fight ultimately have obliged the native elites "to create mass parties or movements. . . . The democracy which they originally feared or scorned, save as a remote ideal, comes to be a political necessity for their further advance." Over time, "the general trend in Asian and African countries appears to be in the direction of a continued narrowing of the gap between leaders and people."[18] Eventually, it seems, the national idea does percolate down to the nation itself.

The nations of the contemporary Third World are not the only ones that can be traced back to the efforts of a distinct set of intellectuals and political activists. Indeed, as Seton-Watson remarks, only a handful of modern nations do *not* conform to this pattern. Very few of our existing political communities began in the distant past and developed wholly unself-consciously, he notes; the vast majority originated in the last two hundred years and were the deliberate creations of "small educated . . . elites" who utilized "propaganda among their own populations, designed to implant in them a national consciousness and a desire for political action."[19] This appears, in fact, to be the commonest method of beginning a nation. Nationalism starts as elitism and ends as populism.

The foregoing considerations are highly relevant to a discussion of the argument of Publius and the intent of the American Founders. *The Federalist* was written at a time when the national identity of our ancestors was not yet wholly firm. One option, membership in the transatlantic British nation, had long since been discarded. Other choices, however, remained: we comprised either a single continent-wide American nation; or thirteen smaller nations, each based on a former colony; or perhaps two or three confederacies. Most Americans seem to have even then preferred the first of these alternatives, although not invariably or very clearly. Provincial loyalties were still strong. The argument of Publius is a statement on behalf of an extensive American nationality and an exploration of the various implications of that national choice for our federal government. Hamilton, Madison, and Jay felt that a strong central regime was needed to solidify their country, and their reasonings in that regard would sound quite familiar to the political leaders of the Third World today.

The Founders were the articulate elite who created the American nation. In terms of their social status, education, access to the government, and political ideology, they plainly fit the pattern. It is true that their fellow Americans were not in general quite so politically underdeveloped as the masses of the Third World today. The American peasantry was already Westernized, indeed of European stock, was used to the process of popular self-government, and was not impoverished, but relatively prosperous, by eighteenth-century standards. Yet in some ways the Americans of that period were not unlike the less developed populations of the modern globe. They were rural and agricultural, and therefore of somewhat limited horizons. They were all too susceptible to local and particularistic appeals in politics. They had some sense of American nationhood, but it was vague and theoretical. The movement for the new Constitution, like most nationalistic efforts, began in the cities and was not at first accepted in the countryside. As spokesmen for the nation, the Founders upheld an entity derived from the people, yet one that the people themselves did not entirely appreciate.

And Hamilton, Madison, and Jay operated under a disadvantage that has not affected subsequent nation-builders, for they were obliged to do without the benefit of any previous statement of the nationalist political theory. The components of this conception had been in circulation for many years preceding 1787, but had never been assembled into a coherent whole. The nationalism of the Publii was largely an original creation.

Nationalism is such an all-pervasive feature of the modern world that we tend to take its presence for granted. Yet, as already noted, the nationalist point of view had only been in existence for about two hundred years. This ideology developed gradually over time, as the coming together of a number of separate influences. Four of these are particularly important.

The first, and most venerable, of these influences was the idea of the classical Greek *polis*: a self-governing community of free citizens who find personal fulfillment through their participation in the affairs of the society. This ideal is perhaps best stated in Pericles' funeral oration, as recorded by Thucydides. The speaker begins by praising the Athenians of former days: "There has never been a time when they did not inhabit this land, which by their valour they have handed down from generation to generation." The people of Athens are free, yet "reverence pervades our public acts; we are prevented from doing wrong by respect for authority and for the laws." Indeed, Athenians "regard a man who takes no interest in public affairs . . . as a useless character." Pericles boasts of the achievements of Athens, and adds that, "in magnifying the city," he is eulogizing those citizens "whose virtues made her glorious." He concludes with a passionate outburst: "I would have you day by day fix your eyes upon the greatness of Athens, until you become filled with your love of her."[20] This exaltation of communal values over private concerns is typical of the Hellenic age.

In general, it may be said that ancient Greek political thought does not recognize any actual conflict between the needs of the individual and the imperatives of social life. As George H. Sabine has pointed out, in the classical scheme of things the "citizen has rights, but they are not attributes of a private personality; they belong to his station. He has obligations, too, but they are not forced on him by the state; they flow from the need to realize his own potentialities."[21] This idea of a community composed of persons whose true essence is defined collectively, and who therefore genuinely express themselves through conformance to group norms, has unquestionably been carried over into nationalism. Like present-day nationalists, the old Greeks presumed that the laws and customs of a polity determined the characters of its members.

Yet in one vitally important respect, the political thought of antiquity was quite unfavorable to nationalism. True, the ancient Greeks were by no means unacquainted with nationalistic sentiments: they believed that their own national culture was unique and wholly superior to the cultures of other peoples, and they were proud of their ability to maintain their national independence in the face of overwhelming odds. But not only did the Greeks fail to construct a nation-state of their own, they did not even regard such a thing as desirable. Their allegiance was given to a wholly different form of government: the city-state. They were well aware of the disadvantages of their favorite governmental type—above all that it fostered the division of their country—but they could not devise an alternative they trusted to maintain their freedom. Because Western political thought essentially derives from ancient Greek ideas, their views on this matter were still generally regarded as definitive two thousand years later, when *The Federalist* was written.

The reasons for the Greek attitude were cogently explained by Aristotle. A polity, said the philosopher, should be composed of "freemen" of equal status and similar condition, who are united by "friendship and good fellowship." And it appears that "such a community can only be established among those who live in the same place and intermarry." Their propinquity will tend to nurture social ties: "family connections, brotherhoods, common sacrifices, amusements which draw men together." Extensive states are too impersonal to give rise to such feelings. To begin with, "a very great multitude cannot be orderly." Moreover, when citizens no longer "know each other's character," then "both the election to offices and the decision of lawsuits will go wrong." Also, "in an over-populous state foreigners . . . will readily acquire the rights of citizens, for who will find them out?" Aristotle goes so far as to "require that the land as well as the inhabitants . . . should be taken in at a single view, for a country which is easily seen can be easily protected."[22] This was the virtually universal stance of the ancient Greeks: the personal political participation of the citizen was seen as the indispensable cement of the community.

It was to say the least inconvenient for Publius that the ideas of the founders of Western civilization thus clearly contradicted the nation-state concept. "If respect is to be paid to the opinion of the greatest and wisest men who have ever thought or wrote on the science of government," noted Publius's antagonist, Brutus, "a free republic cannot succeed over a country of such immense extent . . . as that of the whole United States."[23] Hamilton, Madison, and Jay were well aware that the weight of classical authority did indeed support the anti-Federalists on this point.

The second component of the nationalist political theory that was prominent during the late eighteenth century was the growing tendency of individuals to identify with their nation, culturally and politically. During the Middle Ages in Europe, nations in the present-day sense hardly existed. The dialect of a locality was unintelligible to peasants living in the very next province, and whether one's feudal overlord spoke the same tongue as oneself was not considered a significant fact. In any case, all educated people used Latin. The development of extensive areas of uniform, although distinct, speech and culture did not come about until the invention of the printing press and the consequent stimulation of a vernacular literature. This eventuality divided educated Europeans into national segments, tended to assimilate the literati to the peasantry of their regions, and reduced the differences of dialect among the common people. The participation in a national culture, through reading and writing, served the same function as the interpersonal contact that had been possible in the archaic *polis:* the arousing of a communal spirit. Yet not for some time did national similarities come to be widely considered the natural basis for a political connection.

The sense of national identity in early modern Europe developed according to the uneven pattern seen today in the Third World: such sentiments first appeared among the social elite, and only later in the population at large. Kohn points out that "in the seventeenth and eighteenth centuries, 'nation' . . . indicated the conscious and active part of the people, whereas 'people' denoted the politically and socially more passive masses." The commonalty, "especially outside the great cities and the small educated classes, even in France," remained locked in their traditional ways. "Nationalism certainly had no hold over the masses," says Kohn. One noble writer, Henri de Boulainvilliers, explicitly defined the French nation as the aristocratic descendants of the Germanic Franks. The Celtic peasantry he viewed as a subject race, outside the national bounds. Only "the revolutions of the eighteenth century," notes Kohn, "brought the integration of the people into the nation, the awakening of the masses to political and social activism."[24] More specifically, it was the French Revolution that achieved this. Thus Publius wrote at a time when nationalism was generally considered the perspective of an elite.

The centralized monarchical regimes that developed in Europe in the sixteenth and seventeenth centuries were the third important influence on the evolution of the nationalist idea. These states tended ultimately to create nations around themselves, in the manner of the French royal government, but they were not originally founded on a national basis. In fact, their populations were often somewhat heterogeneous in the beginning. The "national monarchies" brought a measure of efficiency and order, but they did not usually at first even claim to express a unique popular spirit. Machiavelli seems to have been the first to recommend the creation of a monarchy around an existing cultural and geographic entity, as he did in *The Prince*. It is relatively easy, he notes, for a ruler to unify provinces that are "in the same region and of the same language," but when they are "different in language, customs, and institutions, then difficulties arise." Machiavelli was not a systematic nationalist—or even a consistent centralizer. He was much influenced by classical notions of politics, and he displays in *The Discourses* more than a trace of residual loyalty to the city-state form.[25] But no one else, for centuries, managed to come so close to the national idea.

The most thoroughgoing advocate of royal centralization was Thomas Hobbes, who asserted that, although "men may fancy many evil consequences" to "unlimited . . . Power" in the government, "yet the consequences of the want of it, which is perpetual warre of every man against his neighbor, are much worse." "A multitude," Hobbes noted, "being distracted in opinions . . . do not help, but hinder one another"; they therefore require "a common Power to keep them all in awe." The best regime was that of a single, absolute monarch: "in Monarchy, the private interest is the same with the publique," because "the riches, power, and honour of a Monarch arise only from the riches, strength, and reputation of his subjects." But "in a

Democracy, or Aristocracy, the publique prosperity" may not enhance "the private fortune" of a "corrupt or ambitious" official, as much as "a perfidious advice, a treacherous action, or a Civill Warre." Hobbes acknowledged that political authority could be lodged in the people, and exercised through representatives, but he clearly regarded such an arrangement as quite inferior.[26] He is therefore not a nationalist: the inhabitants of a state obtain cohesion solely through their submission to a common ruler, in his view, not from ties of custom or affection existing spontaneously among the people. Only Hobbe's insistence on the inherent indivisibility of sovereign power links him with later nationalistic thought.

The fourth influence promoting the development of nationalism was the idea and the practice of representation: that is, the election by the people of a body of delegates who confer together and exercise the ultimate authority of the state. The efficacy of representative bodies was shown in seventeenth-century England, in the course of the titanic struggles between the Stuart monarchs and Parliament for predominance within the English polity. That noted contest contributed to the formation of the national outlook in two ways. First, the English people unequivocally established their precedence over their kings by beheading one, chasing away another, and accepting a third only upon conditions. Second, Parliament proved that it was an institution through which the popular will could be exerted over a whole nation—even, when necessary, against the wishes of a powerful hereditary ruler. The ultimate result of this civil conflict was a limited monarchy, however, not a republic, and that outcome may have masked the nationalistic implications of the English revolutionary experience.

An important theoretical statement regarding the propriety of representative institutions is found in the works of John Locke. Government, Locke asserts, ultimately derives from "the Consent of the People." And he is quite specific concerning the appropriate organ for expressing the popular mandate. Abuses, he points out, are "not much to be fear'd in Governments where the Legislative consists . . . in Assemblies which are variable" and "whose Members . . . are Subjects under the common laws of their Country, equally with the rest." Locke here takes a major stride toward the articulation of the national idea, by affirming that a free regime can operate successfully without the personal participation of the whole citizen body. Yet he himself was no nationalist. There are traces of the concept in his writings, but such passages are few. He utterly rejects the idea that valid political connections might arise out of ancestry, or residence in a certain territory, or any other factor besides the free choice of unaffiliated individuals.[27] Locke's concern for property rights has impressed later generations far more than any other part of his teaching. And while classical liberalism and nationalism are sometimes combined in practice, they are two different political theories.

Thus, as the American Founders surveyed the political thought and practice of the Western world in 1787, they found neither clear-cut statements of the nationalist concept nor unequivocal examples of nation-states in action. Even Great Britain, which was perhaps the closest approximation to the latter, was a limited monarchy, not an extended republic. Various components of the national outlook had been expressed by one or another theorist and incorporated into at least some states, but the elements of nationalism had not been combined in the modern manner. Indeed, there seemed to be a certain amount of incompatability between them. Those thinkers who favored popular political institutions frequently assumed that they could not function over a wide territory. Those who preferred a strong centralized government usually disdained republicanism. Sentiments of nationality were recognized, but were not necessarily regarded as providing the basis for a state—certainly not a free state. The underdeveloped condition of the national concept in the eighteenth century is evident in the writings of two leading philosophers of that era, Montesquieu and Rousseau.

There is a sharp disagreement among the authorities concerning Montesquieu's relationship to the nationalistic point of view. Kohn says that he "was not concerned with nations in the modern sense of the word," and that his influence was "negligible on the development of nationalism"; whereas Smith maintains that he was "the first man to deal with nationalism in any systematic manner."[28] The truth appears to be that although Montesquieu does discuss many of the themes relevant to nationalists, he himself does not qualify as one. He sees the existence and importance of national differences. The "general spirit" of a nation, he observes, is "influenced by various causes: by the climate, by the laws, by the maxims of government, by precedents, morals, and customs." It follows that the "civil laws of each nation" must be "adapted in such a manner to the people for whom they are framed that it should be a great chance if those of one nation suit another." Yet Montesquieu did not feel that a nation should necessarily be ruled by just a single state. Ancient Greece had been "a great nation, composed of cities, each of which had a distinct government and separate laws," he notes.[29] But he denies that the Greeks suffered thereby.

Montesquieu was an admirer of popular government, and he flatly declares that such a government is not feasible in a great state. "It is natural," he observes, "for a republic to have only a small territory; otherwise it cannot long subsist." He believes that "in an extensive republic the public good is sacrificed to a thousand private views," whereas "in a small one, the interest of the public is more obvious, better understood, and more within the reach of every citizen." Only in a "small state" will "the body of the people" behave "like a single family"; strong community feelings "cannot be expected in the confusion and multitude of affairs in which a large nation is entangled," Montesquieu asserts.[30]

Montesquieu's opinion in this regard cannot have been welcome to the supporters of the American Constitution, especially because the distinguished Frenchman's reputation as a political sage was at its height in the late eighteenth century. The Founders followed him in many things, but they needed to contest his views on the optimal size for a popular regime. Fortunately, the philosopher himself apparently provided them with a way to do this, in a passage that was quoted *ad nauseum* by both sides in the ratification fight. Montesquieu had identified a "confederate republic" as a means of combining "the internal advantages of a republican, together with the external force of a monarchical, government." The Federalists claimed that this statement validated the plan of the Philadelphia Convention. But their adversaries, probably more correctly, read Montesquieu's comment as merely endorsing a loose system like that which existed under the Articles of Confederation. In any case, the modern idea of a nation-state is not to be found in the Frenchman's work. The premise throughout is that, if not a "despot," at least a "monarch" is needed to completely unify a large area.[31]

Nor is the concept of a nation-state to be found in the work of Rousseau—a lack that may well seem surprising, for there is no doubt that Rousseau had a major influence on the development of the doctrine of nationalism. Thus Sabine has observed that "Rousseau's political philosophy," although "vague," had the effects of stimulating "national patriotism," because of its "adaptation of the ideal of citizenship as it had been in a city-state to the modern national state."[32] Rousseau, in other words, proposed that nations be given the same measure of loyalty and affection that the classical Greeks accorded to their cities. And Rousseau's idea of the general will has been considered favorable to the concentration of governmental authority. Morley, who sees *The Federalist* as a brief for states' rights, regards Rousseau as endorsing the opposite principle of "the denial of local self-government in behalf of centralized power."[33] Yet, although Rousseau may have prepared the way for nationalism, he no more than Montesquieu truly qualifies for the label. Sabine notes that he possesses an "enthusiasm for the democratic city-state."[34] And Morley's reading is precisely wrong: Publius is far more of a centralizer than Rousseau is.

Rousseau's greatest work is *The Social Contract,* wherein he explains why individuals are legitimately subject to the general will. Considered by many the origin of modern nationalist ideas, this book in fact constitutes a celebration of the city-state in words that echo Aristotle. A monarchy, Rousseau observes, "will always rank . . . below republican government," in terms of merit. Among the "many conditions" needed for such a regime, however, is "a very small State, where the people can readily be got together and where each citizen can with ease know all the rest." "The people legitimately assembled as a sovereign body," says Rousseau, "are the aegis of the body politic." "The larger the State, the less the liberty." Representation is no answer. "The moment a people allows itself to be represented, it is no longer free: it no longer exists." Rousseau hints that a confederation of city-states may be a feasible way of combining "good government" with "the resources a great territory furnishes."[35] But he refrains from developing this concept at any length.

Rousseau's most complete treatment of the national question comes in *The Government of Poland,* his last political work, written in 1772. Poland at that point had a remarkably feeble government and was on the verge of being parceled out among the neighboring states. Rousseau recommends that the Poles attain their political salvation by arousing and reinforcing their sense of national identity. He notes that the "legislators of ancient times" worked to strengthen those "ties that . . . bind the citizens to the fatherland and to one another." He calls for the creation of "national institutions" that would give "form to the genius, the character, and the customs of a people." "It is education," he says, "that you must count on to shape the souls of the citizens in a national pattern." "When the Pole reaches the age of twenty, he must be a Pole, not some other kind of man." The Polish nation may then survive even physical conquest, Rousseau argues. "See to it that every Pole is incapable of becoming a Russian, and I answer for it that Russia will never subjugate Poland." "You cannot possibly prevent them from swallowing you; see to it, at least, that they shall not be able to digest you."[36] This all seems very nationalistic. Yet, once again, the idea of the nation-state is absent.

Indeed, Rousseau explicitly rejects the arguments for such a state. He remains committed to the opinion that popular government is practicable only in a small, localized entity. He wishes for Poland to become "a confederation of thirty-three tiny states." He actually proposes that the weak Polish monarch he deprived of some powers he already possessed. He counsels against wholesale changes in the anarchistic aspects of the existing constitution of Poland: "it was anarchy that formed in its bosom the hearts of . . . patriots." And Rousseau quite destroys any resemblance between his proposed confederation and a true national government, by his insistence that delegates to the Polish Diet from the thirty-three petty republics be absolutely bound by detailed instructions from their constituents: "The nation does not send deputies to the Diet to give voice to their own sentiments but to declare the nation's own will."[37] These words may have a nationalistic ring, but it is hollow. The practical effect of such a provision obviously would be to refer national decisions to the provinces, making coordinated policy impossible to achieve. Rousseau appreciates the spirit of nationalism, but he is unwilling to frame institutions through which that spirit can effectively rule.

This, then, was the condition of advanced protonationalistic thought just prior to the writing of *The Federalist*. Of course, there were many eighteenth-century critics who could have pointed out the defects of Rousseau's concept. Indeed, as Wilmoore Kendall notes, Rousseau was writing in opposition to a radically different analysis of Poland's problem. Many of the political leaders of that endangered nation sought the creation of a strong central government with a hereditary ruler and a standing army—a "national monarchy," in other words.[38] Yet these prescriptions fell short of nationalism on the opposite side, for they proposed institutions that were not entirely dependent on the will of the people. No theorist had yet systematically asserted the idea that the spirit of a self-conscious nation could be embodied in a centralized government by means of representative republican institutions. The time was ripe, however, for such a statement. Enter Publius.

4
Jay Describes a Nation

Of the first five *Federalist* papers, all but No. 1 were written by John Jay, constituting four-fifths of his entire contribution to the argument of Publius. In these essays, Jay systematically enumerates the elements of American nationhood, warns of foreign intervention in our internal affairs, points out the advantages of centralized decision making, and praises the wise—and popularly representative—national elite. All the vital aspects of the political theory of nationalism are here blended into a coherent perspective that will underlie the rest of *The Federalist*.

The *Independent Journal,* wherein these essays first appeared, was a biweekly newspaper published on Wednesdays and Saturdays. *Federalist* No. 1 came out on Saturday, October 27, with the others following over the next two weeks. Cato and Brutus were already in the field, while the Federal Farmer surfaced on November 8; all three made prominent reference to "the opinions of many great authors, that free elective government cannot be extended over large territories."[1] In response, Publius gives in these initial papers the rationale for a large-scale government in America, and it is right here, particularly in Jay's No. 2, that he makes his greatest contribution to the development of the national idea.

The first of the *Federalist* papers, by Hamilton, serves merely as an introduction to the series; the argument on behalf of the Constitution actually begins with No. 2. Yet No. 1 is by no means devoid of interest. Hamilton starts by noting the global significance of the crisis at hand: "It seems to have been reserved to the people of this country . . . to decide . . . whether societies of men are really capable or not, of establishing good government from reflection and choice, or whether they are forever destined to depend, for their political constitutions, on accident and force." For this reason, "a wrong election of the part we shall act, may . . . be considered the general misfortune of mankind" (3-7).[2] Thus the notion of a special American mission to transform the politics of the world makes an early appearance here. We will see, however, that this theme is by no means a prominent aspect of the argument of Publius, and indeed rates only two more brief mentions in the essays. The authors are mainly concerned with the welfare of the American people, not the betterment of humanity.

The Constitution, says Hamilton, should be evaluated solely on the basis of the "public good," but it "affects too many particular interests" and "innovates upon too many local institutions" not to stir the "passions and prejudices" of some people. This is clearly a dig at the Anti-Federalists, but Hamilton avoids the intemperate *ad hominem* assaults of Caesar. Without doubt, he admits, "much of the opposition" to the proposed government is "actuated by upright intentions" and consists merely of "the honest errors of minds led astray by preconceived jealousies and fears." He observes that "we upon many occasions, see wise and good men on the wrong as well as on the right side of questions, of the first magnitude to society." Furthermore, "we are not always sure, that those who advocate the truth are influenced by purer principles than their antagonists. Ambition, avarice, personal animosity, party opposition, and many other motives, not more laudable than these, are apt to operate as well upon those who support as upon those who oppose the right side of a question." Thus Hamilton acknowledges that some of his allies may be supporting the Constitution for questionable reasons. He agrees with Beard to some extent, it seems.

It is immediately apparent that Publius is not a simple-minded idealist. Good motives do not guarantee political astuteness, in his opinion, nor is selfishness necessarily incompatible with it. Yet neither is he a moral relativist. He believes in a "right" and a "wrong" in politics, presumably based on the distinction between "the public good" and "particular interests," and he thinks the two can be told apart by those who have "upright intentions" and minds strong enough not to be "led astray" by their preconceptions. Human beings may act from unworthy and mixed motives at times, but some persons, at least, appear capable of rising above their special biases and of offering rational guidance to the whole community. Publius admits that "my motives must remain in the depository of my own breast," but observes that these "arguments will be open to all, and may be judged of by all." The authors of *The Federalist* really believed they were speaking on behalf of the entire American people. They did not regard politics as a totally venal process. They were realists, not cynics.

Publius expresses his regret that the "enlightened zeal for the energy and efficiency of government," shown by the Constitution's supporters, should "be stigmatized as the off-spring of a temper fond of despotic power," and he unflinchingly avows that "the vigour of government is essential to the security of liberty." Publius thus makes quite plain his distance from libertarian notions of politics. Hamilton finds no wisdom in the Jeffersonian adage that the best government governs least; he wants a strong and active government, capable of regulating society for the common welfare. Hamilton states that he is "not unfriendly to the new Constitution," as if there could have been any doubt. Cato, in his first letter, had somewhat lamely posed as an impartial observer.[3] Publius scores crisply on this point: "I will not amuse you with an appearance of deliberation, when I have decided." There follows a short outline of the proposed series of papers, chiefly remarkable for the extent to which it fails to indicate the important divisions of the argument. As it was written, *The Federalist* far outstripped the original conception of its authors.

Hamilton then winds up No. 1 and sets the stage for No. 2 by raising a horrifying specter: the prospect of national division. He has already mentioned, as "among the most formidable of the obstacles which the new Constitution will have to encounter," the interest of state officials in preserving their power, and also "the perverted ambition" of men who will "flatter themselves with fairer prospects of elevation from the subdivision of the confederacy into several partial confederacies, than from its union under one government." Publius observes that "we already hear it whispered in the private circles of those who oppose the new constitution, that the Thirteen States are of too great extent for any general system." He predicts that "this doctrine will . . . be gradually propagated, till it has votaries enough to countenance an open avowal of it." To reject the proposed Constitution would play into the hands of the disunionists. "For nothing can be more evident, to those who are able to take an enlarged view of the subject, than the alternative of an adoption of the new Constitution, or a dismemberment of the Union." Hamilton adds, in a footnote, that "the same idea," of subdividing the union, "tracing the arguments to their consequences, is held out in several of the late publications against the New Constitution." This is a serious charge directed at the Anti-Federalists. But was it really justified? That question is worth consideration.

Most historians have believed that the accusation was unfounded. For example, although admitting that some Anti-Federalist leaders, such as Luther Martin and (probably) Patrick Henry, did prefer disunion, Jackson Turner Main nonetheless emphasizes that this was not the typical attitude of that party. Similarly, Merrill Jensen has argued that the Anti-Federalists saw America as a nation and that they merely "disagreed as to whether the new nation should have a federal or a national government." Herbert J. Storing has taken issue with Main and Jensen on this point, observing that "a debate over whether a nation should have a national government amounts to a debate over whether it shall *be* a nation."[4] Yet even Storing seems not to take the threat of disunity in 1787 very seriously. It is generally presumed that Publius's comments on this issue are merely propaganda, designed to frighten his readers.

Hamilton, however, regarded disunity as a real threat. He was convinced that Gov. George Clinton, for one, secretly contemplated the breakup of the United States. In a private letter to Gouverneur Morris—in which he would have had no reason to disguise his real views—Hamilton asserted that "it is reduced to a certainty that Clinton has in several conversations declared the union unnecessary; though I have the information through channels which do not permit a public use of it." If Clinton did harbor disunionist feelings, he likely would have refrained from expressing them except in what he considered the proper company, so Hamilton's information may well have been correct. Madison also privately declared his opinion that disunion was the object of at least some of the Anti-Federalists.[5] Henry, of whom Madison was very suspicious, made some questionable remarks in Virginia's ratifying convention. He piously observed that "separate confederacies" were "evils never to be thought of till a people are driven by necessity." Yet, he continued, "one Government cannot reign over so extensive a country as this is, without absolute despotism. Compared to such a consolidation, small confederacies are little evils."[6] Support for a dissolution of the Amercan union may have been more widespread in Publius's day than many modern critics have been willing to recognize.

Indeed, Publius did not have to travel very far afield to find quasi-disunionist opinions being openly stated. Such views are found in the letters of Brutus and Cato. Both of these antifederal writers subscribed to the doctrine of small-state republicanism. They gave lip service to the idea of an American federal union, yet they also voiced sentiments that, "tracing the arguments to their consequences," could be taken to imply separation. Thus Brutus notes that "history furnishes no example of a free republic, any thing like the extent of the United States." This was because "in a republic, the manners, sentiments, and interests of the people should be similar." However, "if we apply this remark to the condition of the United States, we shall be convinced that it forbids that we should be one government," Brutus declares.

The United States includes a variety of climates. The productions of the different parts of the union are very variant, and their interests, of consequences, diverse. Their manners and habits differ as much as their climates and productions; and their sentiments are by no means coincident. The laws and customs of the several states are, in many respects, very diverse, and in some opposite; each would be in favor of its own interests and customs, and, of consequence, a legislature, formed of representatives from the respective parts, would not only be too numerous to act with any care or decision, but would be composed of such heterogeneous and discordant principles, as would constantly be contending with each other.[7]

Cato's sentiments are expressed in virtually identical terms. He notes "the immense extent of territory . . . within the limits of the United States," refers to "the variety of its climates, productions, and commerce," and also to the "dissimilitude of interest, morals, and politics" between the states, and ultimately concludes that a "consolidated . . . legislature" would "be like a house divided against itself."[8] Since Cato was possibly Clinton, it is easy to see why the voicing of these disintegrationist opinions might have seemed genuinely ominous to Hamilton, Madison, and Jay.

Moreover, it was not so much what the Anti-Federalists intended to do that was important, in Hamilton's view, but what the effect of their opposition could be. The majority of the Anti-Federalists were probably loyal to the union. Yet retention of the existing Confederation was inconceivable, and a rejection of the new regime might precipitate a dissolution, as the only available alternative to the unacceptable status quo. In a private memorandum written about this time, Hamilton declares that if the Constitution does "not finally obtain, it is probable the discussion of the question will beget such struggles, animosities and heats in the community that this circumstance conspiring with the real necessity of an essential change in our present situation will produce civil war." He adds that "A dismemberment of the Union . . . may be expected."[9] This was certainly Hamilton's sincere opinion. He felt that Clinton was hiding his real purposes and that the Anti-Federalist masses were being gulled. The possibility of disunity was far more than a straw man to Publius.

It is important to remark that the arguments of Brutus and Cato, although seemingly in the classical tradition and obviously tending towards separatism in the immediate context, are actually quite different from the arguments used by the ancient Greeks to justify small-scale government. Aristotle stresses personal participation, not uniformity of custom and interest, in his defense of the *polis*; the state must be local, so that citizens may physically take part in its affairs, he says. But the Anti-Federalist writers neglect the factor of personal participation and mention only homogeneity, which marks a fundamental shift in emphasis. This concentration on uniformity is, in fact, a characteristic of the political theory of nationalism! Brutus and Cato have—probably inadvertently—deserted classical republicanism. They had no choice: as Hamilton would later point out in *Federalist* No. 9, the entities that the Anti-Federalist writers were upholding, the states, were already much bigger in size than the archaic *polis*, (52-53) and indeed themselves functioned by means of representation. Thus the Constitution's foes were obliged to shift the ground of their rejection of an extensive government. We will shortly see how Jay takes brilliant advantage of his opponents' amendment of the classical formulation.

Federalist No. 1 thus gives a foretaste of some of the main themes to come: realism, disinterested leadership, strong government, and national unification. But Publius has just warmed up. With No. 2 the argument begins in earnest.

The second of the *Federalist* papers occupies a most strategic location in the argument of Publius. Whereas No. 1 is a preliminary, No. 2 really commences the brief for the Constitution. It is here that we could reasonably look for a statement of the fundamental axioms underlying the entire treatise. Jefferson enunciated his "self-evident" truths concerning "inalienable rights" and natural equality at the outset of the *Declaration of Independence*, and he went on from there to justify the actions of the colonists in terms of those general ideas. If Publius followed the same logical order, we would expect to find an affirmation of basic principles in No. 2. The authors of *The Federalist* must have attempted some coordination of their efforts, and we may presume that any overall plan was most closely followed in the early stages. No. 2 must reveal what Hamilton and Jay, at least, agreed to be the proper starting point of the discussion. Indeed, the very first words from Jay's pen reveal his intention to take "a very comprehensive . . . view" of the "question" (8-13). This can only mean that he purposes to deal with fundamental issues. Jay then proceeds to lay out the foundation of the suggested system quite explicitly. America needs a new regime, he says, because America is a nation.

Before Jay introduces the national idea, however, he pauses to consider the crucial subject of human rights. He says: "Nothing is more certain than the indispensable necessity of Government, and it is equally undeniable, that whenever and however it is instituted, the people must cede to it some of their natural rights, in order to vest it with requisite powers." That is *all* he says. Not only is this statement quite brief—indeed perfunctory—it actually implies the irrelevance of human rights considerations to the matter under discussion, the division of political power between the national and state levels. Rufus King had made the same point at the convention: "the people having already parted with the necessary powers it is immaterial to them, by which Government they are possessed, provided they be well employed."[10] The Federalists felt there was no need to trace the proper line between individual rights and governmental prerogative at this juncture, since that particular boundary would not be affected by adoption of the Constitution. Publius is not interested in theory for its own sake.

This lack of concern for issues of abstract right is a leading characteristic of *The Federalist*.[11] Thus, although Publius speaks of "rights" and clearly believes in them, he never bothers to define or enumerate them, and he does not appear to use the term with any particular precision or frequency. When Publius finally does deign to pay systematic attention to the question of a bill of rights, at the very end of his case in No. 84, his conclusions are not exactly commendable to a twentieth-century civil libertarian. Dietze's amazing comment that *The Federalist* "can be a treatise on the Union only in a relative sense and must, in an absolute sense, be a treatise for the individual's rights," displays a remarkable lack of perception.[12] If Hamilton, Madison, and Jay were primarily interested in individual rights, in this work, it is odd of them to discuss other matters almost exclusively. In fact, the Publii do believe that a national government would, for various reasons, be protective of certain personal rights. But they wish to preserve and enhance the union for many reasons, of which this is only one, and probably not the main one.

Having virtually denied the relevance of natural rights, Jay now turns to the issue at hand: "whether it would conduce more to the interest of the people of America, that they should, to all general purposes, be one nation, under one federal Government, than that they should divide themselves into separate confederacies." On this point, at least, Publius is clear, copious, and decisive.

It has often given me pleasure to observe, that Independent America was not composed of detached and distant territories, but that one connected, fertile, wide spreading country was the portion of our western sons of liberty. Providence has in a particular manner blessed it with a variety of soils and productions, and watered it with innumerable streams, for the delight and accommodation of its inhabitants. A succession of navigable waters forms a kind of chain round its borders, as if to bind it together; while the most noble rivers in the world, running at convenient distances, present them with highways for the easy communication of friendly aids, and the mutual transportation and exchange of their various commodities.

With equal pleasure I have as often taken notice, that Providence has been pleased to give this one connected country, to one united people, a people descended from the same ancestors, speaking the same language, professing the same religion, attached to the same principles of government, very similar in their manners and customs, and who, by their joint counsels, arms and efforts, fighting side by side throughout a long and bloody war, have nobly established their general Liberty and Independence.

This country and this people seem to have been made for each other, and it appears as if it was the design of Providence, that an inheritance so proper and convenient for a band of brethren, united to each other by the strongest ties, should never be split into a number of unsocial, jealous and alien sovereignties.

Similar sentiments have hitherto prevailed among all orders and denominations of men among us. To all general purposes we have uniformly been one people—each individual citizen every where enjoying the same national rights, privileges, and protection. As a nation we have made peace and war—as a nation we have vanquished our common enemies—as a nation we have formed alliances and made treaties, and entered into various compacts and conventions with foreign states.

A strong sense of the value and blessings of Union induced the people, at a very early period, to institute a Federal Government to preserve and perpetuate it.

Thus John Jay comments on the foundation of the American union. This is a remarkable statement, for a number of reasons.

Obviously, this passage is, to say the least, strong evidence for the nationalist interpretation of *The Federalist*. We have here a perfect description of a nation, combined with the assertion that a government should be based on this nation—that is, in a nutshell, the political theory of nationalism. The location of this statement at the very beginning of the argument of Publius, as the centerpiece of a "comprehensive" discussion, and its fullness, particularly by comparison with Jay's slight mention of natural rights, testify to its crucial significance for this treatise. The concept of American nationhood underlies the whole case for the Constitution. Yet this is not the only importance of the passage.

Jay plainly was writing in response to Brutus and Cato. The two Anti-Federalists stressed the dissimilarities of Americans, and their opinions appeared in print at the precise moment when Jay must have been composing his essays. He wishes to confute their arguments on the subject of small-scale government, and he astutely realizes that they have phrased the issue in a way that allows him an effective answer. Brutus and Cato used a modern conception, the need for uniformity of custom and interest in a state, to defend an old idea, local government. But Jay points out that national similarities can, in fact, exist over a wide area. By choosing to rest their case on homogeneity rather than personal participation, Brutus and Cato have unwittingly undermined the whole case for small-state republicanism and have accidentally entered the era of nationalism, where Jay is happy to be.

Primarily, Jay's rejoinder is one of simple contradiction: the American people are very diverse, say Brutus and Cato; no, they are very much the same, Publius replies. Jay emphasizes two factors that his adversaries have neglected: the geographical unity of the country and the subjective emotions of togetherness that Americans feel. And he shrewdly manages to turn one of the Anti-Federalist arguments to his advantage. Brutus noted that the "variety of climates" in America fostered variant "productions." Jay admits this and observes that the several parts of America can therefore carry on a profitable and useful trade with each other—which he construes as an argument for a common political authority. Thus, while Americans may have some differences, these can be harmonized on the national level. Here, incidentally, we have a hint of the economic nationalism that would be espoused in greater detail by Hamilton in later papers.

It must be admitted that the Federalists were in some respects on rather uncertain ground here. The Americans were not, in fact, a very uniform people. Cultural differences between North and South and between the seaboard and the frontier were great. Religious divisions ran deep. Ethnic purity was a lost cause. Jay himself, the very man who penned those words about our common ancestors, had not a drop of English blood in his veins: he was five-eighths Dutch and three-eighths French. One of his polemical tracts of the Revolutionary War period had to be published in a bilingual edition—English and German—for the benefit of the many Americans of Teutonic stock.[13] Moreover, it took a certain amount of brass for Jay to refer to the "succession of navigable waters" around our borders, binding us into one. He had touched off a major political squall a year earlier when, as secretary of foreign affairs, he had proposed the infamous Jay-Gardoqui treaty, which would have permitted Spain to continue to block Americans from navigating the Mississippi River in return for commercial advantages for his own region, the East. The treaty was never ratified, but some westerners threatened secession on that occasion. Those navigable waters could as easily pull us apart as bring us together.

Yet there were consolidating forces at work. Given America's relative isolation from the nations of Europe, it did make sense to regard the United States as a geographic unit. The spirit of '76 lingered on. Political values and institutions were very much the same throughout the country. And the governing elite was perhaps more homogeneous than the general population. Unification, although not inevitable, was obviously feasible, since it happened. The truest view was expressed by Elbridge Gerry at Philadelphia: "We were neither the same Nation nor different Nations."[14] America in 1787 could undoubtedly have gone either way. Jay's picture of the American nation was based as much on future hopes as on existing realities.[15]

However, the real significance of Jay's description is not found in its literal applicability to eighteenth-century America, but in the general idea of nationhood that it embodies. Clearly, Jay possesses a systematic, coherent concept of what a nation is. He presents the factors most methodically: a connected territory, a potentially integrated economy, an objectively uniform population with a subjective desire to be associated together, and a common political history. His delineation is indeed equal to the best efforts of a later day, as seen by comparing it to one that is widely regarded as a classic: the "important" definition by Francis Lieber, framed in 1868, that, notes Carlton Hayes, "has been quoted again and again down to the present day." According to Lieber:

The word "nation," in the fullest adaptation of the term, means, in modern times, a numerous and homogeneous population . . . permanently inhabiting and cultivating a coherent territory, with a well-defined geographic culture, and a name of its own— the inhabitants speaking their own language, having their own literature and common institutions which distinguish them clearly from other and similar groups of people, being citizens or subjects of a unitary government, however subdivided it may be, and having an organic unity with one another as well as being conscious of a common destiny.[16]

There are, to be sure, some differences between Jay's statement and Lieber's. Lieber's notion of an "organic unity" of the people seems to imply a *Volkisch* bond that Jay does not really suggest, but Lieber omits the factor of a shared economy that Jay has included. These dissimilarities are not insignificant, yet the differences seem less important than the obvious likenesses. Jay expresses an entirely modern version of the national idea.

To grasp the full magnitude of Jay's achievement, we must recall that the political theory of nationalism had not been unequivocally stated as of 1787. Previous concepts of what constitutes nationhood seem sketchy by today's standards. Machiavelli, Montesquieu, and Rousseau, for example, are all seen as precursors of nationalism, yet none of them had ever defined the meaning of the term *nation* with anything approaching the precision and comprehensiveness that Jay attains in *Federalist* No. 2. To be sure, these theorists and others had employed the term, perhaps more vaguely, but not inconsistently with Publius's sense. Yet, at a remarkably early date, Jay presents this conception carefully and explicitly in its modern, fully developed form. *Federalist* No. 2 constitutes a milestone in the development of the national idea.

But it is a milestone that has been somewhat overlooked. True, many critics have commented on the fervency of Jay's nationalist convictions at this juncture. Thus, Dietze, who erroneously regards the nationalism of Publius as a mere device for the protection of individual rights, nonetheless admits concerning No. 2 that "it is doubtful whether in American political literature there can be found a similarly strong confession of faith in the Union." Clinton Rossiter includes *Federalist* No. 2 among the "cream" of the papers and calls his readers' attention to Jay's celebration of "the physical, cultural, linguistic, and sentimental oneness of the American people." Hans Morgenthau uses this passage to show that a "pre-existing community" underlay the United States Constitution.[17] Previous commentators, however, appear not to have realized that in the context of the relatively underdeveloped condition of nationalist thought in 1787, Jay's statement is not only strong, but also quite advanced. When it appeared, it was probably the most lucid description of a nation that had ever been penned.

The rest of this essay consists of praise of the Philadelphia Convention—and also of "the Memorable Congress of 1774," to which the constitutional conclave is likened, and of which Jay himself had been an active member. Publius sees an essential continuity between the American revolutionary movement and the later movement for the Constitution. The American people have felt "the value . . . of Union" from the beginning, he notes; they well know that their "liberty" can only be secured by an adequate "national government." So, when they detected the inadequacy of the Articles of Confederation, they summoned "as with one voice" their best and most trusted chiefs to Philadelphia, to devise an appropriate arrangement.

This convention, composed of men, who possessed the confidence of the people, and many of whom had become highly distinguished by their patriotism, virtue and wisdom, in times which tried the minds and hearts of men, undertook the arduous task. In the mild season of peace, with minds unoccupied by other subjects, they passed many months in cool uninterrupted and daily consultations: and finally, without having been awed by power, or influenced by any passions except love for their Country, they presented and recommended to the people the plan produced by their joint and very unanimous counsels.

Jay stresses that "this plan is only *recommended,* not imposed" and that the people themselves would therefore have the last word. This proposal deserves their "sedate and candid consideration"—although, alas, such an eventuality is "more to be wished than expected," he pessimistically adds.

Jay now recalls the First Continental Congress. That body had "recommended certain measures to their constituents, and the event proved their wisdom; yet it is fresh in our memories how soon the Press began to teem with Pamphlets and weekly Papers against those very measures." Opposition had come from officers of the existing governments and from others suffering from "the undue influence of former attachments" or harboring ambitions inconsistent "with the public good." Having thus neatly equated the Anti-Federalists of 1787 with the Tories of 1774, Jay proceeds to laud the Continental Congress in terms identical to those he had used with regard to the convention. The American people followed the leadership of Congress because:

They considered that the Congress was composed of many wise experienced men. That being convened from different parts of the country, they brought with them and communicated to each other a variety of useful information. That in the course of the time they passed together in enquiring into and discussing the true interests of their country, they must have acquired very accurate knowledge on that head. That they were individually interested in the public liberty and prosperity, and therefore that it was not less their inclination, than their duty, to recommend only such measures, as after the most mature deliberation they really thought prudent and adviseable.

Jay also emphasizes that "some of the most distinguished members of that Congress . . were also members of this Convention." It is most characteristic of Jay that he would so glowingly praise bodies of which he and his colleagues had been conspicuous members. Undue modesty was not among the faults of our Founders.

As with Jay's picture of the American nation, some overstatement has crept into this image of a sagacious leadership cadre. Both the Continental Congress and the Constitutional Convention were deeply divided and their deliberations marred by bitter factional debate. The diaries of John Adams provide a useful corrective to Jay's rosy recollections of the events of 1774. "In Congress, nibbling and quibbling as usual," says Adams. "These great wits . . . these learned lawyers, these wise statesmen, are so fond of showing their parts and powers, as to make their consultations very tedious."[18] Jay also somewhat magnifies the overlapping of membership between the two bodies: of the fifty-six members of the First Continental Congress, exactly six were also among the fifty-five delegates at Philadelphia, and only one of these, Roger Sherman, played a really important role.[19] Publius was a propagandist, as well as an analyst.

Yet, with these exaggerations duly noted, it nonetheless remains true that, allowing for a bit of poetic license, Jay's depiction of the early American ruling class is not entirely inaccurate. For all their many quirks, the Founders were certainly very able men. The existence of this network of enlightened, realistic, and determined politicians was undoubtedly a principal factor contributing to the success of the American Revolution. The continuity of leadership noted by Jay did exist in a general way. Perhaps just a handful of the constitutional Framers had been present at the first session of Congress, but only twelve of them had *not* been elected to Congress at one time or another.[20] Few of them were new to public life. They perfectly exemplified the elite group that had been guiding American politics since 1774.

As with Jay's national portrait, his description of the American ruling class is valuable less for its correspondence with mundane fact than for what it tells us about the outlook of *The Federalist*. The Founders may, in some respects, have fallen short of the model pattern of deliberation that is shown here, but that was clearly the way in which they thought vital political decisions ought to be made. The people should select able and experienced representatives who meet together in a central place; these leaders should exchange information and strive to understand each other's viewpoint; they should consider only the overall interest of the country; they should devise a rational course of action that can win the support of all sincere citizens; and the people should in some fashion approve the final result. Publius presumes, throughout *The Federalist*, that the American political process will to some extent approach this ideal. Ordinarily, he expects, the populace will ratify the suggestions of their wise governors, unless deceived by carping critics, and society will proceed, well regulated, for the benefit of the whole community.

This decision-making process combines the advantages of competence with the advantages of centralization. The elite will propose judicious measures because they are intelligent and well-motivated—and also because their access to information from all parts of the country has given them a comprehensive point of view. This procedure has a superficial resemblance to the method of bargain and compromise enjoined by modern pluralists, but the differences are more significant than the similarities. Jay does not see the rulers as engaged in mere horsetrading between special interests, but as seeking to harmonize their partial perspectives through the promotion of a general interest shared by them all. The objective is not simply to reach agreement, as such, but to agree on a logical plan to advance the welfare of the nation, considered as a corporate body. Factionalism, shortsightedness, and ignorance are the great impediments to good government, Publius feels.

A great deal of time has been spent on *Federalist* No. 2 because the view of politics presented therein also underlies the remainder of the argument of Publius. Nationalism, centralization, and the wise, representative elite comprise the main elements of the creed of *The Federalist*. This outlook may appear somewhat archaic because of its reliance on virtuous leaders. Yet the process described by Jay could, without any real stretching of the term, be deemed a form of "democratic centralism"—although with a more heartfelt emphasis on democracy than is usual in twentieth-century regimes employing that method of rule. Governing officials in many of today's Third World countries would not find those sentiments irrelevant to their own situation. And Publius's case is based on a wholly modern concept of the nation. All important aspects of the political theory of the nation-state are explicitly stated or clearly implied in No. 2, and Publius has barely begun.

Jay often asserts the existence of a uniformity of opinion among the Americans and their representatives. Thus the people called for the convention "as with one voice," and the delegates put forth "the plan produced by their joint and very unanimous counsels." The measures of the First Continental Congress were approved, not just by a majority, but by a "great majority," of Americans—indeed, by all of them who were not "deluded." He feels that the Americans form a coherent body with a general will. Indeed, not only Jay, but Hamilton and Madison as well, habitually and repeatedly refer to the American populace as though they form a single undivided mass: the people. If the Publii truly regarded the Americans as inherently split by state citizenship or interest-group affiliation, they would hardly have so often chosen words indicating the exact opposite.

Jay concludes this paper by observing that "not only the first, but ever succeeding Congress, as well as the late convention, have invariably joined with the people in thinking that the prosperity of America depended on its Union." Like Hamilton, he deprecates the suggestion of separate confederacies and warns that the rejection of the new Constitution "would put the continuance of the Union in the utmost jeopardy." He ends with the cry of Shakespeare's fallen Wolsey. "Whenever dissolution of the Union arrives, America will have reason to exclaim, in the words of the poet: 'Farewell! A long farewell to all my greatness.' "

The next three papers, by Jay, all aim to show the horrendous consequences of American disunity on our country's relations with foreign powers. The themes that have been aired in No. 2 are further explored in these essays.

Federalist No. 3 begins with the observation that "the people of any country (if like the Americans intelligent and well informed) seldom adopt, and steadily persevere for many years in, an erroneous opinion regarding their interests" (13-18). Publius, as we shall see, is quite concerned about sudden bursts of popular foolishness, but he respects the mature, considered opinions of the nation. In this case, the astute and long-standing public view is that the Americans should continue "firmly united under one Fœderal Government, vested with sufficient powers for all general and national purposes." Jay realistically notes that "among the many objects to which a wise and free people find it necessary to direct their attention, that of providing for their safety seems to be the first." Therefore, he now considers the effect of the adoption of the Constitution on the "dangers from foreign arms and influence."

Jay inquires "whether so many *just* causes of war are likely to be given by *United America,* as by *disunited* America." Wills remarks that it is indicative of Jay's regard for virtuous behavior that he thus early raises the possibility that his own compatriots might be wrong in some future military confrontation.[21] There is, indeed, a tone in No. 3 that suggests the professional diplomat, at home in foreign chanceries, eager to smooth over disputes, and less than impressed with bursts of chauvinistic enthusiasm emanating from the home population. Jay's nationalism was of the polycentric sort. He notes that "America has already formed treaties with no less than six foreign nations" most of them "able to annoy and injure us," and he adds that "it is of high importance to the peace of America, that she observe the laws of nations towards all these Powers." To him it is "evident that this will be more perfectly and punctually done by one national Government"

than by separate states or distinct confederacies. He also feels that a single
national regime would tend to repress "direct and unlawful violence" by
Americans toward foreigners, thus preserving our peace.

The considerations urged by Jay to support his view are already familiar
to us. Characteristically, he first turns to the notion of the wise elite. He
evidently expects the sterling qualities found in the First Continental Congress and the Constitutional Convention to continue in the new national
government. The American people, it seems, know how to pick good
leaders.

When once an efficient national government is established, the best men in the
country will . . . generally be appointed to manage it; for altho' town or county, or
other contracted influence may place men in state assemblies, or senates, or courts
of justice, or executive departments; yet more general and extensive reputation for
talents . . . will be necessary to recommend men to offices under the national
government—especially as it will have the widest field for choice, and never
experience that want of proper persons . . . not uncommon in some of the States.
Hence it will result, that the administration, the political counsels, and the judicial
decisions of the national Government will be more wise, systematical and judicious,
than those of individual States, and consequently more satisfactory . . . to other
nations, as well as more *safe* with respect to us.

This presumption of the superior ability of national officials, by comparison
with those on the state level, runs through the whole of *The Federalist*.

Publius now considers the advantages of centralization. Under the new
national government, he notes, "treaties and articles of treaties, as well as
the laws of nations, will always be expounded in one sense, and executed in
the same manner." This would not be true under multiple confederacies,
which would each be differently influenced by "local laws and interests."
Also, "the prospect of present loss or advantage, may often tempt the
governing party in one or two States to swerve from good faith and justice;
but those temptations not reaching the other States, and consequently
having little or no influence on the national government, the temptation will
be fruitless, and good faith and justice to be preserved." This passage offers
a foretaste of Madison's argument in No. 10. The states bordering on foreign
territories might, "under the impulse of sudden irritation, and a quick sense
of apparent interest or injury," start an untimely conflict, but the "wisdom
and prudence" of the central authorities "will not be diminished by the
passions which actuate the parties immediately interested." The national
regime will be somewhat distant, and therefore free from that "pride of
States as well as of men" that "naturally disposes them to justify all their
actions, and opposes their acknowledging, correcting or repairing their

errors and offences." This contrast of shortsighted passion with long-term wisdom is a favorite motif of Publius.

If in *Federalist* No. 3 Jay appears as an advocate of international comity, he assumes a rather different guise in No. 4, where the main idea is the inevitable conflict of nations. He notes: "It is too true, however disgraceful it may be to human nature, that nations in general will make war whenever they have a prospect of getting any thing by it, nay that absolute monarchs will often make war . . . for reasons entirely personal, such as, a thirst for military glory . . . ambition or private compacts" (18-23). Regrettably, American interests must clash with those of other countries. Publius lists numerous instances of unavoidable antagonism. "With France and with Britain we are rivals in the fisheries," he says, and also "with them and most other European nations . . . in navigation and the carrying trade." Our prosperity will be their misfortune, and they will consequently be hostile to us: "as our carrying trade cannot encrease, without in some degree diminishing their's, it is more their interest and will be more their policy, to restrain, than to promote it." Thus "Spain thinks it convenient to shut the Mississippi against us on the one side, and Britain excludes us from the St. Laurence on the other." We must expect these malevolent attentions to continue. "The . . . cabinets of other nations" will not "regard our advancement . . . with an eye of indifference and composure."

American unity is essential to forestall foreign intervention. "Whatever may be our situation," Publius declares, other countries "will know and view it exactly as it is; and they will act towards us accordingly." If we are well governed and united, "they will be much more disposed to cultivate our friendship, than provoke our resentment." But if "they find us either destitute of an effectual Government . . . or split into three or four independent and probably discordant republics or confederacies, one inclining to Britain, another to France, and a third to Spain, and perhaps played off against each other by the three, what a poor pitiful figure will America make in their eyes! How liable would she become not only to their contempt, but to their outrage."

When Jay discusses the ability of a single government to repel a foreign invasion, he sounds the familiar notes of centralization and the sagacious elite. They are clearly his favorite tune.

One Government can collect and avail itself of the talents and experience of the ablest men, in whatever part of the Union they may be found. It can move on uniform principles of policy—It can harmonize, assimilate, and protect the several parts and members, and extend the benefit of its foresight and precautions to each. In the formation of treaties it will regard the interest of the whole, and the particular interests of the parts as connected with that of the whole. It can apply the resources and power of the whole to the defence of any particular part, and that more easily and expeditiously than State Governments, or separate confederacies can possibly do, for want of concert and unity of system.

Obviously, we have here Publius's paradigm for intelligent decision making in the United States.

The latter part of No. 4 contains many comments on the utility of "one government watching over the general and common interests, and combining and directing the powers and resources of the whole." Jay refers to the British navy and points out that "if one national Government had not so regulated the navigation of Britain as to make it a nursery for seamen—if one national Government had not called forth all the national means and materials for forming fleets, their prowess and their thunder would never have been celebrated." It should be remarked that he here praises the British Navigation Acts, classic mercantilist legislation. Hamilton subsequently argues at length along these lines. Jay finishes with the comment that "when a people or a family so divide, it never fails to be against themselves." The comparison of the Americans to a family seems revelatory of Jay's attitude.

The main thrust of *Federalist* No. 5 is the same as that of No. 4— American division will facilitate the interference of outsiders in our internal affairs. The essay is divided into two parts: the first briefly considers the nationhood of Great Britain; the second expounds on the dangers of separate confederacies in America. These comments will help to clarify Publius's understanding of the concept of a national community.

Jay clearly believes that the British example is applicable to the situation of the United States. "Altho' it seems obvious to common sense, that the people of such an island, should be but one nation," and "notwithstanding their true interest, with respect to the continental nations was really the same," he observes, "yet we find that they were for ages divided into three, and that those three were almost constantly embroiled in quarrels and wars with one another" (23-27). He does *not* mention a similarity of language and custom as reasons for a British union—probably because such a similarity did not originally exist in that instance. Apparently, geography and a common material interest can, by themselves, provide the basis for a viable nation, in Jay's view.

The same opinion is evident in Jay's discussion of the effects of an American schism. It is vain to hope that unconnected states will join to repel a foreign invader, he declares. "The proposed confederacies will be *distinct nations*. Each of them would have its commerce with foreigners to regulate by distinct treaties; and as their productions and commodities are different . . . so would those treaties be essentially different. Different commercial concerns must create different interests, and of course different degrees of political attachment to . . . foreign nations." Thus, continues Jay, "the foreign nation with whom the *Southern* confederacy might be at war," could "be the one, with whom the *Northern* confederacy would be the most desirous of preserving peace and friendship." Feelings of American togetherness could be negated by the operation of the profit motive. A commercial interest backed by a government can be the kernel of a distinct new nation, it seems.

Thus, Jay's wonderful national description notwithstanding, he apparently does not really think that the American people constitute a preordained fellowship. Our unity will be facilitated by our various commonalities, but the presence of these factors does not automatically ensure the emergence of an American national regime. New communal sentiments could coalesce around governments founded on a more partial basis. Americans can either be one nation or many. The former choice would be preferable, Jay feels, for the reasons he discusses, but the latter is, unfortunately, entirely conceivable. Our similarities of language and culture, and the emotions left over from the years of revolutionary struggle, help to cement us together, but if these feelings are not reinforced by a centralized political authority, and by a concrete plan to promote our material welfare in a coordinated fashion, they will prove, by themselves, insufficient to preserve the American union. Publius is a practical and realistic nation-builder, dealing with a people whose national sentiments have not entirely jelled.

This pragmatic undercurrent runs not only through the argument in No. 5 but also through Jay's other papers—in fact, of course, it runs through the whole of *The Federalist*. Thus, when Jay notes the nationalistic tendencies of the American public, he does not say that we hold our country dearer than our fortunes, he says that "it has until lately been a received and uncontradicted opinion, that the prosperity of the people of America depended on their continuing firmly united" (8). Our nationhood, in other words, is conceived to be a tool for the promotion of our economic well-being—not a very idealistic view, although perhaps genuinely expressive of American values. The union in Jay's opinion will also serve other, perhaps more noble, purposes including the preservation of our liberty and peace, yet in these cases as well, the nation is regarded as a means to some other end. This pragmatic attitude is by no means contrary to the true spirit of nationalism. Many nations, as noted in the last chapter, have been created for very practical reasons of government.

Moreover, we should not think that Jay has a wholly instrumental perception of the nation. When he calls the American people a "band of brethren," deprecates their separation into "unsocial, jealous and alien sovereignties," and likens them to a "family," it is clear that he has something of an emotional attachment to his compatriots. Practical considerations may predominate in Publius's argument, but sentimental considerations are not absent.

As we proceed with *The Federalist,* it becomes increasingly apparent that these early papers by Jay highlight crucial features of the argument of Publius. Jay maintains that the American people are, or at least should consider themselves, a nation; that they have a common material interest; that this interest can be most reliably discerned by a set of sagacious and patriotic statesmen conferring together on a comprehensive plan; that the intervention of foreign powers in the internal affairs of America must not be allowed; that we require a strong central government to manage our concerns; and that the people should select the rulers and approve their work. All the important points of the political theory of nationalism are present here, along with an appreciation of the role of a national elite and a realistic assessment of the important part played by existing governmental powers in the formation of a national entity. These four papers by Jay are a highly impressive performance; issues of nation building are discussed in terms that have not lost their relevance.

Because Jay's papers are so few in number and because he was a slightly less eminent historical figure than Hamilton or Madison, his contributions to *The Federalist* have not received the attention that their intrinsic importance seems to warrant. Wills goes so far as to say that Jay's withdrawal from the enterprise was in fact "a blessing for us. It would be revealing to have papers on the judiciary written by the man who became the first chief justice under the Constitution. But it is hard to see how Hamilton's work in Nos. 78 and 81 could be bettered; and Madison would not have contributed so heavily if Jay had remained close to the project."[22] We would surely not wish for less from Madison—or from Hamilton, for that matter—but Jay expresses a clear-cut national vision that provides the master key to the entire argument of Publius and also comprises a major advance in the development of the concept of the nation-state. Hamilton and Madison do not depart from this stance, but neither do they declare it with quite the crystal clarity attained by Jay in these early papers. Perhaps there would be less misunderstanding of the message of *The Federalist* if Jay had written more of the work.

5
Hamilton Aims to Centralize

The next thirty-one papers, No. 6 through No. 36, further establish the need for a strong and centralized American national government. The great majority of these essays were written by Hamilton. Only five were penned by Madison, but these include the most celebrated of them all, *Federalist* No. 10. The articles were published between November 14, 1787, and January 9, 1788, usually at the rate of four per week. Most first appeared in one of two newspapers, the *New-York Packet* or the *Independent Journal*. They were widely reprinted. This was the pattern of publication until near the end of the series. Publius's chief antagonists, Brutus and Cato, were both active during this period, although Cato's seventh and last letter came out on January 3. Thus one of the most notable of the Anti-Federalist authors tired of the contest at a juncture when Publius had already produced five times as many papers, yet was not half done. The authors of *The Federalist* possessed an energy level their opponents could not match even when they cooperated, as Brutus and Cato seem to have done. (The two published on alternate Thursdays.) Brutus continued writing after Cato stopped. Indeed, he stayed with Publius until the very end, but he rarely managed to produce more than one essay every other week.

The essays written by Hamilton and Madison during this period are considered separately here in order to facilitate an examination of the contention that Publius has a "dual personality." It is true that these two sets of papers are in certain respects oriented quite differently. The articles by Hamilton are mostly directly relevant to the specific problems of eighteenth-century America and are the least abstract and theoretical portion of Publius's case. Madison's offerings, however, are notably more philosophical and are somewhat removed from the immediate concerns of the day. This variety of approaches has been matched by the disparate reactions of posterity. The papers by Hamilton are perhaps the most neglected part of *The Federalist*, whereas Madison's, particularly No. 10, are the most praised and commented upon. The two authors' views, however, are basically the same. Hamilton's papers are examined in this chapter, Madison's in the next.

Although the twenty-six essays by Hamilton comprise the great bulk of Publius's case for a more potent national government, they have not always been accorded great weight by later critics. Dietze provides the most striking case of disdain for this portion of *The Federalist*. At one point in his study, he frankly admits he has "omitted to mention some of the more technical aspects and details of the administration that are discussed by Hamilton, Madison, and Jay," and then he blandly proceeds to assure his readers that these trivialities do "not seem to have a bearing upon an over-all evaluation of the *Federalist*."[1] No portion of Publius's argument contains more administrative detail than that now being considered, and no part more clearly shows the incorrectness of Dietze's already mentioned assertion that *The Federalist* concerns national unity only "in a relative sense," incidental to the "absolute" safeguarding of the rights of the individual. It is evident that Publius prized unification as a positive instrument for the active promotion of American well-being, not just for negative reasons concerning the protection of private rights. Indeed, were we to judge by the relative amount of space Publius gives to these topics, we would conclude the former to be by far the more significant.

The basic viewpoint expressed here by Hamilton is essentially the same as that voiced by Jay in the preceding essays. Hamilton feels that America comprises a national community with a general interest that overrides all more partial interests. He thinks that the American people should be governed by a sagacious elite, chosen by popular election, acquainted with the needs of their compatriots, and qualified by education and experience to discern the long-term good of all. And most important, he thinks that this national elite should rule through centralized political institutions that will give them the power they need to comprehensively manage the resources of the country. The virtues of centralization are indeed his favorite topic, to which he repeatedly returns. The national government in· his view must possess an unlimited power of taxation, as well as the authority to create a standing army. Hamilton warns of the danger of foreign intervention, yet he appears equally if not more concerned about the possibility of domestic revolts. Uniting the American nation will apparently require more than just drafting a constitution and holding free elections.

Hamilton recommends a policy of economic nationalism in these papers. He praises our native "spirit of enterprise," but he is not an advocate for free trade, except domestically. Like Jay, he feels that separate countries are to a certain extent inevitable economic antagonists, and he therefore regards the systems of controls by which nations try to exclude foreigners from their home markets as normal and legitimate. He suggests that America use retaliatory tariffs in an effort to force down the barriers to our goods abroad. The American economy is, in his view, a mutually dependent ensemble of interests, naturally congruent, but requiring a certain amount of supervision by the national rulers to coexist harmoniously. He sees the promotion of commerce as a prime governmental responsibility. Although he does not specifically propose anything like the great program of tariffs and subsidies, leading toward industrialization, that he later outlined in his famous *Report on Manufactures* of 1791, what he says here is more than enough to demonstrate that he was not a laissez-faire purist.

More than any other segment of *The Federalist*, these essays deal with the mundane side of government: unglamorous topics such as administrative efficiency, revenue policy, and the stimulation of economic activity. Yet they are not lacking in merit, nor are they trivial aspects of Publius's case.

Hamilton begins where Jay left off, with a discussion of the inadvisability of a separation of the states. *Federalist* No. 6 through No. 14 examine this topic. Whereas Jay has dealt with the dangers of foreign intervention, Hamilton considers the possibility of conflict between the disunited states themselves.

In No. 6, Publius examines his subject in light of "the accumulated experience of ages (28-36). He observes that only a person "far gone in Utopian speculations . . . can seriously doubt, that . . . the subdivisions" of a fragmented America "would have frequent and violent contests with each other. To presume a want of motives for such contests," he declares, "would be to forget that men are ambitious, vindictive, and rapacious." Hamilton quotes that Abbé de Mably: "Neighbouring nations are naturally enemies of each other." He recounts, with a certain relish, some celebrated historical cases of political folly leading to conflict. It may be a reflection of Hamilton's own life experiences that several of his examples involve women, usually of somewhat questionable character.[2] All in all, Publius feels that "momentary passions and immediate interests have a more active and imperious controul over human conduct than . . . remote considerations of policy, utility, or justice."

Hamilton does not say that all human beings are always passionate and selfish, he only contends that these undesirable characteristics will inevitably be present in human affairs to a large extent. Like Jay, Hamilton believes that some persons are sufficiently sagacious and impartial to be able to offer disinterested leadership to the whole nation.

Hamilton's mercantilist tendencies are prominently displayed in this essay. He derides the "visionary" hope that commerce between the American states would promote "a spirit of mutual amity and concord," in the event of their political disconnection. "Has commerce hitherto done any thing more than change the objects of war? Is not the love of wealth as domineering and enterprising a passion as that of power and glory?" Hamilton observes that many trading republics of the past were frequently at war and that the conflicts between Britain and France have "in a great measure grown out of commercial considerations." The inevitable opposition of national economic interests is, of course, a cardinal mercantilist tenet. And Hamilton shows sympathy with the efforts of nations to protect their domestic markets from foreign penetration; he regards the "desire of sharing in the commerce of other nations, without their consent," as "culpable," and he labels as "unjustifiable" and "illicit" certain violations of Spanish restrictions by British traders that led to war between those countries. The doctrine of free trade is by no means sacred to Publius.

Some reservations concerning democracy are also evident here. "Are not popular assemblies," Hamilton observes, "frequently subject to the impulses of rage, resentment, jealousy, avarice, and of other irregular and violent propensities?" Americans are intrinsically no more virtuous than any other people: "Is it not time to awake from the deceitful dream of a golden age, and to adopt as a practical maxim for the direction of our political conduct, that we, as well as the other inhabitants of the globe, are yet remote from the happy empire of perfect wisdom and perfect virtue?" Jay has praised the settled convictions of the people, but Hamilton here affirms that their "impulses" may be unsound.

Federalist No. 7 discusses possible "sources of hostility" between the American states (36-43). It is a lengthy list. Redistribution of the western lands, state jealousies, interfering commercial regulations, and the apportionment and extinguishment of the public debt, among other things, could lead to conflict without an "umpire or common judge to interpose between the contending parties," Hamilton says. New York's impost and "the enormities perpetrated by the legislature of Rhode-Island" on out-of-state creditors are prominently noted as examples of state actions that could provoke war. The previous close relations of the Americans would only worsen the situation. "The habits of intercourse, on the basis of equal privileges, to which we have been accustomed . . . would give a keener edge to those causes of discontent, than they would naturally have. . . . We should be ready to denominate injuries those things which were in reality the justifiable acts of independent sovereignties consulting a distinct interest." Finally, Hamilton warns of the possibility of foreign interference. "Incompatible alliances" could cause the states to be "entangled in all the pernicious labyrinths of European politics and wars. . . . *Divide et impera* must be the motto of every nation, that either hates or fears us," he concludes.

In *Federalist* No. 8, Hamilton introduces the subject of standing armies (44-50). The critics of the Constitution were complaining that the new charter contained inadequate safeguards against those pernicious institutions. Yet, says Hamilton, the likelihood of standing armies would be far greater were the states "subject to those vicissitudes of peace and war . . . which have fallen to the lot of all neighboring nations not united under one government." Being contiguous, the disunited American states would be direct military threats to one another, and the security requirements of the separated governments would necessarily spawn permanent military establishments. "Safety from external danger," says Hamilton, "is the most powerful director of national conduct. Even the ardent love of liberty will, after a time, give way to its dictates."

Standing armies were regarded as undesirable because they were felt to be, in Publius's words, "engines of despotism." Hamilton considers that Great Britain's freedom is mainly due to its "insular situation," which, by "guarding it in a great measure against the possibility of foreign invasion," thereby eliminates "the necessity of a numerous army within the kingdom." He applies this observation to the circumstances of America. "If we are wise enough to preserve the union," he says, "we may for ages enjoy an advantage similar to that of an insulated situation. Europe is at a great distance from us. . . . Extensive military establishments cannot, in this position, be necessary to our security." However, "if we should be disunited . . . our liberties would be a prey to the means of defending them." Like Jay, Hamilton regards geography as a powerful argument for American nationhood. Liberty and union, as Webster would say half a century later, are one and inseparable.

Federalist No. 9 begins with a momentous assertion: "A Firm Union will be of the utmost moment to the peace and liberty of the States as a barrier against domestic faction and insurrection (50-56). This idea, of course, is famous as the central theme of Madison's No. 10. Jay has already given us a foretaste of the notion in No. 3, where it is noted that "temptations" which might cause one state to "swerve from good faith and justice" will be unlikely to extend over the entire country, and that national policies will therefore tend to be wiser than those of a single province (15-16). In No. 9, Hamilton makes a full-scale assault on the small-state republican idea. He deplores the turbulence of "the petty Republics of Greece and Italy"—their "perpetual vibration, between the extremes of tyranny and anarchy." He contends, however, that such disorders may be prevented by new "discoveries" in the "science of politics." Among these novelties are expedients such as separation of powers, checks and balances, an independent judiciary, and popular representation. And Hamilton wishes to add another: "the enlargement of the orbit within which such systems are to revolve either in respect to the dimensions of a single State, or to the consolidation of several smaller States into one great confederacy."

Brutus, Cato, and other Anti-Federalists had quoted Montesquieu on the topic of small-state republicanism.[3] Publius now turns that very battery upon them. First, Publius notes that the Frenchman "had in view . . . dimensions, far short of the limits of almost every one of these States." In order to actually follow Montesquieu's advice, we should be forced to subdivide our existing states "into an infinity of little jealous, clashing, tumultuous commonwealths." Cato seemed to sugggest such a measure in his third letter. "The extent of many of the states of the Union," Cato said, "is at this time almost too great for the superintendence of a republican form of government, and must one day or other revolve into more vigorous ones, or by separation be reduced into smaller and more useful, as well as moderate ones."[4] Hamilton cannot resist a thrust at his provincial-minded antagonist: "Such an infatuated policy, such a desparate expedient, might by the multiplication of petty offices, answer the views of men, who possess not qualifications to extend their influence beyond the narrow circles of personal intrigue, but it could never promote the greatness or happiness of the people of America," he declares.

Publius invokes the French philosopher on behalf of his own position: "So far are the suggestions of Montesquieu from standing in opposition to a general Union of the States, that he explicitly treats of a confederate republic as the expedient for extending the sphere of popular government and reconciling the advantages of monarchy with those of republicanism." Hamilton inserts a long quotation from that writer. A federal republic "prevents all manner of inconveniencies," according to Montesquieu. "Should a popular insurrection happen, in one of the confederate States, the others are able to quell it. Should abuses creep into one part, they are reformed by those that remain sound" (54). Local factions will not be able to prevail over a whole nation, in other words. Montesquieu's idea is not quite the same as the famous argument of No. 10, but it points in the direction of Madison's great insight.

It should be observed that neither Montesquieu nor Hamilton suggests here that the individual states per se have a useful role to play in the quashing of faction; indeed, Hamilton specifically says that the advantages of an extended territory will accrue in a unitary government, as well as in a confederation. Publius considers America as a whole to be relatively insulated from the ravages of faction not because it is politically subdivided, but because the somewhat irresponsible provinces may be controlled by the larger and more levelheaded nation.

Finally, Hamilton maintains that the Constitution will create a true confederacy. This had been denied by the Anti-Federalists, who contended that a genuinely federal system would operate only on and through the state governments, in the manner of the Articles, not directly on individuals, like the new scheme. Hamilton again turns to Montesquieu, who, he says, defines a confederation merely as "an assemblage of societies" (55). Hamilton notes that this vague phrase will easily cover the new charter. "The proposed Constitution, so far from implying an abolition of the State Governments, makes them constituent parts of the national sovereignty by allowing them a direct representation in the Senate, and leaves in their possession certain exclusive and very important portions of sovereign power." Moreover, Montesquieu had commended the Lycian confederation, the "common council" of which "had the appointment of all the judges and magistrates of the respective cities," who, of course, would then directly act on the people. Hamilton therefore concludes that "the distinctions insisted upon were not within the contemplation of that enlightened civilian."

Epstein points out that the translation of Montesquieu followed here by Hamilton is faulty, and that the French philosopher really does seem to envision an arrangement like that of the Articles, in which the states are acted upon in their corporate capacities only. True, Montesquieu's praise of the Lycian confederation lends some plausibility to Hamilton's interpretation. But, on the whole, the Anti-Federalist view of the question seems to be more accurate, and as Epstein observes, this was certainly the prevalent perception in 1787.5 In any case, Hamilton's argument is only a verbal quibble. Even if previous usage of the term *confederation* was vague enough to justify its application to the Constitution, the employment of the same word for both the old and new regimes in America veiled the fact that the two governments were not really organized on the same pattern. The Anti-Federalists were quite correct to insist on this difference, whereas Hamilton was somewhat disingenuous in attempting to obscure it. We will see that Madison conspicuously disagrees with his colleague on this point. Incidentally, our modern usage distinguishes between the terms *federal* and *confederal*, applying the former to a system such as that under the Constitution and the latter to one like that of the Articles. Diamond notes, however, that this distinction was unknown in the eighteenth century.6 *The Federalist* equates the two terms.

There is some excuse for Hamilton's verbal shuffling here. He was perhaps a bit misleading in his use of the word *confederacy*, but he no doubt considered his comments to be substantially valid. The proposed government may not have been a true federation by the standards of the day, but as Hamilton points out, the states nevertheless retain a degree of authority that amounts to partial sovereignty. He sincerely believes this power is enough to enable the provinces to maintain their position within the American polity and, indeed, to often frustrate the plans of the central rulers. He certainly regards the suggested charter as significantly less than a full national unification.

Following Madison's No. 10, Hamilton presents three papers showing the practical advantages of union: a centralized government would be able to promote our common economic interests more effectively and administer our affairs more efficiently than separate states or lesser confederacies can do, he says.

The commercial importance of the union, notes Hamilton in No. 11, is agreed on by all "who have any acquaintance with the subject (65-73). Foreign nations have already marked "the adventurous spirit, which distinguishes the commercial character of America," and they would "naturally" adopt "the policy of fostering divisions among us and of depriving us as far as possible of an active commerce in our own bottoms." National unity, hoever, would enable us to overcome these unfriendly machinations. "Under a vigorous national government, the natural strength and resources of the country, directed to a common interest, would baffle all the combinations of European jealousy to restrain our growth." By the enaction of "prohibitory regulations, extending at the same time throughout the States, we may oblige foreign countries to bid against each other, for the privileges of our markets." Most important, "the establishment of a fœderal navy" would "enable us to bargain with great advantage for commercial privileges." And such a navy, "as it would embrace the resources of all, is an object far less remote than a navy of any single State, or partial confederacy, which would only embrace the resources of a part." The more southerly of the American states produce the most "solid and lasting" timber, whereas our "seamen must chiefly be drawn from the Northern hive." These comments obviously echo the previous remarks of Jay on the British fleet.

Hamilton also contends at some length that the elimination of domestic trade barriers would stimulate our economy: "unrestrained intercourse between the States themselves will advance the trade of each." But this would not happen if the states separate. "An unity of commercial, as well as political interests, can only result from an unity of government," Publius observes.

The policy recommended here is obviously a version of economic nationalism, or neomercantilism. General free trade is endorsed only in the domestic sphere, where it can receive the appropriate supervision by a centralized government. In relation to foreign countries, Publius speaks of the American economy as a single entity with a coherent interest, which must be promoted according to some sort of coordinated plan. In particular, he maintains that other nations should not be allowed into our home market unless they provide counterbalancing advantages to us. As J.W. Horrocks has pointed out, such retaliatory tariffs have been standard features of the neomercantilistic programs of the twentieth century, and a navy to defend merchant vessels was "an essential element in the English Mercantile System."[7] All in all, Publius's prescriptions are a far cry from the undiluted free market.

Federalist No. 11 is notable not only for what it says, but also for what it fails to say. There is no mention here of the erection of tariff barriers against foreign manufactures to protect infant industries in the United States— indeed, there is a suggestion that America, as a country "addicted to agriculture," would continue to import finished goods for some time. Yet Hamilton, as secretary of the treasury, proposed such tariffs within a very few years. The probable explanation for this omission is that Hamilton, in No. 11, was attempting to appeal to the mercantile interest in America, and the merchants could be expected to oppose tariffs for any purpose other than the promotion of trade. There was no industrial interest to speak of in the United States in 1787, and hence no need to raise that subject. Discretion was not Hamilton's strongest suit, but in this instance he knew what not to say.

The essay concludes with an arresting conception of the future foreign policy of the United States: "our interests prompt us to aim for an ascendant in the system of American affairs." Europe, says Hamilton, "by her arms and her negociations, by force and by fraud," has "extended her dominion" over the rest of the globe. "Africa, Asia, and America have successively felt her domination." It is the rightful destiny of the people of the United States "to vindicate the honor of the human race, and to teach that assuming brother moderation." Publius goes on to call for the erection of "one great American system, superior to the controul of all trans-atlantic force or influence, and able to dictate the terms of the connection between the old and new world." This seems to prefigure not only the Monroe Doctrine, but something even more grandiose, although the actual meaning of these words is—probably deliberately—obscure. Some aspects of this topic, says Hamilton, are "not proper for a Newspaper discussion." We should recall that Hamilton was a close friend of Francisco de Miranda, who was even then promoting a Latin American revolt against the Spanish Empire.[8]

This last passage is one of the very few in *The Federalist* that indicate an interest on Publius's part in anything transcending the affairs of the United States. By contrast with the superficially similar remarks in No. 1, the focus here is on an assertive American foreign policy, rather than on the general betterment of humanity. The Third World flavor of the passage is notable.

Federalist No. 12 is ostensibly about the collection of public revenues.

Hamilton argues that taxes would be less burdensome under a unified American government than under separate states or partial confederacies. He asserts that the wealth of the community would be increased, rendering the payment of taxes easier; and that the evasion of import duties—which are, in his view, the least oppressive taxes—would be far more difficult under a single national regime than under a system of independent adjacent states. One central government, Hamilton notes, "having the same interests to provide against violations every where," could plug all loopholes. This dry discussion of public administration contains two ideas of key importance to Hamilton's outlook (73-79).

First, this essay demonstrates that Hamilton fully shares the vision of American nationhood expressed by Jay in No. 2. America is a geographically distinct region, says Publius in No. 12, and its people are inherently bound together. Hamilton notes "the relative situation of these States, the number of rivers, with which they are intersected, . . . the facility of communication in every direction, the affinity of language, and manners, the familiar habits of intercourse," along with our distance from Europe, as factors that serve to unite our people. Moreover, he says, the seemingly diverse interests of this nation are really related in a harmonious way: "The often-agitated question, between agriculture and commerce, has from indubitable experience received a decision, which has silenced the rivalships, that once subsisted between them, and has proved to the satisfaction of their friends, that their interests are intimately blended and interwoven." Furthermore, there exists in America a characteristic "genius of the people," consisting of a special love of freedom, which seems to distinguish us from other lands. These factors are not systematically arranged as in Jay's great definition, but together they comprise a clear description of a nation.

Second, if No. 11 is addressed to the merchants, No. 12 constitutes an appeal to the agricultural interest. In a sense, this essay gives us Hamilton's answer to Jefferson—his explanation of why even the farmers should favor the growth of a commercial economy in America. The argument on this point is contained in two statements. First: "It has been found . . . that in proportion as commerce has flourished, land has risen in value." Second: "Revenue . . . must be had in all events. In this country, if the principal part be not drawn from commerce, it must fall with oppressive weight upon land." Clearly, the appeal is purely a financial one. Compare this to Jefferson's statement on the moral superiority of the agricultural way of life: "Those who labor in the earth are the chosen people of God, if ever he had a chosen people, whose breasts he has made his peculiar deposit for substantial and genuine virtue."[19] It was Hamilton's guess that the farmers would rather be rich than virtuous. We see, once again, that Publius conceives the common good in somewhat materialistic terms.

The following paper, No. 13, considers the factor of economies of scale. "If the States are united under one government," observes Hamilton, "there will be but one national civil list to support; if they are divided into several confederacies, there will be as many different national civil lists to be provided for; and each of them, as to the principal departments coextensive with that which would be necessary for a government of the whole" (80-83). It would, therefore, be more economical to manage our affairs on the basis of a single centralized government than through these lesser entities. This argument seems to apply to virtually anything capable of being handled on a national scale, and it certainly militates against such ventures as President Reagan's New Federalism.

This essay contains a passage that once again underscores the extent to which Hamilton shares the nationalistic view of politics. He observes that should the American union collapse, the thirteen states would probably "league themselves under two governments"—a northern and a southern. These lesser federations would take shape on the basis of "geographical and commercial considerations, in conjunction with the habits and prejudices of the different States,"—that is, from "all the causes that form the links of national sympathy and connection." Pennsylvania would "join the northern league" because "an active foreign commerce on the basis of her own navigation is her true policy, and coincides with the opinions and disposi-tions of her citizens." The southerners, "from various circumstances, may not think themselves much interested in the encouragement of navigation," and "Pennsylvania may not choose to confound her interests in a connection so adverse to her policy." Also, she would rather have her flank turned towards "the weaker power of the southern, rather than towards the stronger power of the northern confederacy. This would give her the fairest chance to avoid being the Flanders of America." The customs of the people combined with geographical, economic, and strategic considerations are the founda-tion of nations, it seems.

This passage is worth remarking for three reasons. First, it stamps Hamilton as a systematic adherent of the nationalist theory, because he finds governments originating in national ties. Second, it admits that, in spite of Publius's staunch assertion of a "sacred knot" uniting the Americans (89), there are natural divisions within the community that can only be overcome by governmental centralization. Third, it previews the sectional disputes over economic policy that marked the early history of the United States. Hamilton had a keen eye for the main point.

Madison's *Federalist* No. 14 wraps up Publius's examination of the advantages of the American union, and the horrendous consequences should we dissolve it. With No. 15, Hamilton commences a discussion of the shortcomings of the Articles of Confederation that extends over the next eight essays. He maintains that a national authority acting on individuals is essential to the welfare of America, and that the Articles are incurably deficient in that regard. In the opinion of Publius, the states should not have any direct role whatsoever in the conduct of our national affairs.

Federalist No. 15 notes the many problems then facing the American people (89-98). It is a very long list. "We may indeed with propriety be said to have reached almost the last stage of national humiliation," declares Publius. Our government's "engagements" to foreign powers and to "our own citizens" remain chronically unfulfilled. We have made no provision for the payment of our public debts. The British still occupy our western territories, in violation of the treaty of peace, and we are unable to remove them—or "even . . . to remonstrate with dignity," owing to our own delinquencies. Spain excludes us from navigation of the Mississippi. Our public credit seems to have been "abandoned . . . as . . . irretrievable." Our commerce is languishing. Other countries treat our ambassadors as "the mere pageants of mimic sovereignty." The price of improved land is far too low. Private investment capital is scarce. In short, we are faced with a "dark catalogue of . . . public misfortunes." Publius reveals his priorities by mentioning the public debt twice, yet he has not forgotten the landed interest. These evils are all blamed on "defects in the scheme of our Fœderal Government."

One of these defects stands out: "The great and radical vice in the construction of the existing Confederation is in the principle of legislation for States or governments, in their corporate or collective capacities . . . as contradistinguished from the individuals of whom they consist." Because of this fatal flaw, the decrees of our national authorities are "in practice . . . mere recommendations, which the States observe or disregard at their option." The United States, says Hamilton, can be either a single government or a set of petty sovereignties. The latter option would be disastrous, as Publius has been shown in previous essays. But if we mean to be the former, we must invest our national rulers with the power to enforce their resolutions on individuals. "It is essential to the idea of a law, that it be attended with a sanction; or in other words, a penalty or punishment for disobedience." Individuals can be coeced through the court system; states can only be coerced by war. If the central regime is forced to govern through the states, "military execution must become the only instrument of civil obedience." This "can . . . not deserve the name of government," Hamilton declares.

Federal systems like the United States are prey to centrifugal forces, notes Hamilton: "in every political association which is formed upon the principle of uniting in a common interest a number of lesser sovereignties, there will be found a kind of excentric tendency in the subordinate or inferior orbs, by the operation of which there will be a perpetual effort in each to fly off from the common center." The reason for this is that "there is in the nature of sovereign power an impatience of controul." The states, being partly sovereign, naturally resent the national regime that tries to control them and often do not cooperate voluntarily. "The rulers of the respective members, whether they have a constitutional right to do it or not, will undertake to judge of the propriety of the measures themselves." And, Hamilton observes, "this will be done . . . in a spirit of interested and suspicious scrutiny, without that knowledge of national circumstances and reasons of state, which is essential to a right judgement, and with that strong predilection in favour of local objects, which can hardly fail to mislead the decision." It has proven impossible to obtain coordinated action under the Articles. "Each State yielding to the persuasive voice of immediate interest and convenience has successively withdrawn its support, 'till the frail and tottering edifice seems ready to fall upon our heads," Hamilton laments.

These words should be marked. Publius contends that federal governments always have an intrinsic tendency to fall apart; that this regrettable circumstance results specifically from the portion of sovereign power which has been left with the states; that the states will attempt to pass judgement on national measures, whether constitutionally allowed to do so or not; and that their views will be of limited scope. These destructive tendencies are especially strong under the Articles because of the need for state approval of Confederation policies, but they are said to be characteristic of federal systems in general. As Hamilton uses the term, this would naturally include the new Constitution as well. He has explicitly affirmed that the states would retain a degree of sovereignty under the proposed scheme, yet he here asserts that state sovereignty is inherently destructive of the unity of the nation, upon which the welfare of the American people has been said to essentially depend. Federalism has innate disadvantages, it seems.

Federalist No. 16 repeats many previous contentions. It is evident that "the principle of legislation for States" will lead to chronic "delinquencies in the members of the Union," says Hamilton, "and that whenever they happen, the only constitutional remedy" will be "civil war" (99-105). Such an event would invite intervention by "foreign powers," would inflame "the passions of men," and "would probably terminate in a dissolution of the Union." Although, to be sure, given "the genius of this country," it is more likely that the federal regime will just dissolve. A central government acting solely on the states, like the existing Confederation, can succeed only if backed by a standing army, which "would instantly degenerate into a military despotism," Hamilton claims.

Matters would, however, be otherwise under a system such as that embodied in the new Constitution. "If the execution of the laws of the national government, should not require the intervention of the State Legislatures; if they were to pass into immediate operation upon the citizens themselves, the particular governments could not interrupt their progress without an open and violent exertion of an unconstitutional power." Mere evasions or refusals to act would not suffice, as under the Articles. If a state did attempt to behave in such an unjust fashion, it would be checked either by the judiciary or the people. The judges would declare the measures of the state to be "unconstitutional and void," and the people, "as the natural guardians of the constitution, would throw their weight into the national scale." Hamilton expresses confidence that the American public would be "enlightened enough to distinguish between a legal exercise and an illegal usurpation of authority." The people would support irregular actions on the part of their states only "in cases of a tyrannical exercise of the Fœderal authority."

We have here an explicit rejection of the doctrine of nullification, which was concocted nearly half a century later by John C. Calhoun: Hamilton says, in so many words, that a state cannot interpose itself constitutionally to prevent the implementation of a law enacted on the national level. We have, on the other hand, a clear affirmation of judicial review—at least with regard to the exertion of national authority over the states. And the notion that the states might forcibly resist a threatened despotism by the national regime has been broached. This latter contention should be kept in mind.

Federalist No. 17 begins with an amusing expression of Hamilton's attitude towards the states. It is not likely, he says, that the national government will intrude on the "residuary authorities" left by the Constitution to these subordinate polities (105-10). The reason for this is that the subjects "which are proper to be provided for by local legislation" are too unimportant and boring to be worth the effort. Hamilton avoids "tedious and uninteresting" details, but he observes that the "administration of private justice between the citizens of the same State, the supervision of agriculture and of other concerns of a similar nature, . . . can never be desirable cares of a general jurisdiction." He gladly leaves such dull matters in the hands of George Clinton and his ilk. "The regulation of the mere domestic police of a State appears to me to hold out slender allurements to ambition," Hamilton observes. "Commerce, finance, negociation, and war seem to comprehend all the objects, which have charms for minds governed by that passion", he notes, "and all the powers necessary to these objects ought in the first instance to be lodged in the national depository."

Yet, although the allotted sphere of the states will be limited to provincial concerns under the new Constitution, these entities will not for that reason lack influence with the people. In fact, they are far more likely to "encroach on the national authorities," than to be themselves encoached upon, in Hamilton's opinion. "It will be well," he declares, if the states do not interfere with the "legitimate and necessary authority" of the union. The "ordinary administration of criminal and civil justice," which will remain in the hands of the states, will "ensure them so decided an empire over their respective citizens, as to render them at all times a complete counterpoise and not unfrequently dangerous rivals to the power of the Union." Once again, he points out that there is, in general, "an inherent and intrinsic weakness in all Fœderal Constitutions," and he specifically affirms that the proposed new government would have its share of these defects.

Hamilton feels the natural tendency of the people will be to identify with their home states. "Upon the same principle that a man is more attached to his family than to his neighbourhood, to his neighbourhood than to the community at large," he says, "the people of each State would be apt to feel a stronger byass towards their local governments than towards the government of the Union." Only the political elite will adequately appreciate the importance of the nation, Hamilton believes. He asserts that the "operations of the national government, falling less immediately under the observation of the mass of citizens . . . will chiefly be perceived and attended to by speculative men. Relating to more general interests, they will be less apt to come home to the feelings of the people, and, in proportion, less likely to inspire a habitual sense of obligation and an active sentiment of attachment," than will the activities of the states. Hamilton does express a hope for a gradual evolution in the attitudes of the public. He notes that the people's preference for the states could "be destroyed by a better administration" on the part of the national regime. But he admits that the nation is still an abstraction to most Americans.

Hamilton's opinion here is in line with the conventional wisdom of his day. It was then widely assumed that only local governments could be truly popular and that the national view would usually be confined to an aristocracy. The French Revolution was the first clear instance of intense national feeling pervading a whole people, so it is not surprising that Hamilton, in 1787, would consider this prospect unlikely. Today we might simply say that *The Federalist* appeared at an early stage in the formation of the American nation, when national feelings had not yet spread to the commonalty.

Following the next three papers by Madison, Hamilton returns to the fray in *Federalist* No. 21 (129-35). The existing Confederation, he notes, possesses no explicit "sanction to its laws"; nor can one be derived by implication from the Articles without directly contradicting the section reserving to the states all powers "not expressly delegated to the United States in Congress Assembled." Moreover, under the Articles there is no national guarantee of popular government at the state level, as would be established under the Constitution. He observes that a despotism established in one state could threaten the liberties of the rest. Political homogeneity is essential to a national union, in his view. And Hamilton condemns the method "of regulating the contributions of the States to the common treasury by quotas." Indeed, this was an egregious example of the weakness of the Articles. Congress under the Confederation could not levy taxes on its own authority; it could only make requisitions on the states, which they frequently, in practice, ignored. This difficulty can be overcome, Hamilton says, only "by authorizing the national government to raise its own revenue in its own way."

Hamilton begins *Federalist* No. 22 by deploring the Confederation's lack "of a power to regulate commerce" (135-46). He asserts that "there is no object . . . that more strongly demands a Fœderal superintendence." Without a strong central government, economic nationalism was proving to be impossible. Foreign nations, like Britain, were deriving economic benefits from American divisions. "Several States have endeavoured by separate prohibitions, restrictions and exclusions, to influence the conduct of that kingdom," Hamilton observes, "but the want of concert, arising from the want of a general authority, and from clashing, and dissimilar views in the States, has hitherto frustrated every experiment of the kind; and will continue to do so as long as the same obstacles to an uniformity of measures continue to exist." The states were even aiming economic ordinances against each other. "The interfering and unneighbourly regulations of some States contrary to the true spirit of the Union, have in different instances given just cause of umbrage and complaint to others; and it is to be feared that examples of this nature, if not restrained by a national controul, would . . . become not less serious sources of animosity and discord, than injurious impediments to the intercourse between the different parts of the confederacy." If this goes on much longer, inhabitants of different states may come to regard one another as "foreigners and aliens," Hamilton warns.

Publius now attacks the provision in the Articles for "raising armies," which "is merely a power of making requisitions upon the States for quotas of men." This method inevitably involves chronic uncertainty and lack of coordination, as was proven during the War of Independence. "The states near the seat of war, influenced by motives of self preservation, made efforts to furnish their quotas, which even exceeded their abilities, while those at a distance from danger were for the most part as remiss as the others were diligent in their exertions," Hamilton recalls.

He then proceeds to indict the equal vote of the states in the Confederation Congress. "Its operation contradicts that fundamental maxim of republican government, which requires that the sense of the majority should prevail," Hamilton says, meaning the majority of the people. (He does not remind his readers that the Senate under the proposed Constitution would feature the same provision.) And the Articles have compounded this undemocratic aspect by providing that "two thirds of the whole number must consent to the most important resolutions." Indeed, Hamilton notes, in some instances unanimity has been required: "A sixtieth part of the Union, which is about the proportion of Delaware and Rhode-Island, has several times been able to oppose an entire bar to its operations." He condemns this, too, on majoritarian grounds. "To give a minority a negative upon the majority (which is always the case where more than a majority is requisite to a decision) is in its tendency to subject the sense of the greater number to that of the lesser number," he disapprovingly declares. Such democratic purism seems on the surface inconsistent with Hamilton's usual elitist proclivities.

Some of his further comments, however, appear more in character. The requirement for extraordinary majorities, or unanimity, greatly hampers decisive government action, he notes: "Congress from the non-attendance of a few States have been frequently in the situation of a Polish Diet, where a single veto has been sufficient to put a stop to all their movements." In such a situation, "a pertinacious minority" can prevent any forward movement. "Hence tedious delays—continual negotiation and intrigue—contemptible compromises of the public good. And yet in such a system, it is even happy when such compromises can take place: For upon some occasions, things will not admit of accommodation; and then the measures of government must be injuriously suspended or fatally defeated." It is true, Hamilton admits, that in this case "nothing improper will be likely *to be done*; but we forget how much good may be prevented, and how much ill may be produced, by the power of hindering the doing what may be necessary." At critical junctures, he says, "there is commonly a necessity for action. The public business must in some way or other go forward." Better a vigorous majoritarian regime than a weak and divided minorities veto scheme, it appears.

This passage must certainly perplex those critics who perceive *The Federalist* as an argument for a passive government solicitous of minorities. The merely negative aim of a preventing the passage of bad laws is deprecated. And a political system in which special-interest groups are allowed to occupy key points in the legislative process, and block all governmental proposals they do not favor, is here censured in the most unsparing terms. Publius, as we will see, has no objection to at least temporarily frustrating the will of the majority when this is done by officials, such as the president or members of the Senate, who are presumably acting on behalf of the long-term welfare of the whole nation. But he shows no desire to do this for the benefit of purely self-regarding factions. His remarks here on compromise are noteworthy. He obviously does not regard it as a desirable end per se. He admits that it is sometimes necessary in this imperfect world, but he plainly considers it a mild form of corruption, not a positive good.

Hamilton proceeds with some remarks on the comparative merits of republics and monarchies. "One of the weak sides of republics, among their numerous advantages, is that they afford too easy an inlet to foreign corruption," he declares. "In republics, persons elevated from the mass of the community, by the suffrages of their fellow-citizens . . . may find compensations for betraying their trust, which to any but minds animated by superior virtue, may appear to exceed the proportion of interest they have in the common stock, and to over-balance the oligations of duty." He uses this regrettable circumstance as another argument against a political system that allows minorities to hamstring a majority—because under such a system a foreign power may, with "bribes and intrigues," immobilize our government by gaining a few key individuals. On the other hand, "a hereditary monarch, though often disposed to sacrifice his subjects to his ambition, has so great a personal interest in the government, and in the external glory of the nation, that it is not easy for a foreign power to give him an equivalent for what he would sacrifice by treachery to the State." For this reason, Hamilton some-what cynically remarks, "the world has . . . been witness to few examples of this species of royal prostitution, though there have been abundant specimins of every other kind."

Hamilton's comments on monarchies are strikingly reminiscent of Hobbes's *Leviathan*, with this difference: Hobbes asserts a general superi-ority of monarchies over republics, whereas Hamilton limits this superiority to just one aspect, the relative freedom from foreign corruption, and other-wise expresses no great reverence for kings. The passage is vintage Hamilton in its lack of illusion concerning human motivations in general, its stress on the need for unusually virtuous leaders in the republic, its appreciation of the advantages of an untrammeled government—and even in the somewhat gratuitous reference to sexual conduct.

Hamilton observes that the Articles have failed to create a centralized national judicial power. This, he says, has resulted in great confusion. "We often see not only different courts, but the Judges of the same court differing from each other," he points out, adding that "if the particular tribunals are invested with a right of ultimate jurisdiction, besides the contradictions to be expected from difference of opinion, there will be much to fear from the bias of local views and prejudices, and from the interference of local regulations." Hamilton concludes this important essay by noting that "it has not a little contributed to the infirmities of the existing fœderal system, that it never had a ratification by the people," but only by the legislatures of the states. Unfortunately, this fact has encouraged those bodies to claim too much authority. "The fabric of American Empire ought to rest on the solid basis of the consent of the people," he affirms. "The streams of national power ought to flow immediately from that pure original fountain of all legitimate authority."

So much for the existing, inadequate Confederation. Hamilton now turns to an examination of the powers that would be required by a truly competent national regime.

Federalist No. 23 lists the "principal purposes to be answered by Union" and asserts that an unlimited authority over these matters should be granted to the federal government (146-51). The thirteen essays immediately following, all of them by Hamilton, discuss military and financial subjects. The new Constitution would give the federal rulers control over the sword and purse of the nation, and Publius explains the necessity for this.

According to No. 23, the primary ends of the union are national defense, internal peace and security, the regulation of commerce, and the conduct of foreign relations. All these would benefit from national supervision. "Who [is] so likely to make suitable provisions for the public defense," inquires Hamilton, "as that body . . . which, as the center of information, will best understand the extent and urgency of the dangers that threaten—as the representative of the whole will feel itself most deeply interested in the preservation of every part . . . and which, by the extension of its authority throughout the States, can alone establish uniformity and concert in the plans and measures, by which the common safety is to be secured?" The advantages of centralization are negated when national officials are obliged to work through the states, Hamilton points out, noting the experience of the Confederation: "Is not a want of co- operation the infallible consequences of such a system?"

In general, Hamilton takes the somewhat Hobbesean position that "it is both unwise and dangerous to deny the Fœderal Government an unconfined authority, as to all those objects which are entrusted to its management." His reasoning is that "it is impossible to foresee or define the extent and variety of national exigencies, or the correspondent extent & variety of the means which may be necessary to satisfy them. The circumstances that endanger the safety of nations are infinite; and for this reason no constitutional shackles can wisely be imposed on the power to which the care of it is committed." The misuse of national power is to be guarded against by the "internal structure" of the new regime, says Hamilton, not by limiting its scope. An active government is needed for the United States. "The extent of the country, is the strongest argument in favor of an energetic government; for any other can certainly never preserve the Union of so large an empire."

A passage in this essay provides perhaps the first instance of a misquotation of *The Federalist*—a practice that has unfortunately continued through the ages. Publius commences a sentence thus: "If the circumstances of our country are such, as to demand a compound instead of a simple, a confederate instead of a sole government. . . ." About two weeks after *Federalist* No. 23 appeared, Brutus, in his sixth essay, misquoted the passage by substituting "that" for "if," thus putting Publius clearly on record as favoring federalism.[10] This shift from a conditional to a declaratory statement is by no means a trivial alteration. Indeed, it should be noted that nowhere in *The Federalist* does Publius ever categorically say, in so many words, that a federal system is indispensable in America.

The next six papers all deal with military matters, mainly the question of a standing army. This was an extremely ticklish issue for Publius. In No. 8 and No. 16 he characterizes permanent military forces as "engines of despotism" and suggests that the danger from that source constitutes a strong argument for American unity (45-46, 101-2). Yet the Anti-Federalists were attacking the proposed Constitution on exactly this point. "Will this consolidated republic," Cato warned, "beget such confidence and compliance, among the citizens of these states, as to do without the aid of a standing army? I deny that it will."[11] Indeed, the new charter would grant Congress the power to raise and support troops on its own authority, not just to make military requisitions on the states, as provided by the Articles of Confederation. Hamilton thus needed to argue for a national power to create a standing army, although he admits such institutions may be fatal to the popular liberties.

Hamilton accomplishes his challenging task with great dexterity. He has already observed in No. 8 that the standing army of a united America would be much smaller, and hence more controllable, than the multiple armies of disunited states (47-49). He now notes that, given the realities of international and domestic politics, standing armies are unavoidable evils. We should not wantonly run the risk of a military tyranny, to be sure, but neither should we absolutely debar our democratically chosen rulers from the use of coercion, when appropriate. The protections contained in the Constitution should be adequate safeguards. Publius thus smoothly avoids possible contradiction, illuminating several aspects of his overall argument in the process.

In *Federalist* No. 24, Hamilton first notices the objection to the Constitution "that proper provision has not been made against the existence of standing armies in time of peace" (152-57). He remarks that the proposed charter in fact calls for legislative control of the military purse strings, and that neither the constitutions of most of the states, nor the Articles of Confederation, forbid standing armies in peacetime. He warns that "though a wide ocean separates the United States from Europe; yet there are various considerations that warn us against an excess of confidence or security," among these being "improvements in the art of navigation" which render "distant nations in a great measure neighbours." Total prohibition of a military force in time of peace would therefore be inadvisable. Our isolation is real, but only relative, it seems.

Federalist No. 25 explains why America's defense should not "be provided for by the State Governments" (158-63). A lack of coordination would inevitably result, says Hamilton, and the existence of state military forces would be dangerous to the union. He again affirms the inherent tendency of a federal system to break up. "Reasons have been already given," he notes, "to induce a supposition that the State Governments will too naturally be prone to a rivalship with that of the Union, the foundation of which will be the love of power; and that in any contest between the fœderal head and one of its members, the people will be most apt to unite with their local government." He adds that state armies will tend to engender state rebellions: "it would afford too strong a temptation and too great facility to them to make enterprises upon, and finally to subvert the constitutional authority of the Union."

He is opposed to a flat ban on a national army in peacetime. Such an unrealistic provision would certainly be violated whenever peril appeared imminent. Hamilton observes "how unequal parchment provisions are to a struggle with public necessity" and cautions against placing undue restraints on our chiefs: "Wise politicians will be cautious about fettering the government with restrictions, that cannot be observed; because they know that every breach of the fundamental laws, though dictated by necessity, impairs that sacred reverence, which ought to be maintained in the breasts of rulers toward the constitution of a country, and forms a precedent for other breaches, where the same plea of necessity does not exist at all, or is less urgent and palpable."

Hamilton begins *Federalist* No. 26 with an unreserved plea for an active central regime. Popular freedom, he says, is not by itself sufficient to secure the happiness of the nation. There is a "happy mean, which marks the salutary boundary between power and privilege, and combines the energy of government with the security of private rights" (164-71). In particular, "the idea of restraining the legislative authority, in the means of providing the national defense, is one of those refinements, which owe their origin to a zeal for liberty more ardent than enlightened" He feels, however, that "the citizens of America have too much discernment to be argued into anarchy," and he declares himself to be "much mistaken if experience has not wrought a deep and solemn conviction in the public mind, that greater energy of government is essential to the welfare and prosperity of the community." Again, Publius is no libertarian.

The provision in the proposed Constitution limiting military appropriations by Congress to a period of two years should comprise an ample safeguard against the dangers stemming from a standing army, Hamilton contends. "As the spirit of party, in different degrees, must be expected to infect all political bodies, there will be no doubt persons in the national Legislature willing enough to arraign the measures and criminate the views of the majority." Thus, should this "majority . . . be really disposed to exceed the proper limits the community will be warned of the danger." Moreover, Hamilton notes, "the state Legislature, who will always be not only vigilant but suspicious and jealous guardians of the rights of the citizens, against incroachents from the Fœderal government, will constantly have their attention awake to the conduct of the national rulers and will be ready enough, if any thing improper appears, to sound the alarm to the people and not only to be the voice but if necessary the arm of their discontent." Therefore, it would be safe for the United States to maintain a military force.

The above is a remarkable passage for two reasons. First, it is about the only place in *The Federalist* where any merit whatsoever is ascribed to political parties. Second, it identifies the one truly important function of the states: if the national rulers attempt to set up a military dictatorship, the states can express the people's opposition and, if required, lead the resistance. Besides their petty local administrative responsibilities, this seems to be all the states have been preserved for—to be potential centers for a popular uprising. Hamilton's praise of political parties and the states in this paper has a negative tinge. He seems to imply that although these institutions will be useful for fighting against national tyranny, they are usually detrimental to good government because they are inherently divisive. Parties and states are apparently serviceable only on the eve of a looming military coup, when the usual methods of unified national leadership are no longer appropriate.

Hamilton does not, however, anticipate that there will be many occasions on which the states will need to intervene in national politics. He finds the danger of a central government plot to use a standing army against the popular liberties quite remote. This, he notes, would require a secret conspiracy between the executive and the legislature, a most unlikely prospect in itself and impossible to sustain over a long period of time. "Is it probable," he asks, that such an intrigue "would be persevered in and transmitted along, through all the successive variations in the representative body, which biennial elections would naturally produce in both bodies? Is it presumable, that every man, the instant he took his seat in the national senate, or house of representatives, would commence a traitor to his constituents and to his country?" Hamilton dismisses the possibility. "If such presumptions can fairly be made, there ought to be at once an end of all delegated authority. The people should resolve to recall all the powers they have heretofore parted with out of their own hands; and to divide themselves into as many states as there are counties, in order that they may be able to manage their own concerns in person." The representative system will be protection enough for our freedoms, he thinks.

In *Federalist* No. 27, Hamilton examines the Anti-Federalist claim that the new national government would be too remote from the people to possess their sympathy, and would therefore need a large standing army to enforce its laws (171-75). His view is that the people's "confidence in and obedience to a government, will commonly be proportioned to the goodness or badness of its administration," and he reminds his readers that "various reasons have been suggested in the course of these papers, to induce a probability that the General Government will be better administered than the particular governments." He mentions in this regard "the extension of the spheres of election," which "will present a greater option, or latitude of choice, to the people"; and also the national regime's relative freedom from the "spirit of faction" and from the "occasional ill humors or temporary prejudices and propensities, which in smaller societies frequently contaminate the public councils." All in all, Hamilton maintains, "these circumstances promise greater knowledge and more extensive information in the national councils," and this circumstance should elicit the unforced obedience of the population.

Moreover, says Hamilton, the federal government would gradually expand the scope of its activities and would thereby become more acceptable to the people: "the more the operations of the national authority are intermingled in the ordinary exercise of government; the more the citizens are accustomed to meet with it in the common occurrences of their political life; the more it is familiarized to their sight and to their feelings; the further it enters into those objects which touch the most sensible cords, and put in motion the most active springs of the human heart; the greater will be the probability that it will conciliate the respect and attachment of the community." The current preference of the people for their states, noted in No. 17, thus is not a permanent condition: "The authority of the Union, and the affections of the citizens towards it; will be strengthened rather than weakened by its extension to what are called matters of internal concern; and will have less occasion to recur to force in proportion to the familiarity and comprehensiveness of its agency." Those critics who maintain the "states' rights" interpretation of *The Federalist* must find this passage difficult to explain. Publius here clearly envisions the future expansion of the national government and the widening of its responsibilities to include some "internal" items presumably previously assigned to the states.

Hamilton starts off *Federalist* No. 28 with a forthright statement of political realism: "That there may happen cases, in which the national government may be necessitated to resort to force, cannot be denied" (176-80). Unfortunately, violent upheavals "are . . . maladies as inseparable from the body politic, as tumors and eruptions from the natural body." Experience shows "that the idea of governing at all times by the simple force of law (which we have been told is the only admissible principle of republican government) has no place but in the reveries of those political doctors, whose sagacity disdains the admonitions of experimental instruction." This passage exhibits Publius's admirable willingness to utter unpalatable truths. The Anti-Federalists had charged that a national standing army would be used against the people, and Hamilton replies that, yes, this might sometimes be necessary. Unlawful insurrections might break out on occasion, and they must be put down. However, he has in mind here local revolts, comprising at most "a whole State, or a principal part of it." He does not believe that the national forces would be employed to oppress the whole community.

The fact that the proposed federal government would be a popular one would, of itself, eliminate all danger on that score, says Hamilton: "Independent of all other reasonings upon the subject, it is a full answer to those who require a more peremptory provision against military establishments in time of peace, that the whole power of the proposed government is to be in the hands of the representatives of the people. This is the essential, and after all the only efficacious security for the rights and privileges of the people which is attainable in civil society." In the unlikely event that representation fails, he admits, the people have "no resource left but in the exertion of that original right of self-defense, which is paramount to all positive forms of government." He adds, however, that the popular liberties can be defended "against the usurpations of the national rulers . . . with infinitely better prospect of success, than against those of the rulers of an individual State," and he proceeds to explain why.

The small size and unitary form of the states, says Hamilton, would render the resistance of the people difficult should a state government attempt to violate the rights of their constituents. The usurpers would be "cloathed with the forms of legal authority" and would be able to easily find and defeat their opponents. On a nationwide scale, however, a necessary popular uprising would be more feasible, due largely to the existence of the states. "Power being almost always the rival of power; the General Government will at all times stand ready to check the usurpations of the state governments; and these will have the same disposition towards the General Government," Hamilton notes, and he adds that "the people, by throwing themselves into either scale, will infallibly make it preponderate." The legislatures of the states, being "select bodies of men," will "discover the danger at a distance," and because they will possess "all the organs of civil power and the confidence of the people, they can at once adopt a regular plan of opposition, in which they can combine all the resources of the community." Thus the states can stand against the power of the national regime, if it comes to that. "In a confederacy," says Hamilton, "the people" are truly "masters of their own fate."

This passage comprises the fullest discussion in *The Federalist* of what Publius appears to see as the one truly important role of the states under the new Constitution: to watch the national rulers for indications of incipient military dictatorship, to organize the opposition, and even to rise in revolt if that course of action seems indicated. Because this comprises the only real justification for allowing the states to retain a portion of their sovereignty within a federal system, it will be well to be clear about what is actually being asserted here. Particularly, we should note that Publius does *not* want the states to defend minority interests against a national majority, nor does he wish those entities to be ordinarily involved with the concerns of the United States as a whole.

Hamilton mentions two kinds of state rebellions in this essay. He deprecates the revolt of local factions against the greater part of the nation, and he expects that the standing army would put these down. He is, however, willing to sanction uprisings by the whole body of the people, acting through the state governments, against the tyranny of a ruling faction on the federal level. Thus he envisions the states as instruments of the American majority, albeit on special occasions. Publius never suggests that it is good for the states to uphold particularistic values against the bulk of the nation; indeed, he consistently disapproves such actions. Moreover, the role of the provinces in preserving our liberties is entirely extraconstitutional.[12] The states would safeguard our freedoms by organizing a political opposition and by helping the people exercise their natural right of revolution, not through any legal authority to interfere with the operations of the central government. The fundamental purpose of the Constitution is precisely to preclude, as far as possible, any state intermeddling in national affairs. State intrusion is, in Publius's view, a strong medicine, akin to a poison, to be taken only under unusual circumstances.

Also, Hamilton puts equal stress here on the ability of the national rulers to "check the usurpations of the state governments." The federal system is useful, he says, not just because the states are available to intervene on the national scene, but also because the central regime may intervene within a state to combat despotism there. In either case, he wants the general will of the American people to prevail.

Thus Hamilton's discussion of state revolts in this essay is reconcilable with the nationalistic thrust of his views as a whole. Yet, although there is no flat contradiction, this endorsement of provincial uprisings does seem rather out of character. Publius ordinarily asserts that the fear of a federal despotism is utterly unfounded and that the states are fatally prone to be mistaken when judging of national affairs. It appears incongruous for him to advocate state insurrections of any kind, especially on the basis of what he sees as an unreal problem. Publius probably has an ulterior motive here. When he notes that "the state governments will in all possible contingencies afford complete security against invasions of the public liberty by the national authority," he appears primarily interested in calming the fears of his readers. Had he not been attempting to demonstrate the Constitution's safety, Publius likely would have had little good to say concerning state rebellions. It is not, of course, necessary to convict Hamilton of an actual untruth at this point; he undoubtedly sincerely believed that the states and people together would easily overthrow a national tyrant, in the remote event that one should arise.

Whether Hamilton feels that the states are actually necessary for the prevention of national despotism is, however, most doubtful. The representative system and the sheer size of the country should be enough to defeat any such schemes, he declares. He emphatically asserts that popularly elected federal officials are very unlikely to betray their constituents. Furthermore, "the great extent of the country is a further security," Hamilton contends. "The natural strength of the people in a large community, in proportion to the artificial strength of the government, is greater than in a small; and of course more competent to a struggle with the attempts of the government to establish a tyranny." The entire nation could hardly be conquered at one fell swoop: "The advantages obtained in one place must be abandoned to subdue the opposition in others; and the moment the part which had been reduced to submission was left to itself its efforts would be renewed and its resistance revived." Epstein points out that Hamilton here regards the extent of the country per se as a factor militating against tyranny.[13] The states would reinforce this safeguard, but it would evidently exist even in their absence.

The problematical role of the states in combating a national despotism seems inadequate to justify the federal features of the proposed regime. The powers that would enable the states to stand against purely hypothetical, and improbable, national tyrants would also enable them to frustrate legitimate and necessary national policies. Indeed, the possession of a degree of sovereign power would actually stimulate the states to oppose the nation, Hamilton has said. The drawbacks of federalism appear to be certain and serious, whereas the advantages are doubtful. On the basis of *The Federalist* alone, it is hard to understand why the Founders did not simply establish a unitary national government.

The next essay, No. 29, was originally published as the thirty-fifth in the series, but was moved to its present position in the first bound edition, presumably because its subject, the federal supervision of the militia, seemed to fit with the discussion of military matters. Hamilton notes that "uniformity in the organization and discipline of the militia would be attended with the most beneficial effects," and he adds that "this desirable uniformity can only be accomplished by confiding the regulation of the militia to the direction of the national authority" (181-87). Cato had expressed concern that the militia, in federal hands, might prove dangerous to the public liberties.[14] Hamilton ridicules the notion. "What shadow of danger can there be," he rhetorically asks, "from men who are daily mingling with the rest of their countrymen; and who participate with them in the same feelings, sentiments, habits and interests?"

With this essay, Publius concludes his examination of the need for a national military capability. He now turns his attention to the federal finances—by no means the least reason, in his view, for strengthening the American union.

The Confederation's fiscal system was one of the most clearly inadequate features of the existing regime. The method of state requisitions had proven unreliable, and important national purposes remained without adequate funding—in particular, no start had been made on repayment of the public debt occasioned by the Revolutionary War. Because repayment was essential to establish the credit of the new nation, Publius could derive much support for his case from this topic. At the same time, the subject was one of some delicacy. No one enjoys being taxed, and Publius in effect was arguing that the Constitution should be adopted because it would enable the national authorities to reach deeper into the pockets of the American people. Hamilton understandably felt compelled to justify this aspect of his argument at some length. His task was not an easy one; clarion calls for increased public revenues have not usually been popular with taxpayers, as Walter Mondale found out in the 1984 presidential campaign. Publius does not evade the issue, however. He frankly acknowledges the necessity for an unlimited power of taxation, to be vested in the federal government.

In *Federalist* No. 30, Hamilton states his position in blunt terms: "Money is with propriety considered as the vital principle of the body politic" (187-93). It follows, he adds, that "a complete power . . . to procure a regular and adequate supply of it, as far as the resources of the community will permit, may be regarded as an indispensable ingredient in every constitution." A government without adequate funds, says Hamilton, is a pitiful sight. "How can it ever possess either energy or stability, dignity or credit, confidence at home or respectability abroad? How can its administration be any thing else than a succession of expedients temporizing, impotent, disgraceful? . . . How can it undertake . . . any liberal or enlarged plans of public good?" Some anti-Federalists had suggested limiting the national government only to "external taxation"—that is, "duties on imported articles"—leaving everything else to the states. Hamilton rejects such a limitation because "we could not reasonably flatter ourselves, that this resource alone . . . would even suffice for" the "present necessities" of the nation, while its "future necessities admit not of calculation or limitation."

As long as the requisition system remained in force, the credit of the United States government would not be good: "to depend upon a government, that must itself depend upon thirteen other governments for the means of fulfilling its contracts . . . would require a degree of credulity, not often to be met with in the pecuniary transactions of mankind, and little reconcilable with the usual sharp-sightedness of avarice," Hamilton realistically notes. Especially in time of war, the lack of ability to borrow could have catastrophic results. "Reflections of this kind, may have trifling weight with men, who hope to see realized in America, the halcyon scenes of the poetic or fabulous age; but to those who believe we are likely to experience a common portion of the vicissitudes and calamities, which have fallen to the lot of other nations, they must appear entitled to serious attention," Hamilton concludes.

Publius obviously possesses an expansive view of the taxing and spending capabilities contained in the proposed Constitution. He does not here specify the "liberal or enlarged plans of public good" on which he desires to spend the national revenues, but he clearly does not take an overly passive approach to government.

Federalist No. 31 was the first essay of the new year, appearing on January 1, 1788. Hamilton appropriately begins with a discussion of the initial premises, or "primary truths," of politics (193-98). He affirms that although "it cannot be pretended that the principles of moral and political knowledge have in general the same degree of certainty with those of the mathematics; yet they have much better claims in this respect, than to judge from the conduct of men. . . . The obscurity is much oftener in the passions and prejudices of the reasoner than in the subject." Among the undeniable postulates of politics, says Hamilton, is the precept that "a government ought to contain in itself every power requisite to the . . . complete execution of the trusts for which it is responsible; free from every other control, but a regard to the public good and to the sense of the people." It follows from this that "as revenue is the essential engine by which the means of answering the national exigencies must be procured, the power of procuring that article in its full extent, must necessarily be comprehended in that of providing for those exigencies." The case for an indefinite national revenue was literally axiomatic, from Hamilton's point of view.

He now turns his attention to the argument maintained by Brutus in his fourth and fifth letters,[15] that under the Constitution "the national government might at any time abolish the taxes imposed for State objects, upon the pretence of an interference with its own." Hamilton dismisses this possibility: the new national authority has been carefully designed to guard against "the danger of usurpation." Indeed, he says, "a disposition in the State governments to encroach upon the rights of the Union, is quite as probable, as a disposition in the Union to encroach upon the rights of the State Governments." In the case of a conflict between the two levels, the states would be likely to prevail, he thinks. "As in republics, strength is always on the side of the people; and as there are weighty reasons to induce a belief, that the State governments will commonly possess most influence over them," Hamilton notes, "the natural conclusion is, that such contests will be most apt to end to the disadvantage of the Union." Thus he once again acknowledges the disruptive power of the states under the federal system he is advocating. He hopes, however, that the people "will always take care to preserve the constitutional equilibrium."

The next two essays, No. 32 and No. 33, were originally printed as one number in the newspapers and were only separated at the time of the first bound edition. In No. 32, Hamilton plainly affirms that the new regime will not be a unified nation-state. "An entire consolidation of the States into one complete national sovereignty would imply an intire subordination of the parts; and whatever powers might remain in them would be altogether dependent on the general will," he says (199-203). "But as the plan of the Convention aims at only a partial Union or consolidation, the State Governments would clearly retain all the rights of sovereignty which they before had and which were not by that act exclusively delegated to the United States." Thus, he adds, under the Constitution the states would in all events retain the power of taxation, which could in no legal or proper manner be abridged by the federal government.

In Hamilton's opinion, nation and states possess a "concurrent jurisdiction" with respect to taxation, resulting from "the division of sovereign power." Other than with regard to duties on imports, the taxing authority of the states would be no less than that of the federal government. Hamilton recognizes that problems may arise as a consequence: "It is indeed possible that a tax might be laid on a particular article by a state which might render it inexpedient that a further tax should be laid on the same article by the Union; but it would not imply a constitutional inability to impose a further tax." The two levels of government might sometimes act in mutually frustrating ways: "The particular policy of the national and of the State systems of finance might now and then not exactly coincide, and might require reciprocal forbearance." Publius again admits an inconvenience of federalism.

Yet he does not see the protection of the revenue base of the states as particularly important. "I am of opinion that there would be no real danger of the consequences, which seem to be apprehended to the State governments, from a power in the Union to controul them in the levies of money," Hamilton maintains, "because I am persuaded that the sense of the people, the extreme hazard of provoking the resentments of the State Governments, and a conviction of the utility and necessity of local administrations, for local purposes, would be a complete barrier against the oppressive use of such a power." Hamilton obviously thinks there is a purpose for subnational political units, but he does not see the provinces as, in any real sense, threatened by the expansion of national authority. The central rulers would not want to undermine the states and could be trusted with absolute control over their finances, he feels. This is hardly an argument for federalism.

Federalist No. 33 considers two provisions of the new Constitution: the "necessary and proper" clause (Art. 1, Sec. 8, Para. 18) and the "supreme law of the land" clause (Art. 6, Para. 2). These passages, says Publius, "are only declaratory of a truth, which would have resulted by necessary and unavoidable implication from the very act of constituting a Federal Government, and vesting it with certain specified powers" (203-8). They have been inserted only "for greater caution, and to guard against all cavilling refinements in those who might hereafter feel a disposition to curtail and evade the legitimate authorities of the Union." Hamilton asserts "that the danger which most threatens our political welfare, is, that the State Governments will finally sap the foundations of the Union." These clauses will be useful protections against that peril. But who will determine what is "necessary and proper" for the federal government to do? "The national government, like any other, must judge in the first instance of the proper exercise of its powers; and its constituents in the last." Should the central authority attempt to "make a tyrannical use of its powers," declares Hamilton, "the people . . . must appeal to the standard they have formed, and take such measures to redress the injury done to the constitution, as the exigency may suggest and prudence justify."

Thus Hamilton again suggests popular rebellion as the proper response to unconstitutional actions by the national government. Leonard Levy, who maintains that the Founders did not believe in judicial review, makes much of Hamilton's failure to mention the authority of the courts in this passage. However, Levy misquotes Publius. The scholar reports Hamilton as saying that "Congress in the first instance and the people in the last would judge" issues of constitutionality.[16] In reality, however, *The Federalist* says that "the national government," not Congress, will "judge in the first instance." The Supreme Court, of course, comprises a branch of the national government and could well be the body that is intended to do the judging. Nothing Hamilton says here really precludes that possibility, and we know from other essays that he wholeheartedly endorses judicial review.

In conclusion, Hamilton repeats his observation of the previous essay, that concurrent jurisdiction, although it is constitutionally unassailable, might nevertheless be unwieldy in practice. "As far as an improper accumulation of taxes on the same object might tend to render the collection difficult or precarious, this would be a mutual inconvenience . . . arising . . . from an injudicious exercise of power by one or the other," he notes. He somewhat optimistically adds, however, that "it is to be hoped and presumed . . . that mutual interest would dictate a concert in this respect which would avoid any material inconvenience."

Federalist No. 34 commences with a reiteration of the last point: the "co-equal authority" of nation and states "in the article of revenue" clearly obtains, although it could be disadvantageous. "To argue upon abstract principles, that this co-ordinate authority cannot exist, is to set up supposition and theory, against fact and reality," notes Hamilton (209-15). "However proper such reasonings might be, to show that a thing *ought not to exist*, they are wholly to be rejected, when they are made use of to prove that it does not exist, contrary to the evidence of the fact itself." He goes on to say, however, that concurrent jurisdiction over taxation would probably not be too troublesome because the states should require only very scant revenues: "in practice, there is little reason to apprehend any inconvenience; because, in a short course of time, the wants of the States will naturally reduce themselves within a very narrow compass." It is the federal government that would require a large income, Hamilton points out. "The expenses arising from those institutions, which are relative to the mere domestic police of a State . . . are insignificant, in comparison with those which relate to the National Defense," he declares.

Hamilton's realism is prominently exhibited here. At one point, he refers to the "novel and absurd experiment, in politics, of tying up the hands of Government from offensive war, founded upon reasons of state." In another place, he notes the ubiquity of conflict in human affairs: "To judge from the history of mankind, we shall be compelled to conclude, that the fiery and destructive passions of war, reign in the human breast, with much more powerful sway, than the mild and beneficent sentiments of peace; and, that to model our political systems upon speculations of lasting tranquility, is to calculate on the weaker springs of the human character." Thus the national government would require an ample revenue to meet our military needs.

In No. 35, Hamilton criticizes the Anti-Federalist suggestion that revenue for the national government be limited to import duties. He first notes that such a restriction would weigh heavily on New York, which is "an importing State" (215-22). He then observes that some people have "alleged" that duties on imports "will tend to discourage an extravagant consumption, to produce a favorable balance of trade, and to promote domestic manufactures." However, if such imposts were made the central government's sole revenue resource, they would be carried to a "pernicious" extreme, he says. "Exorbitant duties on imported articles would beget a general spirit of smuggling; which is always prejudicial to the fair trader, and eventually to the revenue itself: They tend to render other classes of the community tributary in an improper degree to the manufacturing classes to whom they give a premature monopoly of the markets: They sometimes force industry out of its more natural channels into others in which it flows with less advantage." Hamilton showed few of these qualms two years later, in his great *Report on Manufactures*, in which he proposed high protective tariffs.

Hamilton now examines an oft-heard objection to the new national regime as a taxing body: "that the house of representatives is not sufficiently numerous for the reception of all the different classes of citizens; in order to combine the interests and feelings of every part of the community, and to produce a due sympathy between the representative body and its constituents." Hamilton contends that a representation of all classes is neither possible nor particularly desirable. He makes reference to the mercantile interest in words that must be quoted at length, because they exemplify his thinking with regard to the wise ruling elite.

Mechanics and manufacturers will always be inclined . . . to give their votes to merchants in preference to persons of their own professions or trades. Those discerning citizens are well aware that the mechanic and manufacturing arts furnish the materials of mercantile enterprise and industry. . . . They know that the merchant is their natural patron and friend; and they are aware that however great the confidence they may justly feel in their own good sense, their interests can be more effectually promoted by the merchant than by themselves. They are sensible that their habits in life have not been such as to give them those acquired endowments, without which in a deliberative assembly the greatest natural abilities are for the most part useless; and that the influence and weight and superior acquirements of the merchants render them more equal to a contest with any spirit which might happen to infuse itself into the public councils unfriendly to the manufacturing and trading interests. . . . We must therefore consider merchants as the natural representatives of all these classes of the community.

By the term *manufacturers* Hamilton means, of course, artisans and crafts-men, not industrial barons—these last did not exist in his day. Hamilton's expectation that the people would be inclined to elect able leaders to public office is surely a source of his faith in strong government.

Hamilton also considers the "landed interest," which he finds "to be perfectly united from the wealthiest landlord to the poorest tenant." He feels this is so because "no tax can be laid on land which will not affect the proprietor of millions of acres as well as the proprietor of a single acre. Every land-holder will therefore have a common interest to keep the taxes on land as low as possible; and common interest may always be reckoned upon as the surest bond of sympathy." Other than merchants and landowners, probably only lawyers would obtain public office, and they would, in effect, mediate between the other two interest groups. Hamilton asks: "Will not the man of the learned profession, who will feel a neutrality to the rivalships between the different branches of industry, be likely to prove an impartial arbiter between them, ready to promote either, so far as it shall appear to him conducive to the general interests of society?" This conception of attorneys as naturally disinterested statesmen may sound peculiar to modern ears, but it is obvious that Hamilton has essentially the same view of the political decision-making process as expressed by Jay in No. 2—wise leaders confer-ring together on the advancement of the common good.

The elite would give proper weight to popular opinion, mainly because they would be chosen by a democratic election. "Is it not natural," observes Hamilton, "that a man who is a candidate for the favour of the people and who is dependent on the suffrages of his fellow-citizens for the continuance of public honors should take care to inform himself of their dispositions and inclinations and should be willing to allow them their proper degree of influence upon his conduct? This dependence, and the necessity of being bound himself and his posterity by the laws to which he gives his assent are the true, and they are the strong chords of sympathy between the representatives and the constituent." The national elite is chosen directly or indirectly by the populace and has the same interest. It should, therefore, act on their behalf.

In *Federalist* No. 36, Hamilton examines the Anti-Federalist claim that "a power of internal taxation in the national Legislature could never be exercised with advantage, . . . from the want of a sufficient knowledge of local circumstances" (222-30). He finds this argument "entirely destitute of foundation." The national rulers would be able to provide each other with information about their respective sections. Moreover, mere minutiae are not necessarily relevant to lawmaking. There is no real need for the national rulers to possess "a minute topographical acquaintance with all the mountains, rivers, streams, high-ways and bye-paths in each State." Should the federal government require an actual valuation of "real property, . . . houses and lands," for purposes of direct taxation, "the execution of the business, which alone requires the knowledge of local details, must be devolved upon discreet persons in the character of commissioners or assessors, elected by the people or appointed by the government for the purpose," Hamilton observes. "And what is there in all this, that cannot as well be performed by the national Legislature as by a State Legislature? The attention of either can only reach to general principles; local details, as already observed, must be referred to those who are to execute the plan."

Thus, through appointment of locally sensitive administrators, the national regime could exercise governmental authority over the entire country. In spite of what Hamilton says of the usefulness of the states for local purposes, he does not seem to think they are actually necessary even on that account. Once again, he envisions a fairly limited role for these entities: "A small land tax will answer the purposes of the States," he asserts.

An advantage to taxation by the national government, Hamilton says, is that it would tend to fall primarily on the affluent: "as far as there may be any real difficulty in the exercise of the power of internal taxation, it will impose a disposition . . . in the national administration to go as far as may be practicable in making the luxury of the rich tributary to the public treasury, in order to diminish the necessity of those impositions, which might create dissatisfaction in the poorer and most numerous classes of the society," he observes. "Happy it is when the interest which the government has in the preservation of its own power, coincides with a proper distribution of the public burthens, and tends to guard the least wealthy part of the community from oppression!" This passage is noteworthy both as a prediction of relatively progressive taxing policies by the federal government and as an endorsement of such a tendency—although it must be admitted that Hamilton only proposes to tax the "luxuries" of the rich, not their income or their working capital. Concerning poll taxes, which fall disproportionately on the poor, he expresses his "disapprobation of them," but he does not think the central government should be forbidden their use, because they might come in handy under some circumstances.

With the conclusion of No. 36, Hamilton had produced some 55,000 words in just over ten weeks. He now passed the pen to Madison for a time. He surely was entitled to a rest, but in fact he suspended his literary labors only to throw himself with greater intensity into other aspects of the struggle. What is the overall impression left by these essays of Hamilton's?

Hamilton's nationalistic orientation is evident. Like Jay, he believes the American people comprise a natural foundation for a government because of their "affinity of langage, and manners"; their geographical situation; and their common interests relative to the rest of the world. It may be that Hamilton's nationalism shows somewhat less emotional content than Jay's, but on the whole their attitudes seem identical. They both want to see the country ruled from the center by a sagacious elite. Indeed, the advantages of centralization are Hamilton's main theme and his constant refrain. Whatever his topic—economic policy, military preparedness, the public revenues, or any other important subject—his sovereign remedy is coordinated management and control on the national level. He calls not only for a centralized government but for a strong and active one as well, equipped with an unlimited power of taxation and a permanent military force. The system of representative democracy should ensure that the new regime would truly promote the interests and desires of the people as a whole, he feels.

These essays constitute an admirable discussion of the various considerations involved in the foundation of a modern nation-state. The mutually reinforcing relationship between national affinities and political authority is quite clearly understood. Like Jay, Hamilton sees that the American nation is not really a preordained unity. Many factors tend to tie us together, but there are also divisions within our social body, such as those between North and South, or between commerce and agriculture. Depending on the political arrangements we adopt, either the unifying or the disintegrative forces may prevail. A potent central government would bolster our commonalities and harmonize our various interests, whereas separate confederacies would exacerbate our differences and lead us into internecine conflicts. The people currently, perhaps inevitably, identify more with their states than with the nation, but after a powerful federal regime has been operating for a few years their loyalty may shift, Hamilton believes. Publius well comprehends the dilemmas and techniques of nation building.

Hamilton's attitude towards the states is extremely hostile. He regards them as useless for all but the most petty governmental purposes, and dangerous as well. State leaders would, he thinks, necessarily tend to take a narrow-minded and shortsighted view of national affairs. They would attempt to second-guess the judgements of the central government and would thereby sabotage a coordinated policy. Thus the state governments should be totally removed from any agency in the handling of significant questions affecting the whole country. Oddly enough, the new federal Constitution would not wholly solve this problem—for the states, as Hamilton admits, have been allowed to retain more than enough authority to be troublesome to the national rulers and perilous to the union. The nationalistic pronouncements of Publius are not entirely congruent with the plan being recommended. It is true that the provinces would be deprived of the commanding position they had held under the Articles of Confederation. But they would retain their corporate identity, the state legislatures would select the U.S. senators, and the local administrative functions of the states would enable them to compete for the allegiance of the people. And, as Publius notes, the states would attempt to interfere in national matters whether they were constitutionally entitled to do so or not. Why have they been suffered to remain so powerful?

Hamilton's only real justification for the preservation of the states as quasi-sovereign entities is that they could be handy for purposes of rebellion, should the national government threaten to become tyrannical or to intrude on the states' rightful sphere. Yet this consideration appears insufficient to warrant retention of the divisive federal system, for he repeatedly stresses that there is no real danger of national despotism. The system of popular election should by itself exclude all danger of tyranny, he contends, and the central authorities would never desire to intermeddle in petty local affairs. The size of the country alone would be an important barrier to plans of usurpation. The advantages of state sovereignty appear to be outweighed by its disadvantages. Publius's case for federalism is actually rather weak.

6

Madison Argues
for a National Regime

Many commentators who concede that Hamilton exhibits no real fondness for federalism in *The Federalist* have maintained that the essays of Madison express a noticeably different point of view. Thus Alpheus T. Mason characterizes Hamilton as a thoroughgoing nationalist who "saw the great size of the country, torn by warring factions, as necessitating a consolidated system with 'unconfined,' 'coercive power,' poised at one center." But Madison, in Mason's view, was a pluralist who "envisaged a counterpoised, confederate system, a 'compound republic' with the power of the people divided between the states and the nation and national power 'sub-divided among distinct and separate departments.' "[1] Certainly the future careers of these two statesmen suggests the possibility of such a variance. Hamilton remained a wholehearted consolidationist until the day he died. Madison, however, became the principal congressional antagonist of his former colleague's nationalizing financial program and joined with Jefferson to lead the states' rights–oriented, agrarian, Republican opposition that eventually toppled the Hamiltonians from power. It is tempting to seek a preview of this conflict within the persona of Publius.

Nor would such a search be wholly unrewarded. As already noted, the two are plainly distinguishable in their manner of argumentation. Hamilton is more forceful and direct and is loath to grant any merit whatsoever to the opposition's case. Madison is more discursive and philosophical and is more ready to acknowledge exceptions and qualifications. It is possible to guess from their respective offerings that Hamilton held most vehemently to the original faith, whereas Madison was the more likely of the pair to be led astray by other considerations. Yet, all in all, charges of a "split personality" appear quite exaggerated. There is no significant contradiction between the two principal Publii, except on the definition of federalism, involving terminology rather than substance. Hamilton and Madison are agreed on the main question before them—the need for a greatly strengthened national regime. They may have diverged on some issues, but they are careful not to let their differences show in *The Federalist*.

Embedded among and immediately following the early essays of Hamilton, so emphatic on the virtues of centralization, are fifteen of Madison's, dealing with the same general topics. If there really is a major contrast between the two principal Publii on this score, it certainly should be apparent in the comparison of these papers by Madison with the twenty-six by Hamilton that were reviewed in the last chapter. In fact, notwithstanding their later disagreements, Hamilton and Madison take fundamentally the same position on the need for a strong national government and on the inadequacies of the states.

Madison's initial contribution, *Federalist* No. 10, was published on Thursday, November 22, 1787, in *The Daily Advertiser.* Undoubtedly, this is the greatest single piece of political analysis ever done by an American. It is not too much to say that for most political scientists No. 10 is *The Federalist*—the main, if not the only, point of the entire work. And the importance that subsequent generations have ascribed to this essay is matched by the obvious care that went into its preparation. Unlike almost every other one of the *Federalist* papers, No. 10 was not hurriedly prepared on the spur of the moment, but had been meticulously crafted over the better part of a year. The central argument of No. 10 is seen in Madison's unpublished memorandum "Vices of the Political System of the United States," dated April 1787; and it also appears in a speech he gave to the Philadelphia Convention two months later on June 6, and in a letter to Jefferson of October 24.[2] By the time No. 10 appeared, he had honed his wording to perfection.

Thus this essay is one that cannot be slighted in any analysis of *The Federalist*. It has a special significance for the present study because it has frequently been interpreted as embodying notions very far from nationalism. Beard was the first critic to pay close attention to this essay, and most later interpretations have tended to follow his lead. William O. Winter enunciates the modern version of this reading when he declares that in No. 10 "Madison gave a clear statement of his *theory of complexity:* that a government functions best when it includes a large and diverse population which is made up of a great many competing interests. It was one of the first expressions of political pluralism, one of the first of many more to come in the ensuing two centuries."[3] Because nationalism stresses the common traits of whole populations and considers division harmful to the community, this reading of No. 10 definitely clashes with the nationalist interpretation of Publius.

Recently, however, certain scholarly critiques have departed from the neo-Beardean rendition of *Federalist* No. 10. Thus Wills and Epstein concur in rejecting the pluralist version, at least as far as it implies an intention on Madison's part to exempt special interests from governmental oversight. These writers choose instead to stress Publius's belief in the rule of a virtuous elite, seeking to achieve "the public good."[4] Neither Wills nor Epstein calls No. 10 specifically nationalistic; yet, because they emphasize Publius's wish to promote the overall welfare of the nation, their interpretations are clearly compatible with that view.

Madison begins with a succinct statement of his thesis: "Among the numerous advantages promised by a well constructed Union, none deserves to be more accurately developed than its tendency to break and control the violence of faction" (56-65). This explicit assertion that factions are turbulent and irregular political phenomena serves to remind the reader of the location of No. 10 within the series of papers: it is included among the essays on the utility of national union for the quelling of uprisings and conflicts among the states. Hamilton, in No. 9, has just observed, quoting Montesquieu, that an attempted usurpation able to subdue part of a confederacy may not be able to conquer the whole, and may therefore be overcome by the remaining forces (53-54). This contention is not exactly identical to the argument of No. 10, but it runs along similar lines and was doubtless meant to lead into Madison's exposition. Significantly, it couches the discussion entirely in terms of the suppression of illicit forms of political behavior. Madison does, in fact, think of factions basically as Hamilton regards local uprisings—as perennial but undesirable features of the political landscape.

What is a faction? Madison says: "By a faction I understand a number of citizens, whether amounting to a majority or a minority of the whole, who are united and actuated by some common impulse of passion, or of interest, adverse to the rights of other citizens, or to the permanent and aggregate interests of the community." He acknowledges that factions are, unfortunately, endemic to republican government. There are only two ways of wholly eliminating faction, he declares: "by destroying the liberty which is essential to its existence" and "by giving to every citizen the same opinions, the same passions, and the same interests." He emphatically rejects the first possibility as a "remedy . . . worse than the disease," noting that "it could not be a less folly to abolish liberty, which is essential to political life, because it nourishes faction, than it would be to wish the annihilation of air, which is essential to animal life, because it imparts to fire its destructive agency." The second possibility—social uniformity—is not so strongly denounced but is "impracticable," he believes.

Contention is inevitable in human affairs, Madison affirms: "As long as the reason of man continues fallible, and he is at liberty to exercise it, different opinions will be formed." Unfortunately, people hold their views passionately and unreasonably. "So strong is the propensity of mankind to fall into mutual animosities," he notes, "that where no substantial occasion presents itself, the most frivolous and fanciful distinctions have been sufficient to kindle their unfriendly passions, and excite their most violent conflicts." To be sure, he observes, material interest is the principal cause of social dissention: "The most common and durable source of factions, has been the various and unequal distribution of property." He adds that from "the possession of different degrees and kinds of property . . . and from the influence of these on the sentiments and views of the respective proprietors, ensues a division of the society into different interests and parties."

Under modern conditions, diverse interests will proliferate. "A landed interest, a manufacturing interest, a mercantile interest, a monied interest, with many lesser interests, grow up of necessity in civilized nations, and divide them into different classes, actuated by different sentiments and views." Each interest constitutes a potential, and probably an actual faction. None are objective concerning themselves. "Shall domestic manufactures be encouraged, and in what degree, by restrictions on foreign manufactures?" This important issue "would be differently decided by the landed and the manufacturing classes; and probably by neither, with a sole regard to justice and the public good." Legislation "ought to hold the balance" equally between the groups. "Yet the parties are and must be themselves the judges; and the most numerous party, or, in other words, the most powerful faction must be expected to prevail." It is not possible to "adjust these clashing interests, and render them all subservient to the public good . . . without taking into view indirect and remote considerations, which will rarely prevail over the immediate interest which one party may find in disregarding the rights of another, or the good of the whole." We see that Madison, like his colleagues, finds the common good in the harmonizing of the material interests of the people.

The most dangerous factions under a republican government are those which comprise a majority of the people, Madison declares. Minorities are naturally prevented from gaining power in a popular regime. "Relief is supplied by the republican principle, which enables the majority to defeat its sinister views by regular vote: It may clog the administration, it may convulse the society; but it will be unable to execute and mask its violence under the forms of the Constitution." Unfortunately, it is possible for the bulk of the people to be seduced by the prospect of short-term gain into actions contrary to their long-run interests or oppressive to a portion of their compatriots. "When a majority is included in a faction, the form of popular government . . . enables it to sacrifice to its ruling passion or interest, both the public good and the rights of other citizens," Madison contends. Unjust legislative measures like those of Rhode Island and outbreaks such as Shays' Rebellion are, in Madison's view, symptoms of the same disease: factiousness.

A government on the city-state model, Madison observes, is unable to solve this problem: "a pure Democracy, by which I mean, a Society, consisting of a small number of citizens, who assemble and administer the Government in person, can admit of no cure for the mischiefs of faction. A common passion or interest will, in almost every case, be felt by a majority of the whole; a communication and concert results from the form of Government itself; and there is nothing to check the inducements to sacrifice the weaker party, or an obnoxious individual." Thus these minuscule polities "have ever been spectacles of turbulence and contention; have ever been found incompatible with personal security, or the rights of property; and have in general been as short in their lives, as they have been violent in their deaths." Madison is critical of those "theoretic politicians, who have patronized this species of Government." He does not say who he means, but Montesquieu and Rousseau are likely possibilities. Madison notes the same tendency toward instability and oppression in the American states: "Many of our heaviest misfortunes," he says, are "chiefly, if not wholly, effects of the unsteadiness and injustice, with which a factious spirit has tainted our public administrations."

However, a government over a wide territory "in which the scheme of representation takes place" provides a cure for the mischiefs of faction, Madison contends. An extended republic is preferable to a smaller one, or a pure democracy, for two reasons.

First, says Madison, the effect of representation is "to refine and enlarge the public views, by passing them through the medium of a chosen body of citizens, whose wisdom may best discern the true interest of their country, and whose patriotism and love of justice, will be least likely to sacrifice it to temporary or partial considerations. Under such a regulation, it may well happen that the public voice pronounced by the representatives of the people, will be more consonant to the public good, than if pronounced by the people themselves convened for the purpose." This is the argument for a wise, although responsive, elite that is already familiar to us from the essays of Hamilton and Jay. Madison points out that a large-sized polity is more "favorable to the election of proper guardians of the public weal," than is a smaller state. "If the proportion of fit characters, be not less, in the large than in the small Republic," he observes, "the former will present a greater option, and consequently a greater probability of a fit choice." The "vicious arts" by which "unworthy candidates" carry elections—presumably the bribery of voters—are more difficult in populous districts than in diminutive ones, he adds.

Second—and "principally"—an extensive republic contains a greater number of interests, which tend to prevent "factious combinations" from forming in the first place. This argument is the culmination of *Federalist* No. 10.

> The smaller the society, the fewer probably will be the distinct parties and interests composing it; the fewer the distinct parties and interests, the more frequently will a majority be found of the same party; and the smaller the number of individuals composing a majority, and the smaller the compass within which they are placed, the more easily will they concert and execute their plans of oppression. Extend the sphere, and you take in a greater variety of parties and interests; you make it less probable that a majority of the whole will have a common motive to invade the rights of other citizens; or if such a common motive exists, it will be more difficult for all who feel it to discover their own strength, and to act in unison with each other. Besides other impediments, it may be remarked, that where there is a consciousness of unjust or dishonorable purposes, communication is always checked by distrust, in proportion to the number whose concurrence is necessary.

Thus it is virtually impossible for factional combinations—which Madison here envisions as covert conspiracies directed against a part of the community—to include the bulk of the American people. Although dangerous within the individual states, popular government would be safe for the whole nation, he feels.

Madison does not contend that it would be impossible for *any* majorities to form on the national level, we should observe. Such a statement would give Publius a split personality indeed. Jay refers to the "great majority" of Americans who are united behind the wise measures of their chiefs (11), and Hamilton speaks of "the people" of America as a unified mass throwing themselves into one or another "scale" (179). Madison himself, in No. 51, notes the possibility that "a coalition of a majority of the whole society" might take place on the basis of "justice and the general good" (353). It is only *factional* majorities—shortsighted or oppressive ones—that he regards as essentially precluded on a nationwide scale. He surely thinks it is possible for the wise representatives of the whole people to agree on a plan to harmonize the varied interests of the country. Judging from Jay's remarks in No. 2 and Hamilton's in No. 35, it seems that this is how nonfactional national majorities would come about: sagacious leaders would evolve a comprehensive policy that would be popularly ratified, if only by the reelection of those who devised it.

Madison concludes with a statement clearly indicating the kinds of factional activities he wishes to suppress. They are principally violent rebellions, religious persecutions, and attempts against the rights of property:

> The influence of factious leaders may kindle a flame within their particular States, but will be unable to spread a general conflagration through the other States;

a religious sect, may degenerate into a political faction in a part of the Confederacy; but the variety of sects dispersed over the entire face of it, must secure the national Councils against any danger from that source; a rage for paper money, for an abolition of debts, for an equal division of property, or for any other improper or wicked project, will be less apt to prevade the whole body of the Union, than a particular member of it.

These words do, to a certain extent, support Beard's thesis, since Madison mentions violations of property rights prominently among the possible "wicked" acts of state majorities. It is no doubt true that a concern for the security of property was among the reasons which induced the Publii to support the Constitution. A distortion arises only when such motivations are made to seem the Founders' sole or main concen. Thus Howard Zinn, in his *People's History of the United States,* quotes just the portion of the above passage that mentions property questions, thereby creating the impression that this was Madison's only care.[5] Actually, the Virginian gave far more energy over the years to fighting religious bigotry than to crusading for the propertied class. His desire in No. 10 is for a safe regime that will be respectful of personal rights generally and solicitous of the overall public good. The protection of property is but one facet of his larger purpose.

This, in summary and leaving aside many interesting but subsidiary points, is the famous argument of *Federalist* No. 10. Several items must now be considered: the importance of this essay to political thought; the sources of Madison's ideas; the extent to which this paper accords with nationalism, states's rights, and pluralism; and the place of Madison's masterpiece within the structure of Publius's case. These all deserve at least a brief discussion.

Federalist No. 10 is important for two reasons. First, it is a direct confrontation of the classical ideal of the city-state with the modern idea of representative democracy, from the standpoint of the latter. A long series of theorists culminating in Rousseau had championed the ancient *polis* and had maintained that the personal participation of the citizen in lawmaking was an essential component of popular government. Other theorists, such as Locke, had argued that a people could be adequately represented by a body of elected legislators. Modern national democracies govern themselves through representative institutions, so it is obvious that Locke's ideas eventually prevailed. But at the time *The Federalist* was written, the question was undecided. Madison makes an original contribution to this ongoing debate by pointing out the impediments to faction inherent in representation and an extended territory.

Second, this essay is the origin of what we today would call the interest-group theory of politics. However, a distinction must be made in this regard. The interest-group theory comes in two guises. On one hand, it is a *descriptive* theory that purports to explain how politics works from a realistic standpoint, but that does not necessarily enjoin the process it finds to exist. In this version, it says only that interest- group clashes, mainly of an economic origin, are the explanation for most political conflicts. We need not applaud this fact, even if we feel obliged to admit it. The interest-group theory, however, can also be seen as a *prescriptive* one that suggests the way in which politics ought to be pursued. This rendition is what is today generally called *pluralism*—the assertion that the activity of special-interest groups is an intrinsically good thing and that responding to these interests is the highest duty of a political leader. Madison created the descriptive version of this theory, but he is not a prescriptive pluralist.

Madison regards the division of society into interest groups as inevitable in civilized nations. His enumeration of the multitude of such interests and his emphasis on economics as their basis have a distinctively modern appearance. He believes that the lawmaking process is principally a matter of adjusting the concerns of groups. "The regulation of these various and interfering interests forms the principal task of modern Legislation, and involves the spirit of party and faction in the necessary and ordinary operations of Government," he observes. But Madison never says that he finds the direct participation of interest groups in politics ("faction") to be a good thing per se. All he says is that if we must have factions, it is best for them to be numerous, small and weak. Clearly, he wants to suppress them as far as possible. Like Hamilton and Jay, he believes that regulation should be carried out by impartial representatives who objectively survey the condition of the nation with an eye to the common good. Certainly these wise leaders will wish to be attentive to the welfare of all segments of the American people. But Madison does not feel that our rulers should heed the clamors of organized special interests.

Madison's opinion of such groups—"factions"—is unremittingly hostile. Organized special-interest groups are to him conspiracies against the community more formally decorous, but really no less reprehensible, than the open assaults of Captain Shays. They may be inevitable, yet they are by no means helpful. Madison does not feel that these groups should be encouraged to participate in politics but, on the contrary, that as far as possible they should be kept from having an impact on the formation of public policy. There is no trace in No. 10 of the pluralist idea that the legislative arena is, and ought to be, a focus for bargain and compromise between the partial spokesmen of the interests. The objective analysis of the representative elite is Madison's political decision-making method of choice. He realistically admits that "enlightened statesmen will not always be at the helm," but he plainly thinks it important that they be here as often as we can manage.

Whence did Madison derive his famous thesis? Adair has argued that "it was David Hume's speculations on the 'Idea of a Perfect Commonwealth,' first published in 1752, that most stimulated James Madison's thought on factions." Hume had observed that "though it is more difficult to form a republican government in an extensive country than in a city; there is more facility, when once it is formed, of preserving it steady and uniform, without tumult and faction." Many other verbal and conceptual parallels further reinforce the conclusion that Madison was influenced by this source. Yet, as Epstein points out, there are also significant differences between Hume's essay and *Federalist* No. 10.[6] For example, "Hume's plan recommends a kind of federalism," but Madison does *not* propose federalism as a remedy for faction. Moreover, unlike Madison, the Scottish philosopher does not mention social and economic diversity as a factor tending to prevent oppression—and that, of course, is the distinctive argument of No. 10. The American statesman certainly borrowed from Hume, but he could hardly have obtained the decisive inspiration for his interest-group theory from him.

Epstein suggests a far likelier derivation for Madison's central insight—his reflections concerning the preconditions for religious freedom.[7] He had shown his dislike of religious discrimination in his first public office, as a delegate to the Virginia Convention of 1776, and his attitude had not varied since that time. Just two years before he wrote *Federalist* No. 10, he had been moved to issue a manifesto in his home state against a proposal to revive compulsory tithing. The idea that the existence of a "variety of sects" could work against the domination of any one of them was an idea which had occurred to him previously. Epstein notes a letter from Madison to Jefferson in which he declares that the mutual dislike of Episcopalians and Presbyterians had rendered them incapable of forming an alliance against the other faiths.[8] And Epstein also observes in this context that Locke had made a similar statement in his *Letter Concerning Toleration,* with which Madison presumably was familiar.

But Epstein does not mention the most conclusive evidence for his suggestion that the thesis of No. 10 originated in a contemplation of the requirements for religious liberty. Madison was fond of repeating the following passage from Voltaire, on the effect of the large number of religions found among the British: "If one religion only were allowed in England, the government would possibly become arbitrary; if there were but two, the people would cut each other's throats; but as there are such a multitude, they all live happy and in peace."9 Without doubt, this argument for religious pluralism, generalized to apply to all competing interests, is the germ of the brilliant insight of *Federalist* No. 10. True, Voltaire's comment in one respect goes beyond anything found in No. 10, for it indicates that many religions are better than a single one. Madison never says in this essay that it would be undesirable to have a wholly unified nation if that were possible.

There is at least one other conceivable source for Madison's notable theory. The American statesman was echoing the sagacity of an ancient political sage—Numa, the second king of Rome. Plutarch records the following strategem of that quasi-legendary lawmaker. The Roman people, says the historian, were at first split into two quarrelsome factions, the Romulians and the Sabines. But Numa was able to quiet their contentions in the following way:

for as the city consisted, or rather did not consist of, but was divided into, two different tribes, the diversity between which could not be effaced and in the meantime prevented all unity and caused perpetual tumult and ill-blood, reflecting how hard substances that do not readily mix when in the lump may, by being beaten into powder, in that minute form be combined, he resolved to divide the whole population into a number of small divisions, and thus hoped, by introducing other distinctions, to obliterate the original and great distinction, which would be lost among the smaller. So distinguishing the whole people by the several arts and trades, he formed the companies of musicians, goldsmiths, carpenters, dyers, shoemakers, skinners, braziers, and potters . . . appointing every one their proper courts, councils, and religious observances. In this manner all factious distinctions began, for the first time, to pass out of use . . . and the new division became a source of general harmony and intermixture.10

Did this ancient tale influence Madison's thinking? We know that he read Plutarch; indeed, he specifically refers to Numa in *Federalist* No. 38 (240). It seems reasonable to suggest that this bit of archaic political wisdom may at least have reinforced his more conventional sources. If so, it is interesting to note that this subdivision of the Roman people was actually calculated to unify them. It should be observed that there is a favorable reference to Numa's strategy in Rousseau's *Social Contract*, which therefore may also be regarded as a precursor of No. 10.11

Let us now consider the argument of No. 10 in relation to each of the three rival interpretations of *The Federalist*. We will find that the essay is far more congruent with the nationalist reading of Publius than it is with the other two.

True, this fact may not be obvious immediately. The national conception is that governments should be based on peoples which are socially uniform, yet Madison affirms that the regime established under the Constitution is desirable because the underlying population is relatively diverse. Indeed, *Federalist* No. 10 is usually interpreted as asserting that social pluralism is a positive good. Madison does not really say this, however. He observes merely that it is "impracticable" to expect a completely homogeneous people in a "civilized" society. He does not consider national uniformity to be objectionable per se. Given that some divisions are inevitable, he thinks it is better to have a lot of little ones than a few big ones, but he never says it is a bad thing to have characteristics that unite the entire citizen body. He believes that under modern conditions a people must be divided in some ways, especially with reference to property, but he does not deny that they may be unified in other ways, or that such unity may be useful. Later papers show that he fully recognizes the problems which pluralism will create for a new nation, and that he acknowledges the value of "homogeneous manners" for keeping a population together (122-23, 237-38).

Madison's thesis that a territorially extensive republic offers significant advantages over the classical city-state is, of course, highly relevant to a justification of nationalism. It is true that he does not specifically say in *Federalist* No. 10 that an extended republic should be formed on a national basis, yet he indicates this clearly enough elsewhere in the papers. And he does, in this essay, stress one theme that is indicative of nationalistic attitude. Throughout No. 10 he presumes that the people of America possess an overriding common interest, and he portrays as illegitimate and foolish any efforts by a part of the people to promote their selfish advantage at the expense of the whole. He regards the apparent conflict of partial interests as resulting from the fallibility of human reason, from an excess of passion and self-love, and from shortsightedness. He anticipates that rational and farseeing chiefs will be able to reconcile these superficial oppositions in a coherent policy to promote the common good. The belief that the national welfare subsumes all lesser considerations is, of course, a fundamental article of the nationalist creed.

On the other hand, Madison's thesis in No. 10 is directly contrary to the states' rights doctrine of the anticonsolidationist school. Yet this fact has not always been thoroughly understood. Indeed, along with the misapprehension that the essay is directed against majority rule as such, there is also a common, equally unfounded, opinion that it proposes the federal system as a barrier to national action against minorities. Mason and Adair, among many others, have lent countenance to this erroneous interpretation. [12] In reality, however, Madison says nothing whatsoever in No. 10 to indicate that he expects the states as corporate entities to play any kind of useful role in opposing factious national majorities. His point is rather that factious national majorities are not likely to form at all. Irresponsible majorities might well exist on the state or local level, he feels, but national majorities, because of the greater variety of interests they must encompass, cannot be narrow-minded or dishonest. This is not an argument for allowing the states great leeway. If anything, it seems to be a reason for concentrating political power on the national level and subjecting the unreliable provinces to the supervision of the central government.

We recall that Hamilton also never recommends that the states act as the defenders of minority interests. He is willing for these bodies to serve as revolutionary instruments of a national majority, forced to rebel against usurping federal rulers, but that is the sole significant function he assigns to them. Whenever he considers the prospect that the states would express a partial view conflicting with the predominant national will, he finds the prospect distasteful.

It is true that Madison does at one point favorably mention the federal system. He suggests that federal representatives be chosen from large districts—to give them a broad outlook—but he admits that this method will have a disadvantage. "By enlarging too much the number of electors, you render the representative too little acquainted with all their local circumstances and lesser interests"; Madison notes, "as by reducing it too much, you render him unduly attached to these, and too little fit to comprehend and pursue great and national objects." That is where federalism comes in handy: "The Federal Constitution forms a happy combination in this respect; the great and aggregate interests being referred to the national, the local and particular to the state legislatures." Of course, Madison does not here assign the states any particularly exalted function. They would handle the issues that otherwise might distract the national representatives from readily important matters: a convenient, but hardly glorious, role.

Nor is *Federalist* No. 10 truly an argument for what is currently called pluralism. Madison does see modern society as divided into various economic interests, and he does believe that lawmaking is mainly the regulation of these interests. But he does not think that interest groups should directly participate in the political process, nor does he show the slightest indication of believing that legislation should consist of nothing more than a compromise of their diverse selfish demands. Madison agrees with Hamilton and Jay that the political system is properly functioning when government is in the hands of wise and patriotic representatives, chosen by the people, and ruling on behalf of the national good. He does not seek to protect interests from governmental regulation, but rather to ensure that regulation is carried out fairly and intelligently. He believes all partial views to be fully reconcilable in the larger unity of the nation. Thus his outlook is a far cry from that of twentieth-century pluralism.

The place of No. 10 within the overall argument of Publius is an interesting question. Prior to Beard's 1913 study, this paper had received little attention from commentators and apparently was not considered critical to an understanding of *The Federalist*. Since Beard's book, however, No. 10 has been generally seen as the pivot of the whole treatise. It is unquestionably the most *original* of the eighty-five papers and a great contribution to political thought, but whether it should be regarded as the keystone of Publius's case is extremely doubtful. The argument of *The Federalist* considered as a whole seems to place most emphasis on the common interests of the American people and on the necessity for a strongly centralized national government to promote those interests. The fact that the new regime would rule over a great variety of interest groups, which should tend to make factional agitations less dangerous, would be a valuable quality of that government, but Publius hardly sees this as the principal reason to adopt the proposed Constitution. The care that Madison took in preparing this essay would seem to indicate that he was quite proud of his novel and weighty argument. Yet for all its profundity and subsequent influence, No. 10 is nevertheless a somewhat subsidiary point in Publius's scheme.

Madison's next essay, No. 14, is basically a discussion of various aspects of nationhood. Madison refutes the "objection, that may be drawn from the great extent of country which the union embraces" (83-89). He finds this "error" to result from "the confounding of a republic with a democracy." He repeats his notion of the distinction between these two: "in a democracy," he says, "the people meet and exercise the government in person; in a republic they assemble and administer it by their representatives and agents. A democracy consequently will be confined to a small spot. A republic may be extended over a large region." He refers to representation as the "great mechanical power in government, by the simple agency of which, the will of the largest political body may be concentrated, and its force directed to any object, which the public good requires"; and he observes that "America can claim the merit of making the discovery the basis of unmixed and extensive republics." If representation has worked for the states, Madison implies, it should work for the nation as well. He computes the size of the territory of the United States to the nearest fraction of a mile and points out that the United States is no larger than many of the countries of Europe.

It should be noted, by the way, that Madison's definitions of the terms *republic* and *democracy* have never been widely accepted. Hamilton coined the phrase "representative democracy" to mean what Madison calls a republic,[13] and it is that formulation which has come into general usage. It should also be remarked that Madison's conception here of the American people as a "political body" with a "will" to be "concentred" has an obvious affinity to the political theory of nationalism.

Madison suggests that the continued existence of the states to handle local interests of the people should put to rest all worries about the possible remoteness of a territorially extensive national regime. Under the proposed Constitution, he observes, "the general government" would be "limited to certain enumerated objects," whereas the "subordinate governments . . . will retain their due authority and activity. Were it proposed by the plan of the Convention to abolish the governments of the particular States, its adversaries would have some ground for their objection," he acknowledges, "though it would not be difficult to shew that if they were abolished, the general government would be compelled by the principle of self-preservation, to reinstate them in their proper jurisdiction." What Madison no doubt means by his "self-preservation" comment is that a single central agency would be likely to fail and alienate the populace if it tried to manage all the petty concerns of the American people. Local bodies have their advantages, he thinks.

This may be the most positive assertion of the governmental utility of the states in *The Federalist*. Yet it should be noted that nothing in this passage implies a necessity for the states to retain any sovereignty. As Diamond points out, Madison here argues the inevitability of "decentralization, but not necessarily *federal* decentralization."[14] Indeed, the contention that the central rulers would, in the absence of the states, willingly create subnational units to deal with local issues seems, if anything, to suggest that state sovereignty is unnecessary. Nor is there any conflict with Hamilton; the New Yorker also says that the national authorities would be happy to leave certain lesser matters in the hands of the provinces. And, like Hamilton's favorable comments on the states, Madison's remarks here are designed to convince the reader of the safety of a strong central government.

Madison notes that America will gradually be bound together more tightly by better means of transportation and communication: "the intercourse throughout the union will be daily facilitated by new improvements," he observes. "Roads will every where be shortened, and kept in better order; accommodations for travellers will be multiplied and meliorated; and interior navigation on our eastern side will be opened throughout . . . the whole extent of the Thirteen States. Communication between the western and Atlantic districts . . . will be rendered more and more easy by those numerous canals with which the beneficence of nature has intersected our country, and which art finds it so little difficult to connect and complete," he says. Madison appears to foresee the internal improvements that later appeared so prominently on the Hamiltonian agenda and in the programs of Hamilton's ideological successors. It is true that Madison does not specifically say the national government will build the roads and canals—indeed, as president he vetoed such a bill on constitutional grounds—but he clearly looks forward to the unification of America by these means.

In an eloquent, if somewhat rhetorical, conclusion Madison lets fall a number of phrases with a definite nationalistic tinge. The American people are "knit together . . . by . . . many chords of affection." They are "members of the same family" and "the mutual guardians of their mutual happiness." In Madison's opinion, "the kindred blood which flows in the veins of American citizens, the mingled blood which they have shed in defense of their sacred rights, consecrate their union, and excite horror at the idea of their becoming aliens, rivals, enemies." We see that Madison's nationalism possesses the emotional component which is also found in Jay's. Thus, according to No. 14, geography, fellow feeling, common interests, ancestry, and a shared history all serve to render a union of the American people natural and practicable. True, Madison admits, "the experiment of an extended republic" will be an innovation; but, he says, "the most alarming of all novelties, the most wild of all projects, the most rash of all attempts, is that of rending us into pieces, in order to preserve our liberties and promote our happiness." This last remark does not sound very pluralistic.

The final paragraph of No. 14 features one of the infrequent suggestions from Publius that America's revolution may alter the politics of the globe. "Posterity will be indebted" to the founding generation "for the possession, and the world for the example" of our new institutions, Madison predicts. "Happily for America, happily we trust for the whole human race," the patriots of 1776 were not bound by precedents, he observes. We note that Madison sees America leading the world by "example" only. And it is significant that this country's innovative contribution to politics is perceived to be, not popular government per se—which indeed existed in ancient times—but our extended republics, which prove that popular rule need not be limited to a small local area. The idea of the *polis* is directly challenged by modern nationalist conceptions in this essay.

Madison's next three papers, No. 18, No. 19, and No. 20, examine certain celebrated confederations of the past and present and assert that every one has failed through lack of central power.

Two federations of the ancient Greeks, the Amphyctionic Council and the Achaean league, are dealt with in No. 18 (110-17). Madison notes that the first of these "bore a very instructive analogy to the present confederation of the American states." The affiliated city-states "retained the character of independent and sovereign States, and had equal votes in the federal council." That body, however, did have apparently impressive prerogatives, which Madison lists, such as the right "to decide in the last resort all controversies between the members" and "to employ the whole force of the confederacy against the disobedient." Madison observes that "in theory and upon paper, this apparatus of powers, seems amply sufficient for all general purposes." Yet appearances, he says, are in this case deceiving. "Very different . . . was the experiment from the theory. The powers, like those of the present Congress, were administered by deputies appointed wholly by the cities in their political capacities; and exercised over them in the same capacities. Hence the weakness, the disorders, and finally the destruction of the confederacy," which Madison mournfully recounts. Foreign powers availed themselves of the "pleasing opportunity . . . of intermeddling in their affairs," and "intervals of foreign war, were filled up by domestic vicissitudes, convulsions, and carnage," he relates.

Madison is substantially more positive concerning the Achaean league: "The Union here was far more intimate, and its organization much wiser, than in the preceding instance. It will accordingly appear, that though not exempt from a similar catastrophe, it by no means equally deserved it," he says. Yet this government, as he describes it, seems more or less the same as the other: "The cities composing this league, retained their municipal jurisdiction . . . and enjoyed a perfect equality." The difference between the two unions turns out to concern not constitutional provisions but the cultural uniformity of the underlying population. Of the Achaean federation, Madison says:

It appears that the cities had all the same laws and customs, the same weights and measures, and the same money. But how far this effect proceeded from the authority of the Fœderal Council, is left in uncertainty. It is said only, that the cities were in a manner compelled to receive the same laws and usages. When Lacedaemon was brought into the league by Philopoemen, it was attended with an abolition of the institutions and laws of Lycurgus, and an adoption of those of the Achaeans. The Amphyctionic confederacies of which she had been a member, left her in the full exercise of her government and her legislation. This circumstance alone proves a very material difference in the genius of the two systems.

Thus, Madison says the Achaean league was superior because it either reflected or created a homogeneity of customs and manners among its people. He obviously regards national commonalities as the proper foundation for a federal union. Even the Achaean league ultimately collapsed, however, thus demonstrating, in Madison's opinion, "the tendency of fœderal bodies, rather to anarchy among the members, than to tyranny in the head."

The next essay, No. 19, also shows Madison's appreciation for the national concept (117-23). He discusses at some length "the federal system which constitutes the German empire." Again, he discovers a long list of superficially imposing authorities—a Diet with, among other things, "the general power of legislating for the empire," conjoined with an emperor whose "prerogatives . . . are numerous." Once again, "the natural supposition would be" that such a regime is effective. Yet: "Nothing would be farther from the reality. The fundamental principle, on which it rests, that the empire is a community of sovereigns; that the Diet is a representation of sovereigns; and that the laws are addressed to sovereigns; render the empire a nerveless body; incapable of regulating its own members; insecure against external dangers; and agitated with unceasing fermentations in its own bowels." And Poland, which had just been partitioned, is another "government over local sovereigns" that demonstrates "the calamities flowing from such institutions."

Madison now turns to Switzerland, where he finds very little to admire in the government: "The connection among the Swiss Cantons scarcely amounts to a confederacy," he says. Yet he admits that the Swiss have managed to stay together over the years. He enumerates a number of circumstantial reasons for this, such as "the peculiarity of their topographical position," the "few sources of contention among a people of such simple and homogeneous manners," and "their joint interest in their dependent possessions." Thus geography, uniform social customs, and a common interest have helped solidify this people. Once again, Madison shows a sensitivity to national factors The Swiss, with their four languages and deep religious divisions, may not be the best example of "homogeneous manners," but Madison is probably thinking of them as an uncorrupted, pastoral people without great disparities of property. Recall that in No. 10 he contends that social differentiation and faction mainly arise in "civilized"—that is, economically developed—nations. In any case, he clearly believes that national commonalities tend to suppress domestic conflict.

Federalist No. 20 concerns that "celebrated Belgic confederacy," the United Netherlands (124-29). Once again, we see a parade of seemingly potent powers counteracted by the members' retention of their entire sovereignty, and the familiar outcome: "Imbecility . . . discord . . . foreign influence and indignities," and so forth. Madison observes that the Dutch national authorities have frequently been obliged to overstep their constitutional bounds. He notes the danger in this: "Whether the usurpation, when once begun, will stop at the salutary point, or go forward to the dangerous extreme, must depend on the contingencies of the moment. Tyranny has perhaps oftener grown out of the assumption of power, called for, on pressing exigencies, by a defective constitution, than by the full exercise of the largest constitutional authorities." Hamilton makes the same point in *Federalist* No. 25 (163). No. 20 concludes with the observation that "experience is the oracle of truth," and that it "unequivocally pronounces . . . that a sovereignty over sovereigns, a government over governments, a legislation for communities, as contradistinguished from individuals; as it is a solecism in theory; so in practice, it is subversive of the order and ends of civil polity, by substituting *violence* in place of *law,* or the destructive *coertion* of the *sword,* in place of the mild and salutary *coertion* of the *magistracy.*"

With the discussion of the preceding five papers by Madison, our examination of the first half of *The Federalist*—the portion up to and including No. 36, comprising volume 1 of the M'Lean edition—is complete. It is clear that Madison's views on the national question do not particularly differ from those of his colleagues. He regards America as a nation with a coherent interest; he believes a central government acting on individuals is required to hold a confederation together; he sees the representative system as a way to concenter the general will while refining it; he considers the states to be factious and divisive; and he wants political decisions made at the less-volatile national level. With *Federalist* No. 37, Publius, that is Madison, begins assessing the specific provisions of the suggested charter. Any lingering doubts about the Virginian's nationalistic outlook are soon dispelled.

Beginning with No. 37, Madison composed twenty-four of the next twenty-seven essays. No. 37 through No. 46 appeared during a three-week period starting January 11, 1788. They consider the fundamental nature of the proposed government and ask whether the Constitution would give too much power to the national regime. Madison asserts that the amount of authority provided under the new plan is no more than is needed to properly attend to the affairs of the American people. If his words sound familiar, this is because he frequently repeats arguments already presented by Hamilton and Jay. Indeed, from the current reader's standpoint, much of what Madison says in these papers seems redundant in the extreme. He himself acknowledges that some of his comments have been "anticipated, in another place" (204). Yet, of course, since Madison could not presume that his audience on any given day had read the earlier articles, this reiteration was not necessarily a bad idea at the time. It is also convenient for the purposes of this study, because we can see the extent to which his views are identical to those of his colleagues.

Madison begins *Federalist* No. 37 by noting that the Constitution "touches the springs of so many passions and interest" that it is not likely to receive "a fair discussion and accurate judgement of its merits" (231-39). He unsparingly criticizes the motives of the carping critics, and notes that "a faultless plan was not to be expected." He enumerates the manifold perplexities that the Convention had to face, such as the "novelty of the undertaking." And he includes a lengthy dissertation on the numerous inexactitudes involved with analyzing "objects, extensive and complicated in their nature," which provides a nice contrast to Hamilton's opinion of politics as similar to mathematics in its certainty. Three of the obstacles to a proper constitution that Madison mentions here are especially significant to the argument of Publius.

Madison points out the difficulty of "combining the requisite stability and energy in Government, with the inviolable attention due to liberty, and to the Republican form." Governmental energy, he says, "is essential to . . . security against external and internal danger, and to . . . prompt and salutary execution of the laws," whereas "stability . . . is essential to national character, and to . . . repose and confidence in the minds of the people." Unfortunately, a popular regime may be inclined to slight these valuable qualities. "The genius of Republican liberty, seems to demand on one side, not only that all power should be derived from the people; but, that those entrusted with it should be kept in dependence on the people, by a short duration of their appointments; and, that, even during this short period, the trust should be placed not in a few, but in a number of hands," he notes. "Stability, on the contrary, requires, that the hands, in which power is lodged, would continue for a length of time, the same." Moreover, "energy in Government requires not only a certain duration of power, but the execution of it by a single hand." The great problem of the nation-state—the meddling of centralization with populism—could not be better put.

Madison also discusses, with admirable candor, "the interfering pretentions of the larger and smaller States." The former would naturally demand a "proportioned" representation in the new regime, while the latter would be for state equality. Madison notes that the "struggle could be terminated only by compromise" and that each side will have tried to assign the primary powers of the proposed regime to "the branches, in . . . which they had respectively obtained the greatest share of influence." So far as this has been the case, says Madison, "the Convention must have been compelled to sacrifice theoretical propriety to the force of extraneous circumstances." This point is different from the contention, stated in other places by Publius, that "theoretic politicians" may propose impractical ideas. Madison implies here that the proposed charter has features that are inferior to certain alternatives, but that were adopted because of the need to secure agreement. In other words, there apparently are some features of the Constitution that Publius does not like.

Finally, Madison refers to the thesis of No. 10: "the different parts of the United States are distinguished from each other, by a variety of circumstances . . . And although this variety of interests, for reasons sufficiently explained in a former paper, may have a salutary influence on the administration of the Government when formed; yet every one must be sensible of the contrary influence which must have been experienced in the task of forming it." It seems that pluralism is not always an advantage: it is not easy to construct a polity out of somewhat disparate materials. Madison once again agrees with the nationalistic idea that governments are most readily based on uniform populations.

In No. 38, Madison notes that in "antient history" the drafting of a constitution was usually assigned to only one man: "the fears of discord and disunion among a number of Counsellors, exceeded the apprehension of treachery or incapacity in a single individual" (239-49). The success of the Convention thus was quite fortuitous, and it would be unwise to force a repetition of the experiment by rejecting the Constitution, he says, especially since the opponents of the new charter disagree among themselves. "A patriot in a State that does not import or export, discerns insuperable objections against the power of direct taxation. The patriotic adversary in a State of great exports and imports, is not less dissatisfied that the whole burden of taxes may be thrown on consumption," Madison observes. He admits that the Constitution may not be "perfect," but he adds that the confederation is "more imperfect" and realistically asserts that "no man would refuse to give brass for silver or gold, because the latter had some alloy to it." Once again, Publius hints that he may not be wholly pleased with the proposed scheme.

Federalist No. 39 considers the question of "whether the general form and aspect" of the new plan is "strictly republican" (250-57). Madison says that "no other form would be reconcilable with the genius of the people of America." He defines a republic as "a government which derives all its powers directly or indirectly from the great body of the people; and is administered by persons holding their offices during pleasure, for a limited period, or during good behavior." This is a fairly inclusive definition that does not wholly agree with his discussion in No. 37, where he declares that lengthy terms for public officials are contrary to the republican principle (234). He notes that the Constitution "is in the most rigid sense conformable" to the relaxed standard of the present essay. The "most decisive" sign of republicanism, he claims, is the "absolute prohibition of titles of nobility." He then turns to the question that occupies him for the remainder of this essay. Is the suggested regime a true "confederacy of sovereign states," or is it a "national government" formed by "a consolidation of the States?"

The contrast of a confederation with a consolidation was early made by the Anti-Federalists. Brutus's first letter contains a very able discussion of this issue. Brutus notes that under the new Constitution "there is no need for any intervention of the state governments, between the Congress and the people, to execute any one power vested in the general government, and . . . the constitution and laws of every state are nullified and declared void, so far as they are or shall be inconsistent with this constitution, or the laws made in pursuance of it, or with treaties made under the authority of the United States. The government then, so far as it extends, is a complete one, and not a confederation." Brutus admits that "this government is limited to certain objects, or to speak more properly, some small degree of power is still left to the states." But he contends that "although the government reported by the convention does not go to a perfect and entire consolidation, yet it approaches so near to it, that it must, if executed, certainly and infallibly terminate in it."[15] This will be a limited national regime at best, and the limitations will probably not be too effective. Madison sets out to combat this argument in No. 39.

Hamilton has already dealt with this topic in No. 15. His comments there are unimpressive, depending as they do on a mistranslation of Montesquieu, and in any case amounting to the mere assertion that previous usage of the term *federal* has been vague enough to apply even to the proposed government. Madison simply ignores his colleague's inadequate sallies. He assumes a stance halfway between Brutus and Hamilton; the new charter, he says, sets up a mixed system. "The proposed Constitution therefore is in strictness neither a national nor a federal constitution; but a composition of both," Madison affirms. In other words, it is not really accurate to call the United States under the Constitution an unqualifiedly federal government, any more than it would be correct to call it, without qualification, a nation-state. Madison as much as admits here that his party's use of the term *federalist* to describe itself is something of a misappropriation.

This is the only notable inconsistency between Hamilton and Madison in *The Federalist*, and it simply concerns a question of nomenclature. The two principal Publii do not disagree concerning what the proposed government will do, but what it should be called.

For the remainder of No. 39, Madison attempts to show that what he considers the federal features of the Constitution are at least as significant as the national aspects. He calls federal all parts of the new government that in any way involve the states as corporate entities or that treat them as equal bodies regardless of population. This is a much more inclusive definition than that of Brutus: the Anti-Federalist writer regards the interposition of the states between the national government and the citizenry as the essence of federalism. Of course, there is precious little of that in the Constitution. Madison labels as national all parts of the union that are arranged proportionately to population or that stem immediately from, or act immediately upon, the American people. The new plan, it appears, is a very mixed bag.

The establishment of the Constitution, says Madison, "will be not a national, but a federal act." This is beause the deed will "result from the unanimous assent of the several States that are parties to it," rather than "from the decision of a majority of the people of the Union." But "the sources" of the "ordinary powers of government" are composite. The House of Representatives derives from the people, and thus it is national; the Senate derives from the states, and so it is federal; the president, due to the complex nature of the Electoral College and the other presidential election procedures, has a motley origin. On the other hand, the central government operates directly on the people, without the intervention of the states except in a few minor ways. This is nationalistic. Madison observes, in this regard, that "the national countenance of the Government on this side seems to be disfigured by a few federal features. But this blemish is perhaps unavoidable in any plan." The characterization of federalism as a "blemish" is perhaps more revealing of Madison's attitude than he intended!

Respecting the "extent" of the new government's powers, however, Madison finds nationalism less pervasive. "The idea of a national Government involves in it, not only an authority over the individual citizens; but an indefinite supremacy over all persons and things, so far as they are objects of lawful Government," he notes. "Among a people consolidated into one nation, this supremacy is compleatly vested in the national Legislature." But the Constitution does not allow the Congress any such sweeping authority. "In this relation then the proposed Government cannot be deemed a national one; since its jurisdiction extends to certain enumerated objects only, and leaves to the several States a residuary and inviolable sovereignty over all other objects." Madison acknowledges that the rights of the states are subject to the rulings of the national Supreme Court. "It is true that in controversies relating to the boundary between the two jurisdictions, the tribunal which is ultimately to decide, is to be established under the general Government," he admits. "But that does not change the principle of the case. The decision is to be impartially made, according to the rules of the Constitution; and all the usual and most effectual precautions are taken to ensure this impartiality." The independent national judiciary is the guardian of states' rights, it appears.

Finally, says Madison, the power to amend the Constitution is "neither wholly national, nor wholly federal." The two principles seem to be inextricably intertwined throughout the proposed regime, according to its main architect.

As Diamond points out, Madison's discussion tends to somewhat exaggerate the federalism of the new government.[16] Thus he counts the ratification procedure as a federal element, thereby lending credence to the "compact" theory of the Constitution's origin.[17] Yet he does not deduce any practical consequences from this theory, and his use of it here seems to be merely a debating tactic. The advocates of nullification later argued, on the basis of the compact idea, that no state can ever be bound to a constitutional provision without its own consent. But Madison explicitly rejected nullification and never explained, in this essay or elsewhere, how the states derive meaningful power from the process of ratification, once it is complete. Also, he calls the circumscribed nature of the central government's authority a federal trait of the system, but this is stretching the term, since the states as sovereign entities have no constitutional role to play in limiting the national rulers. This, Madison admits, is the responsibility of the United States Supreme Court, a national political institution. He clearly wants to disarm criticism of the new plan by overemphasizing its federalism. Yet he at least shows that the proposed government would not be a unitary nation-state. To call it "a composition" is not unreasonable.

It would, however, have been far less composite, if Madison had had his way. He opposed most of the constitutional provisions that he here characterizes as federal. He intensely disliked the idea of equal representation of the states in the Senate, fought the notion tooth and nail at the Philadelphia Convention,[18] and was apparently never reconciled to it, since he could not bring himself to praise that aspect of the plan even when he wrote as Publius. He did not approve of the election of senators by the state legislatures.[19] With regard to the choosing of the chief executive, he contended at the Convention that "the people at large was . . . the fittest in itself" to perform this function,[20] by his standards a nationalistic viewpoint. Nor did Madison favor the notion of the Supreme Court as the guardian of states' rights. The Virginia Plan, as we have seen, gave the national Congress the right to veto all acts by the state legislatures.[21] Madison was extremely unhappy when this method of resolving disputes between the two levels was eliminated from the scheme—partly because he was not enamored of the idea of a strong judiciary.[22] It is quite obvious that his recommendation would in practice have given the national Congress "an indefinite supremacy over all persons and things."

Madison's tendency to exaggerate the federal features of the Constitu-

tion does not signify that he is necessarily prevaricating when he speaks of
the power of the states under the proposed regime. Both Madison and
Hamilton seem genuinely to believe that the states would remain, if anything, *too* strong under the new government. The power of the state legislatures to elect the United States senators would alone be enough to protect
the position of the states, Madison says (416). He stretches the term *federal*
somewhat, but he sincerely feels that the provincial governments would
retain much influence, should the Constitution be ratified.

Federalist No. 40 deals with the issue of "whether the Convention were
authorized to frame and propose this mixed Constitution" (258-67). It is
true, admits Madison, that the congressional authorization of the Philadelphia meeting specifically mentioned only "revising the articles of confederation," but it also called for "a firm national government," and he
declares the latter consideration to be the more vital one. He rhetorically
asks "whether it was of most importance to the happiness of the people of
America, that the articles of confederation should be disregarded, and an
adequate government be provided, and the Union preserved; or that an
adequate government should be omitted, and the articles of confederation
preserved?" Madison observes that "the hopes and expectations of the great
body of citizens, throughout this great empire," have been concentrated on
the outcome of the Convention, and that the proposed scheme is only a
recommendation which will be "of no more consequence than the paper on
which it is written" unless the people approve it. The designers of the
Constitution, he remarks, "must have reflected, that in all great changes of
established governments, forms ought to give way to substance." Had they
acted otherwise, they would have deserved the condemnation of "every
virtuous citizen."

Madison claims that the proposed charter, like the existing one, retains
the sovereignty of the states: "In the new government as in the old, the
general powers are limited, and . . . the States in all unenumerated cases,
are left in the enjoyment of their sovereign and independent jurisdiction."
Madison likes to stress the enumerated nature of the federal prerogatives
under the Constitution. Yet, because he believes in implied powers, his
conception of enumeration is not in fact a very stringent one, as we shall see.

In the next essay, No. 41, Madison commences the discussion of a topic
that will occupy him for four papers: "Whether any part of the powers
transferred to the general Government be unnecessary or improper?" (268-
78). He notes that the Anti-Federalists stress the dangers stemming from
"the extensive powers of the Government," but they neglect to consider
"how far these powers were necessary means of attaining a necessary end."
He observes that "cool and candid people will at once reflect, that the purest

of human blessings must have a portion of alloy in them . . . and that in every political institution, a power to advance the public happiness, involves a discretion which may be misapplied and abused." Thus if a power is "necessary," it must be "conferred," he says; and thereafter it only remains "to guard as effectually as possible against a perversion of the power to the public detriment." Madison's realistic attitude and his praise of strong government are most Hamiltonian.

Madison divides the powers of the national government into a number of classes, "as they relate to . . . different objects." First, he considers those prerogatives that pertain to "security against foreign danger." He reiterates many of the arguments that have appeared in previous essays. The central regime must possess "an indefinite power" of providing for the common defense, because it is not possible to "limit the force of offence." Unrealistic legal "barriers" against actions that might be militarily unavoidable would merely create occasions for "necessary usurpations of power" that would set harmful precedents. Standing armies are obligatory, although "inauspicious" to liberty. The way to limit the risk from that source is to unify the American people, thus eliminating the chance of war between the states. If America divides, the meddling Europeans will intervene in our internal affairs. The United States especially needs a strong navy. Publius repeats himself.

Madison argues against those critics who suggest that the new national government should be restricted to "external" taxation—import duties. Such levies might be productive at the present, he admits, but they probably will not be for all time. "As long as agriculture continues the sole field of labour, the importance of manufactures must increase as the consumers multiply." Yet "as soon as domestic manufactures are begun by the hands not called for by agriculture, the imported manufactures will decrease. . . . In a more remote stage, the imports may consist in considerable part of raw materials, which will be wrought into articles for exportation, and will therefore require rather the encouragement of bounties, than to be loaded with discouraging duties." Thus Madison predicts a Hamiltonian future for the United States and recommends that national economic and revenue policies be shaped in accord with the imperatives of the developmental process: "discouraging duties" at one conjunction, "bounties" at another. Free trade does not appear to be an option—at least the contrary is presumed.

Towards the end of No. 41, Madison attempts to refute what he deems to be a "misconstruction" on the part of the Anti-Federalists with regard to Article I, Section 8 of the Constitution, which says that Congress shall have the power "to lay and collect taxes, duties, imposts, and excises, to pay the debts and provide for the common defense and general welfare of the United

States." Madison observes that the Constitution's opponents have claimed that this provision "amounts to an unlimited commission to exercise every power which may be alledged to be necessary for the common defense or general welfare." But he notes that a list "of the objects alluded to by these general terms, immediately follows; and is not even separated by a longer pause than a semicolon." Why, he asks, would such an "enumeration" have been included if the phrase "general welfare" actually covers every possible example? Madison seems to make a plausible case, yet the view he expresses here is not considered orthodox today. The currently favored interpretation is that this section of the Constitution does indeed give the national government the power to raise and spend money for any reason said to be for the general welfare—a view that is not precisely the same as the one Madison is attacking, but that is inconsistent with the one he is maintaining. Posterity has not followed Publius here.

Ironically, however, posterity *has* followed one of the authors of *The Federalist,* for the currently accepted interpretation was first definitively stated by Hamilton, although he does not, as Publius, put forth this opinion or even mention the "general welfare" clause.[23] It was probably no accident that Hamilton left this point to his colleague. Because of his circumspection in this regard, Publius has no split personality on the question.

In *Federalist* No. 42, Madison discusses two categories of national government powers: "those which regulate" America's "intercourse with foreign nations," and "those which provide for the harmony and proper intercourse among the States" (279-87). The first class "forms an obvious and essential branch of the federal administration," says Madison. "If we are to be one nation in any respect, it clearly ought to be in respect to other nations." The provisions of the Articles of Confederation "leave it in the power of any indiscreet member to embroil the confederacy with foreign nations" by means of irregular actions. The new Constitution, on the other hand, will tend to promote "certainty and uniformity" in this area. The second set of powers mainly involves the regulation of interstate commerce. Without some sort of general superintendence, declares Madison, the states will inevitably discriminate against each other with their fiscal and commercial regulations. Such practices would "nourish unceasing animosities," he notes. And he puts in a word on behalf of "the power of establishing postroads," noting that "nothing which tends to facilitate the intercourse between the States, can be deemed unworthy of the public care."

Federalist No. 43 examines a number of miscellaneous powers and makes several comments relevant to the nationalist theme. The power of "exclusive legislation . . . over . . . the seat of the Government of the United States," says Madison, is designed to free the central rulers from any dependence on the particular state in which the national capital might happen to be located (288-98). The guarantee of a republican form of government to every state will be needed in order to cement the American union: "Governments of dissimilar principles and forms have been found less adapted to a federal coalition of any sort, than those of a kindred nature." Or, in other words, a degree of political homogeneity is essential to such a government. Madison notes that violent factions within a state may prevail because of "secret succors from foreign powers," and he declares that should disorders occur within a state, the conflict may be conveniently mediated by the other states: "To the impartiality of Judges they would unite the affections of friends." The national tie, it seems, is sentimental as well as pragmatic.

On the delicate question of the nation's right to disregard the provisions of the Articles of Confederation, Madison appeals "to the absolute necessity of the case; to the great principle of self-preservation; to the transcendent law of nature and of nature's God, which declares that the safety and happiness of society are the objects at which all political institutions aim, and to which all such institutions must be sacrificed." The welfare of the nation outweighs legalistic considerations, says Publius.

The next essay, No. 44, examines the restrictions placed on the states by the Constitution. Several of those involve the external relations of America and are "fully justified," Madison says, "by the advantage of uniformity in all points which relate to foreign powers; and of immediate responsibility to the nation in all those, for whose conduct the nation itself is to be responsible" (299-308). The "right of coining money" is denied the states in order to avoid the multiplication of "expensive mints" and an awkward diversity "of the circulating pieces." State mints are convenient, Madison allows, but he feels that "the end can be as well attained, by local mints established under the general authority." He bitterly denounced "the pestilent effects of paper money" and points out that "had every State a right to regulate the value of its coin, there might be as many different currencies as States; and thus the intercourse among them would be impeded; retrospective alterations in its value might be made, and thus the citizens of other States be injured; and animosities be kindled among the States themselves." Also: "The subjects of foreign powers might suffer from the same cause, and hence the Union be discredited and embroiled by the indiscretions of a single member." Thus, like Hamilton (42-43), he gives a nationalistic twist to the argument on behalf of creditors.

Madison observes that the constitutional prohibition of state laws "impairing the obligation of contracts" is a response to the "fluctuating" policies of those subordinate entities. The "sober people of America," he declares, "have seen . . . that sudden changes and legislative interference in cases affecting personal rights" have "become jobs in the hands of . . . speculators; and snares to the more industrious and less informed part of the community." There is a clear need, he says, for a "thorough reform . . . which will banish speculations on public measures, . . . and give a regular course to the business of society." These remarks are directed against certain recent actions by state legislatures, but the dislike of wheeling and dealing that Madison reveals here was a principal reason for his later break with Hamilton, whose financial program also appeared to encourage such corruption.

Having thus disposed of the states, Madison turns to the part of the new plan that allows the national rulers "to make all laws which shall be necessary and proper for carrying into execution the foregoing powers, and all other powers vested . . . in the government of the United States." This clause, he notes, has been "assailed with . . . intemperance," but he regards it as "compleatly invulnerable." To have limited the national government to those powers "expressly" mentioned in the controlling document, he claims, would have been too restrictive and would inevitably have spawned many violations of the Constitution. A "positive enumeration" of all the granted powers would have been impossible: the government, says Madison, must be able to adjust to changing conditions by adopting new ways. A negative enumeration of all forbidden powers would have been "no less chimerical." And, besides, "had the Constitution been silent on this head, there can be no doubt that all the particular powers, requisite as a means of executing the general powers, would have resulted to the government, by unavoidable implication." Should the national legislature "misconstrue" this clause, redress may be had from the "executive and judiciary departments, which are to expound and give effect to the legislative acts," and from the people, who can elect "more faithful representatives."

Madison's discussion of implied powers in this essay puts his strict constructionism in perspective. He is fond of stressing the fact that the authorities of the national regime are enumerated, and hence limited, by the proposed Constitution. Yet he clearly affirms here that the central government cannot be restricted only to those prerogatives that have been specified in the new charter, but must inevitably be allowed additional—unlisted—powers. Later events showed Hamilton willing to go much further in this direction than Madison, but the Virginian appears quite supportive of vigorous government in *The Federalist*. His reading of the Constitution is not overrigid. It should be noted that by labeling as "chimerical" the attempt to "enumerate the particular powers not necessary or proper for carrying the general powers into execution," he is in effect arguing against a bill of rights.

Also, we should observe that Madison considers judicial review a protection against improper congressional actions.

Madison also defends the provision that declares "this Constitution and the laws of the United States which shall be made in pursuance thereof, and all treaties made, or which shall be made, under the authority of the United States, shall be the supreme law of the land, and the Judges in every State shall be bound thereby, any thing in the Constitution or laws of any State to the contrary notwithstanding." Had the states been rendered supreme, he notes, "the world would have seen . . . a system of government founded on an inversion of the fundamental principles of all government; it would have seen the authority of the whole society every where subordinate to the authority of the parts; it would have seen a monster in which the head was under the direction of the members." After a few more remarks, he declares his overall conclusion: "no part of the power" given by the new plan "is unnecessary or improper for accomplishing the necessary objects of the Union."

The next two essays consider "whether the whole mass" of powers granted to the national government "will be dangerous to the portion of authority left in the several States" (308-14). Not that Madison seems really to care. Thus he commences No. 45 by asking, "If . . . the Union be essential to the happiness of the people of America, is it not preposterous to urge as an objection to a government without which the objects of the Union cannot be attained, that such a Government may derogate from the importance of the individual states?" Our revolution was fought, he says, "that the people of America should enjoy peace, liberty and safety." We did not rebel from the British merely to enable the states to "enjoy a certain extent of power, and be arrayed with certain dignities and attributes of sovereignty." The states were made for the people, not vice versa. "Were the plan of the Convention adverse to the public happiness," avows Madison, "my voice would be, reject the plan." And similarly, he adds, "as far as the sovereignty of the States cannot be reconciled to the happiness of the people, the voice of every good citizen must be, let the former be sacrificed to the latter."

Yet Madison does not feel the states will be undermined by the Convention's scheme. If anything, he says, the "balance" is more likely to be disturbed by them than by the new federal regime: "We have seen," he says, "in all the examples of antient and modern confederacies, the strongest tendency continually betraying itself in the members to despoil the general Government of its authorities, with a very ineffectual capacity in the latter to defend itself against the encroachments." Under the recommended design, "each of the principal branches of the federal Government will owe its existence more or less to the favor of the State Governments, and must consequently feel a dependence, which is much more likely to beget a disposition too obserquious, than too overbearing towards them." Moreover, "the powers delegated by the proposed Constitution to the Federal Government are few and defined," while "those which are to remain in the State Governments are numerous and indefinite." Like Hamilton, he fears the states will be, if anything, too strong under the new system.

Madison commences the following paper, No. 46, by observing that the national and state governments all derive their authority from the American populace as a whole: "Notwithstanding the different modes in which they are appointed, we must consider both of them, as substantially dependent on the great body of the citizens of the United States," he says (315-23). "The Fœderal and State Governments are in fact but different agents and trustees of the people, instituted with different powers, and designated for different purposes." Therefore, it belongs to the citizenry to determine "whether either, or which of them, will be able to enlarge its sphere of jurisdiction at the expense of the other." Madison notes that it has already been shown "that the first and most natural attachment of the people will be to the governments of their respective States." Thus, he says, if "the people should in future become more partial to the fœderal than to the State governments, the change can only result, from such manifest and irresistible proofs of a better administration, as will overcome all their antecedent propensities. And in that case," he adds, "the people ought not surely to be precluded from giving most of their confidence where they may discover it to be most due." We should remark that Madison here emphatically speaks of the American people as a corporate unity and that he is by no means opposed to an extension of the power of the national government.

Madison also contends that, in any case, "the State governments could have little to apprehend, because it is only within a certain sphere, that the fœderal power can, in the nature of things, be advantageously administered." Once again, *The Federalist* asserts that the central rulers will never attempt to invade the domain of local government. Like most of Publius's statements concerning the usefulness of the states, the effect of this passage is to allay fears of the power of the national regime.

Publius now proceeds to discuss the influence of the states within the new federal system and reaches some interesting conclusions. "The prepossessions which the members themselves will carry into the Federal Government, will generally be favorable to the States," he observes; "whilst it will rarely happen, that the members of the State governments will carry into the public councils, a bias in favor of the general government. A local spirit will infallibly prevail much more in the members of Congress, than a national spirit will prevail in the Legislatures of the particular States."

Thus, he says, "Measures will too often be decided according to their probable effect, not on the national prosperity and happiness, but on the prejudices, interests and pursuits of the governments and people of the individual States." Madison recounts the sorry record of the Confederation Congress: "The members have but too frequently displayed the character, rather of partizans of their respective States, than of impartial guardians of a common interest." The political power left to the states by the Consttution, it appears, would largely be exerted for counterproductive, parochial purposes. There evidently are disadvantages to federalism.

Madison hastens to add that the Constitution would at least be an improvement over the current regime. "I mean not . . . to insinuate," he declares, "that the new Fœderal Government will not embrace a more enlarged plan of policy than the existing government may have pursued, much less that its views will be as confined as those of the State Legislatures; but only that it will partake sufficiently of the spirit of both, to be disinclined to invade the rights of the individual States." Thus the residual powers of the subordinate members will be safe. The states will do less damage under the proposed plan than presently—yet their existence will hardly be an unmixed blessing to the nation, even so.

Madison now discusses at some length the ability of the states to defend their rights against national government usurpation. He finds state resources formidable, indeed invincible. Should the central regime attempt to invade the local rights of the citizens, "a few representatives of the people, would be opposed to the people themselves; or rather one set of representatives would be contending against thirteen sets of representatives, with the whole body of their common constituents on the side of the latter," he observes. Even "warrantable" measures by the national rulers could not easily be enforced over the resistance of a state. Madison ridicules the "visionary supposition that the Fœderal Government may previously accumulate a military force for the projects of ambition." It is most unlikely that an "uninterrupted succession" of "traitors" would be elected to national office for a long period, that these untrue representatives would steadily pursue an illegal design, and that neither the people nor the states would detect the plot until it is consummated. Fears of national military despotism, says Madison, "appear . . . more like the incoherent dreams of a delirious jealousy, or the misjudged exaggerations of a counterfeit zeal, than like the sober apprehensions of genuine patriotism."

These last two papers demonstrate that Madison exactly shares both Hamilton's attitude towards the states and his conception of the part they should play under the proposed Constitution. On the one hand, the states are the origin of factious, shortsighted, and particularistic sentiments, contrary to the enlightened pursuit of the overall common interest. On the other hand, they can serve as a barrier to national government usurpation. However, the danger of usurpation of the national government is really minuscule, because of the popular nature of the central regime. The provinces are useful for certain local administrative purposes, but the national rulers would not atempt to exercise those functions in any case and would assign them to local bodies even in the absence of the states. All in all, this is not a convincing argument for federalism, as against a unitary government. The degree of power that has been left to the states seems far more likely, on Madison's own showing to be used for ill than for good.

Madison, like Hamilton, sees the state role against national tyranny as an extraconstitutional one; the federal judiciary, he says, should be the final regular arbiter of the proper extent of the general authority. Nor does Madison see the states as the proper defenders of minority viewpoints. Minority rights would gain protection from the likely moderation of national majorities, he thinks. Madison sees states as far more likely to persecute minorities than to succor them. Like Hamilton, he regards these entities as truly useful only as instruments of the national majority under unusual circumstances. The states must "collect the national will and direct the national force," he says.

With No. 46, we have reached the end of that portion of Publius's argument concerned with justifying the establishment of a strong central government. It is obvious that Madison's opinion on this score is in all significant respects the same as the opinions of Hamilton and Jay. Publius has no split personality on this point. Madison lauds energy and stability in government. He says that the national welfare is more important than legalistic forms, that the central rulers must be given every necessary power, and that standing armies are best contained by political unity. He warns of the meddling of foreign countries in our internal affairs. He calls for a strong American navy, for the unification of the country by means of roads and canals, for an unlimited authority of taxation in th national rulers, and for national regulation of the economy. He is extremely critical of the existing governments of the states. He feels that these entities derive their political legitimacy from the American people as a whole and that the people would be entitled to abolish them entirely, should they wish to do so. He contemplates with equanimity the future expansion of the authority of the central regime. He regards America as a nation and observes that national commonalities help to hold a population together. These are very Hamiltonian sentiments, yet they come from Madison's pen.

Only one significant difference between the two principal Publii has been found: Hamilton asserts that the new government would be a federation without qualification, whereas Madison says it would be a mixture of federal and national elements. Yet this is a mere matter of nomenclature, not substance. Whatever their later disagreements, the two men put up a common front in *The Federalist*.

7

Madison Separates
the Powers

Beginning with *Federalist* No. 47, Madison turns his attention to the
internal arrangement of the various parts of the new national regime. The
fourteen remaining essays by him may be divided into three groups. The
papers through No. 51 discuss various methods of keeping the different
branches in their places, culminating in a renowned exposition of the
principles of separation of powers and checks and balances. No. 52 through
No. 58 make up Publius's analysis of the proposed House of Representatives. And No. 62 and No. 63 begin the examination of the Senate. These
articles appeared during the month of February 1788. On about March 1,
Madison left New York to take part in the ratification contest in Virginia, just
coming to its climax. His friends had been beseeching him for weeks to
return and lead the fight for the Constitution in his home state, but he delayed
his departure until the last possible moment—no doubt because of his
commitment to the project of Publius.

On the surface, much of what Madison now says may seem to clash with
views previously expressed. If nationalism, centralization, and wise leadership have been the main themes hitherto, for the rest of *The Federalist* they
must share pride of place with notions that apparently point in a very
different direction. The argument of Publius so far has stressed the advantages of strong government, but attention is now given to the restraint of
government through the division of its institutions. The integrity and the
patriotism of America's federal officials has earlier been more or less
presumed, but now it is thought necessary to set a regular watch over them.
The reader may feel that the real split in Publius's personality is to be found
not between Hamilton and Madison, but between the earlier and later
portions of their joint work.

Yet even this split is more apparent than real. The Publii have not given
up their desire for a strong national government. They regard the nationalism
of their earlier essays, and the checks and balances of their later ones, as
complementary, rather than contradictory. Hamilton, who was certainly an
advocate of governmental centralization in general, observes in *Federalist*

No. 22 that "a single Assembly may be a proper receptacle of those slender, or rather fettered authorities, which have been heretofore delegated to the fœderal head; but it would be inconsistent with all the principles of good government, to intrust it with those additional powers which . . . ought to reside in the United States" (145). And Pierce Butler of South Carolina had expressed this same opinion at the Philadelphia Convention when he declared, in a favorable reference to Madison's Virginia Plan, "that he had opposed the grant of powers to Congress heretofore, because the whole power was vested in one body. The proposed distribution of the powers into different bodies changed the case, and would induce him to go great lengths."[1] Concern for the possible misuse of power was a natural concomitant of the decision to create a potent central regime.

Thus Publius's call for governmental partitions and checks is in no way inconsistent with his desire that the central authorities wield great prerogatives. Nor does Publius really seem to be especially worried about the danger of a national tyranny. It is clear from previous essays that Hamilton, Madison, and Jay were not, in fact, habitually distrustful of government. They were in the government, and we may presume that they trusted themselves. They show awareness of the human capacity for corruption and depravity, yet on the whole, they appear to have expected that the American people would continue to choose judicious statesmen to serve in the new regime and that the process of free elections would ordinarily ensure the fidelity of the federal representatives. The Publii regard the constitutional division of governmental functions as a fail-safe mechanism—in Madison's word an "auxiliary" (349) precaution—designed to defend the freedoms of the country on those infrequent occasions when the usual protections of American politics are for some reason ineffective. We cannot conclude from this that they wanted a generally passive regime.

The prevention of despotism is emphasized in the famous essay No. 51, but this is only the first of three distinct purposes that, according to *The Federalist*, will be served by the complicated arrangement of institutions within the proposed government. The second of these is the restraint of the popular majority from unjust or imprudent acts. Here, too, the role of the constitutional balances is said to be only an "auxiliary" one (425). The primary safeguard against majority misrule is the multiplicity of interest groups over the whole country, says Madison, echoing the argument of No. 10. Indeed, he thinks that when national majorities form, they will almost always do so on the basis of "justice and the general good," which seems to imply that such majorities will not often need to be checked (353). Yet the Senate will nonetheless provide an extra increment of useful wisdom, Madison contends. A third reason for separation of powers is the enhancement of governmental effectiveness. Here the aim is actually to increase the vigor of the government, by concentrating certain important authorities in the hands of the president and the Senate—particularly those powers that relate to foreign affairs. The theme of centralization is by no means absent from the latter part of *The Federalist*.

The new House and Senate are both representative bodies, but Madison's discussion suggests that they exemplify different concepts of representation. The House follows what J.R. Pole has called "the numerical principle." Members of that body are distributed among the states strictly according to population. Madison feels that the new House will be the most powerful of the agencies of the proposed government, because it is able to speak for "the known and determined sense of a majority of the people."[2] He reveals not a trace of Rousseau's doubts concerning the ability of delegates to serve as adequate embodiments of a community.[3] If anything, Madison feels that the House may be a bit *too* reflective of the populace, mirroring their flaws as well as their virtues, especially their ignorance, instability, and haste. But the indirectly chosen Senate conforms to the logic behind the theory of "virtual representation," wherein the legislature is said to stand "for the general interest of the whole nation, in which all were concerned," and the equal apportionment of members is therefore not seen as necessary.[4] One of the chief virtues of a Senate, says Madison, is that this exalted council will possess "a sense of national character," that is, a special feeling of identification with the American community as a whole, and a particular awareness of our country's responsibilities as a member of the family of nations.

By thus combining two theories of representation, Madison gives expression to the complexity of the nationalist idea. We have already observed in chapter 3 that the concept of the nation can be given two interpretations: the populist and the corporate. The former identifies the nation with the will of the present majority, the latter with a social body existing over time. Both of these views are essential to convey the complete meaning of the term *nation*. Neither the House nor the Senate alone can fully stand for American nationhood. Together, however, they may.

The peculiar structure of America's central regime is formed by an amalgamation of two principles: (1) checks and balances and (2) separation of powers. Although these concepts are found in tandem, they actually denote distinct, even somewhat contradictory, ideas. A preliminary clarification of this point will be helpful for an understanding of Madison's argument.

The first notion, checks and balances, envisions that multiple agencies, each perhaps representative of a different social class, will be given joint responsibility for most governmental activities. Because none can move without the approval of the others, no group can be oppressive. This concept can be traced back to the ancient Greeks and was perhaps best stated by Polybius, who praised the mutual dependency of consuls, Senate, and people in the Roman constitution.[5] *The Federalist* does not associate the branches of the new regime with particular classes, but does maintain that they will check and balance each other. Separation of powers also works against a total concentration of political power, but in a different way, because, under this rubric, governmental authority is divided on a functional basis and parceled out to various institutions, each of which operates wholly independent of the others. In the late eighteenth century, the definitive treatment of this conception was thought to be Montesquieu's. "There would be an end of everything, were the same man or the same body, whether of the nobles or of the people, to exercise those three powers, that of enacting laws, that of executing the public resolutions, and of trying the causes of individuals," that philosopher said.[6]

It is obvious that in spite of their common aim, the prevention of oppression, these two principles really imply quite opposite organizational designs. Checks and balances requires that various political organs all be involved in carrying out the *same* public functions, so that each can interfere with the unconstitutional plots of the others. But separation of powers requires distinct governmental bodies to be accorded *different* spheres of operation and not to be subjected to the interference of other branches. Yet these seemingly contradictory concepts may be readily blended in practice: institutions that are for the most part functionally separate may be given a degree of control over the ordinary duties of the others. This combination of ingredients is a fundamental characteristic of the United States Constitution.

All this seems complex enough, but there is yet another twist, because the separation of powers is not necessarily motivated by a desire to restrain the rulers at all, but may be favored on the grounds that it will promote a more effective performance of the tasks of the government.[7] Montesquieu, although he mainly considers separation of powers to be a protection against usurpation, by no means overlooks the factor of efficiency. He says the "executive power ought to be in the hands of a monarch, because this branch of government, having need of despatch, is better administered by one than by many." And yet, "on the other hand, whatever depends on the legislative power is oftentimes better regulated by many than by a single person."[8] This argument obviously has nothing whatsoever to do with hobbling the government—indeed, insofar as it calls for a concentration of the executive functions, it appears designed to promote energy on the part of the public authorities. Publius often reasons along such lines, as we will see.

Madison's next five papers explore the theoretical issues just discussed. *Federalist* No. 47 answers those critics who charge that the Constitution violates separation of powers. Madison admits, in a famous aphorism, that an "accumulation of all powers legislative, executive and judiciary in the same hands, whether of one, a few or many, and whether hereditary, self appointed, or elective, may justly be pronounced the very definition of tyranny" (323-31). He insists, however, that this principle means only "that where the *whole* power of one department is exercised by the same hands which possess the *whole* power of another department, the fundamental principles of a free constitution, are subverted." The maxim does not signify "that these departments ought to have no *partial agency* in, or no *controul* over the acts of each other." Madison observes that "the celebrated Montesquieu" thought the British constitution to be the "mirrour of political liberty," even though it often violates separation of powers. Madison also examines the constitutions of the thirteen states and points out that each of them contradicts this supposedly essential tenet in various important ways.

In No. 48, Madison takes upon himself "to shew that unless these departments be so far connected and blended, as to give to each a constitutional controul over the others, the degree of separation which the maxim requires as essential to a free government, can never in practice, be duly maintained" (332-38). He observes "that power is of an encroaching nature" and must "be effectually restrained from passing the limits assigned to it." The American states have mainly relied on written prohibitions for this purpose, but these "parchment barriers" have proven unable to prevent the "legislative department" from "every where extending the sphere of its activity, and drawing all power into its impetuous vortex," Madison contends. He notes that the "founders of our republics" appear "never to have turned their eyes from the danger to liberty from the overgrown and all-grasping prerogative of an hereditary magistrate." They forgot that "in a representative republic, . . . the executive magistracy is carefully limited," while "the legislative power is exercised by an assembly, which is inspired by a supposed influence over the people with an intrepid confidence in its own strength." Therefore, "it is against the enterprising ambition" of the legislative branch, "that the people ought to indulge all their jealousy and exhaust all their precautions," Madison declares.

Federalist No. 49 examines a suggestion by Jefferson that breaches of a constitution can be cured by occasional popular conventions called specifically for that purpose (338-43). Madison acknowledges that "the people are the only legitimate fountain of power" and that "a constitutional road to the decision of the people, ought to be marked out, and kept open, for certain

great and extraordinary occasions." But he points out that "as every appeal to
the people would carry an implication of some defect in the government,
frequent appeals would in a measure deprive the government of that venera-
tion, which time bestows on every thing, and without which perhaps the
wisest and freest governments would not possess the requisite stability." He
concedes that in "a nation of philosophers, this consideration ought to be
disregarded. A reverence for the laws, would be sufficiently inculcated by
the voice of enlightened reason." However, "a nation of philosophers is as
little to be expected as the philosophical race of kings wished for by Plato.
And in every other nation, the most rational government will not find it a
superflous advantage, to have the prejudices of the community on its side."

This slightly cynical although realistic comment by Madison has a
complex relationship to the nationalist idea. The respect shown for "the
prejudices of the community" has nationalistic overtones, but the fear of an
appeal to the people seems to indicate a contrary, more elitist, perspective.
This passage perhaps serves to indicate what kind of a nationalist Publius is:
a leader with a corporate vision, rather than a fervent populist.

Madison points out that another disadvantage of a special appeal to the
people is that it may stir the emotions of the community and lead to
disturbances. He notes "that all the existing constitutions were formed in the
midst of a danger which repressed the passions most unfriendly to order and
concord; of an enthusiastic confidence of the people in their patriotic
leaders, which stifled the ordinary diversity of opinion on great national
questions; of a universal ardor for new and opposite forms, produced by a
universal resentment and indignation against the antient government; and
whilst no spirit of party, connected to the changes to be made, or the abuses
to be reformed, could mingle or leaven in the operation." In the future,
conditions might not be so favorable: "The experiments are of too ticklish a
nature to be unnecessarily multiplied." Such questions should not be decided in an atmosphere of public excitement: "It is the reason of the public
alone that ought to controul and regulate the government. The passions
ought to be controuled and regulated by government," he asserts.

Madison here indicates that the kind of harmony between virtuous
leaders and respectful masses that Jay and Hamilton have seemingly almost
taken for granted (10-12, 219-22) may not be an automatic or even an
ordinary occurrence, and may need the spur of a special crisis to come into
existence. Indeed, he has already admitted in No. 10 that "enlightened
statesmen will not always be at the helm" (60). Yet while Madison thus
appears rather more pessimistic than his colleagues concerning the prospect
for sagacious elite guidance of American public affairs, he equally believes

with them that such guidance is advisable. Thus he here notes the desir-
ability of settling the American government at a time when wise direction is
available and the danger of doing it under less favorable conditions.

Finally, Madison repeats his observation "that the tendency of republican governments is to an aggrandizement of the legislative, at the expense of
the other departments," and adds that this branch would probably prevail in
a contest for the hearts of the average citizens. "The members of the
executive and judiciary departments, are few in number, and can be personally known to a small part only of the people," he notes. Moreover, these
officials are "generally the objects of jealousy: And their administration is
always liable to be discoloured and rendered unpopular." There are a great
many legislators. They will "dwell among the people at large" and will have
"connections of blood, of friendship and of acquaintance" with "a great
proportion of the most influencial part of the society." As a rule, they will be
regarded as "the confidential guardians of the rights and liberties of the
people." They would most likely be elected to any special conventions,
where they would simply confirm their own usurpations. Something else
will be required to keep the legislators in line with the Constitution.

Federalist No. 50 takes up the possibility of periodical, rather than
occasional, appeals to the people. Such a provision exists in the state
constitution of Pennsylvania, Madison observes, where the conflict of "two
fixed and violent parties" has served to render it worthless. Nor can we hope
for a decline of these vehement partisan feelings in the future, he says,
"because an extinction of parties necessarily implies either a universal alarm
for the public safety, or an absolute extinction of liberty" (343-47). Parties
are undesirable but perennial aspects of politics, it appears.

Madison commences No. 51 by asserting that, "as all these exterior
provisions are found to be inadequate, the defect must be supplied, by so
contriving the interior structure of the government, as that its several
constituent parts may, by their mutual relations, be the means of keeping
each other in their proper places" (347-53). This scheme implies the
"separate and distinct exercise of the different powers of government";
which would appear, in strictness, to require "that all the appointments for
the supreme executive, legislative, and judiciary magistrates, should be
drawn from the same fountain of authority, the people, through channels,
having no communication whatever with one another." Madison acknowledges that a bending of this rule is allowable for reasons of practicality and
efficiency. The crucial necessity, he maintains, is that each branch of the
government be afforded a regular legal check on the actions of the others.
Madison states his thesis in a memorable passage that, well known though it
is, deserves to be fully quoted. Almost every sentence could be an aphorism.

But the great security against a gradual concentration of the several powers in the same department, consists in giving to those who administer each department, the necessary constitutional means, and personal motives, to resist encroachments. . . . Ambition must be made to counteract ambition. The interest of the man must be connected with the constitutional rights of the place. It may be a reflection on human nature, that such devices should be necessary to controul the abuses of government. But what is government itself but the greatest of all reflections on human nature? If men were angels, no government would be necessary. If angels were to govern men, neither external nor internal controuls on government would be necessary. In framing a government which is to be administered by men over men, the great difficulty lies in this: You must first enable the government to controul the governed; and in the next place, oblige it to controul itself. A dependence on the people is no doubt the primary controul of the government; but experience has taught mankind the necessity of auxiliary precautions.

Thus, according to Madison, officeholders will identify with their offices and, in protecting their own prerogatives, will naturally oppose usurpations by the other branches. Counterbalancing forces will prevent the rise of a despot.

The foregoing is surely a brilliant political conception. Two observations are, however, immediately in order. First, we remark that these interfering jurisdictions are labeled only an "auxiliary" safeguard for republican government, whereas the principal protection of liberty is said to be the central government's "dependence on the people." Free elections, not governmental divisions, are the most important barriers to tyranny, in Madison's opinion. Second, we note that in No. 51 checks and balances are presented strictly as a security for the people in general against usurpations by their rulers and are never said to be a restraint on a factious majority. Nor is the issue of governmental effectiveness mentioned in this essay. These latter points do not appear until subsequent numbers. Madison evidently wishes to stress only the most populistic of the reasons for separation of powers in this key paper.

Madison repeats his previous contention that the legislature may require checking. "In republican government," he points out, "the legislative authority, necessarily, predominates." He declares that the "remedy for this inconveniency is, to divide the legislature into different branches; and to render them by different modes of election, and different principles of action, as little connected with each other, as the nature of their common functions, and their common dependency on the society, will admit." The executive branch needs strengthening, however: "As the weight of the legislative authority requires that it should be thus divided," notes Madison, "the weakness of the executive may require, on the other hand, that it should be fortified." He rather nebulously suggests that the upper legislative house could be joined with the executive in some "qualified" fashion and thereby be led to support the latter's rightful authority. Thus the desire for political balance implies a partition of Congress and enhancement of the presidency.

Madison now considers two further aspects of "the federal system of America." These are federalism and the multiplicity of special-interest groups discussed in No. 10. His observations on both these points require some examination.

Madison's comments concerning federalism at this stage are often taken to epitomize the philosophy behind the proposed Constitution and are therefore quoted here in their entirety.

In a single republic, all the power surrendered by the people, is submitted to the administration of a single government; and usurpations are guarded against by a division of the government into distinct and separate departments. In the compound republic of America, the power surrendered by the people, is first divided between two distinct governments, and then the portion allotted to each, subdivided among distinct and separate departments. Hence a double security arises to the rights of the people. The different governments will controul each other; at the same time that each will be controuled by itself.

Anticonsolidationists are fond of this quotation. Morley, for example, who portrays Madison as an advocate of states' rights, sees it as in effect the Virginia statesman's answer to the centralizing and democratic ideas of Rousseau.[9] Yet, despite its significance in the eyes of later critics, there are problems with this passage. Careful consideration reveals that Madison's assertion is, to say the least, overdrawn.

As Epstein points out, Madison here "develops a parallel between the division of power into departments of the government, and the division of power between the state and federal governments." Yet, as Epstein also observes, Madison's parallel between the separation of powers and federalism is not quite accurate.[10] Under the new charter, each of the three branches of the federal government will possess a regular constitutional check on the other two. That is, each is assigned the legal right to restrain the other departments from carrying out their functions. Were the states really invested with such an authority over the national government, they would have to possess some sort of power to suspend or nullify federal laws. But this is not the case. Indeed, it is quite clear from the early *Federalist* papers that Publius wishes above all else to preclude the states from that kind of involvement in our national affairs. The proposed federal rulers have been placed under no constitutional requirement to work in conjunction with the states or to obtain their approval for national policies. The states, therefore, cannot be said to "controul" the national government as the three branches of that government "controul" one another.

True, as Madison has pointed out in No. 45, "the State Governments may be regarded as constituent and essential parts of the federal Government." Specifically, the provincial legislatures will have a major voice in the choosing of presidential electors and will elect the members of the new Senate (311). However, these prerogatives will provide them an indirect influence at most. The senators are not intended to be mere state delegates. They are national officials, chosen by the provinces to be sure, but holding their positions by a lengthy tenure that renders them relatively independent of the bodies that appoint them. In any case, Madison in No. 51 speaks of federalism as an *additional* protection to that already provided by checks and balances on the national level. Any "controul" exerted by the states *through* one of the national branches, like the Senate or the presidency, obviously cannot be said to comprise a further safeguard. Insofar as the authority of the states simply results from their participation in the institutions of the national regime, they cannot be a second line of defense for popular liberty. So what does Madison mean here?

Publius has, in fact, previously indicated a number of other ways in which the states can make their presence known under the Constitution. The proposed charter does not give them a regular legal check on the acts of the general government, but it preserves them as corporate entities and permits them to retain control of local affairs. The people will identify with their home states and will tend to support them in any controversies with the federal regime. The states will be capable, therefore, of leading a popular uprising against a threatened despotism. The possibility of state revolts will no doubt tend to restrain the national chiefs, and in this sense can be said to "controul" them. Still, it is rather misleading for Madison to equate this extraconstitutional source of state influence to the prerogatives of the three national branches in relation to each other—especially because in this very essay he proclaims the importance of giving our institutions "the necessary *constitutional* means" to "resist encroachments" (349, emphasis added). The national branches have the legally recognized right of mutual obstruction, but the states possess no such authority over the central rulers. The two kinds of "controul" are not really comparable.

Our final conclusion, then, must be that Madison's statement is loosely expressed, rather than incorrect—but loosely expressed it certainly is. As he has done before, Madison somewhat overstates the federalism of the new design.

Madison begins his restatement of the thesis of No. 10 with a very interesting comment. "It is of great importance in a republic," he says, "not only to guard the society against the oppression of its rulers; but to guard one part of the society against the injustice of the other part." This passage plainly implies that Madison does not perceive anything he has hitherto discussed—that is, separation of powers, checks and balances, and federalism—as protection for minorities against the majority, but only as safeguards against a tyranny of the rulers over the whole. Later, as a matter of fact, he calls the Senate a restraint on the majority, and Hamilton contends this of the federal judiciary, but neither of them ever says this of federalism. Something else is needed, Madison suggests in No. 51, to secure the rights of the lesser number.

This goal can be achieved in either of two ways: "By creating a will in the community independent of the majority"—a monarch—or "by comprehending in the society so many separate descriptions of citizens, as will render an unjust combination of the majority of the whole, very improbable."The latter idea will be embodied in the new national government. "Whilst all authority in it will be derived from and dependent on the society, the society itself will be broken into so many parts, interests and classes of citizens, that the rights of the individuals or of the minority, will be in little danger from interested combinations of the majority," Madison contends. Were smaller confederacies to be formed in America, they would undoubtedly need undemocratic political institutions to keep their factional conflicts under control. "Justice is the end of government. It is the end of civil society. It ever has been, and ever will be pursued, until it be obtained, or until liberty be lost in the pursuit." Majorities in a little state can readily behave like factions, necessitating the installation of a monarch. But a national union can avert this evil.

In the course of this discussion, Madison explicitly likens his argument concerning interest groups to the rationale for religious pluralism. "In a free government, the security for civil rights must be the same as for religious rights," he says. "It consists in the one case in the multiplicity of interests, and in the other, in the multiplicity of sects." The link with Voltaire's observation on English religious diversity seems clear. Madison's statement sounds like a ringing endorsement of pluralism, yet he does not deny that there may be some interests that unite all Americans. Nor does he contend that majority rule is impossible in this country. "In the extended republic of the United States," he declares, "and among the great variety of interests, parties and sects which it embraces, a coalition of a majority of the whole society could seldom take place on any other principles than those of justice and the general good." At least sometimes, majorities *will* occur under the proposed Constitution, and when they do, they will probably be based on the common welfare. Madison thinks there is a palpable difference between a factious majority and an enlightened one, and it is only the first kind that he aims to frustrate.

The next seven essays consider various objections to the new House of Representatives. Madison did not know it, but he was here describing the part of the government that would be his political home for most of the next decade. His name was proposed to the Virginia legislature for election to the first United States Senate, but the influence of Gov. Patrick Henry defeated Madison in that arena and obliged him to run for his local House seat. Madison did not have an easy time of it in that contest either. His home district had been gerrymandered to contain an antifederal majority, and his opponent was a very respectable gentleman, one James Monroe. But Madison did win the election and enter the House, where he was recognized as the "first man,"[11] authored the Bill of Rights, and was generally a thorn in the side of his former friend, Hamilton.

In *The Federalist*, Madison predicts that the House will be the strongest agency of the national government under the Constitution. He makes this judgement because it is the legislative branch most immediately under the control of the people, and it therefore may expect to obtain their preference. He reasons no doubt by analogy with the British House of Commons, which had already by the late eighteenth century become dominant in the British political system. Madison devotes most of these seven essays to explaining why the House has not been made even more populistic than it is—why the terms are not even shorter and the number of representatives even larger than provided. The reason, he says, is that the House should be a truly deliberative council, with a modicum of stability and virtue. Except with regard to one issue—augmentation of the number of representatives, where perhaps the machinations of the senators might need to be counteracted—Madison does not seem to perceive the House as a checking body. Because it is the most powerful institution of the new regime, he considers it mainly in the character of an entity that needs to be checked.

Madison begins No. 52 by briefly discussing "the qualifications of the electors and the elected" (353-59). The former have been accommodated to preexisting state regulations; the latter, "being . . . more susceptible of uniformity, have been very properly considered and regulated by the Convention." Madison then examines the question of whether a term of two years for the representatives is too long to be "safe." He admits that "as it is essential to liberty that the government in general, should have a common interest with the people; so it is particularly essential that the branch of it under consideration, should have an immediate dependence on, & an intimate sympathy with the people. Frequent elections are unquestionably the only policy by which this dependence and sympathy can be effectually secured." But he maintains that biennial elections are frequent enough. He gives Great Britain, Ireland, and Virginia before the Revolution, as examples of governments that managed to preserve at least "a degree of liberty" with septennial or octennial legislatures. Long terms are the more acceptable, he says, because "the Fœderal Legislature will possess a part only" of the "supreme legislative authority" and will also be "watched and controuled by the several collateral Legislatures." Thus he repeats the misleading expression of No. 51—and, as usual, presents the power of the states as an argument for the safety of a provision bolstering the national rulers.

In No. 53, Madison argues against annual elections to the House of Representatives (359-66). He notes that members of the House will require longer terms than one year to accumulate the "experience" that is required to become "a competent legislator" on the national level. "In a single state," Madison observes, the legislative process will relate "to the existing laws which are uniform throughout the state, and with which all the citizens are more or less conversant; and to the general affairs of the state, which lie within a small compass, are not very diversified, and occupy much of the attention and conversation of every class of people." But to legislate for the entire United States, he declares, is a very different matter. "The laws are so far from being uniform, that they vary in every state; whilst the public affairs of the union are spread throughout a very extensive region, and are extremely diversified by the local affairs connected with them, and can with difficulty be correctly learnt in any other place, than in the central councils, to which a knowledge of them will be brought by the representatives of every part of the empire." Madison here acknowledges quite a bit of variation within the American nation; but, interestingly enough, that variation seems to him to be a reason for centralized decision making. The national government must base its "uniform laws" on a knowledge of "different . . . local circumstances," he says.

Madison hastens to note that this national diversity will tend to diminish over time: "The affairs of the union," he maintains, "will become more and more objects of curiosity and conversation among the citizens at large. And the increased intercourse among those of different states will contribute not a little to diffuse a mutual knowledge of their affairs, as this again will contribute to a general assimilation of their manners and laws." The American nation is obviously a potentiality that, in Madison's opinion, will be actualized in the years to come.

Madison devotes *Federalist* No. 54 to a very involved explanation of why a slave should be counted as three-fifths of a person for the purposes of representation and direct taxation (366-72). Brutus had held that slaves, "who are not free agents," should not be considered in apportioning members of the House; to do so would only reward the "unfeeling, unprincipled, barbarous, and avaricious wretches" who have kidnapped them and brought them here.[12] Because Publius is writing as a citizen of New York State—and possibly also because Madison was psychologically unwilling to argue directly on behalf of an institution that he in fact detested—he places his contentions in the mouth of a hypothetical representative of the slave-owning states. This puts Madison in the interesting position of being a southerner who is pretending to be a northerner who is pretending to be a southerner. He goes so far as to say that the slaveowner's reasoning "may appear to be a little strained in some points." He maintains that "government is instituted no less for the protection of the property, than of the persons of individuals," and that it is therefore fair for this kind of property to be included in the ratio of representation. He does not explain why slavery should be the only form of property so favored, however.

This, by the way, is Publius's most unequivocal statement of the government's responsibility to protect property rights. It is quite interesting that it should arise in this particular context, where it is obviously nothing more than a rationalization for a somewhat embarrassing provision of the Constitution.

Madison also provides insight here into the techniques of social management common in his day: "If the law allows an opulent citizen but a single vote in the choice of his representative, the respect and consequence which he derives from his fortunate situation, very frequently guide the votes of others to the objects of his choice; and through this imperceptible channel the rights of property are conveyed into the public representation." It is the office of the wise elite to direct the somewhat deferential people. We have heard this sort of thing from Publius before.

In No. 55, Madison asserts that the number of representatives, set by the Constitution at sixty-ive for the first Congress, is not so small as to comprise "an unsafe depositary of the public interest" (372-78). In the course of this discussion, he displays his belief that the House should be a truly deliberative body. He admits "that in all cases a certain number at least seems to be necessary to secure the benefits of free consultation and discussion, and to guard against too easy a combination for improper purposes," but he adds that "on the other hand, the number ought at most to be kept within a certain limit, in order to avoid the confusion and intemperance of a multitude." It is his opinion that "in all very numerous assemblies, of whatever characters composed, passion never fails to wrest the sceptre from reason. Had every Athenian citizen been a Socrates; every Athenian assembly would still have been a mob." In any case, the current smallness of the number of representatives is merely a "temporary regulation," he points out. Within fifty years, he notes, there may be as many as four hundred members of the House.

It is worth remarking that Madison's true views on this subject were

slightly more populistic than the stance he takes as Publius. At the Philadelphia Convention he had proposed that the number of representatives
initially allowed to each state be double the figure finally adopted, and had
seconded a motion to increase the amount just a week before the meeting
adjourned.[13] In the former instance, he asserted that a mere sixty-five
members "would not possess enough of the confidence of the people, and
wd. be too sparsely taken from the people, to bring with them all the local
information which would be frequently wanted." On the latter occasion, he
was supported by his elitist friend, Hamilton, who declared that "he held it
essential that the popular branch . . . should be on a broad foundation. He
was seriously of opinion that the House of Representatives was on so narrow
a scale as to be really dangerous, and to warrant a jealousy in the people for
their liberties." Madison did express a concern lest the membership of the
House become "excessive,"[14] yet on the whole, he and Hamilton seem
really to have believed that, given the existence of the elite Senate, the other
body should be numerous, to speak for the public at large.

In *The Federalist*, however, Madison declares himself "unable to conceive that the people of America in their present temper . . . will chuse, and
every second year repeat the choice of sixty-five or an hundred men, who
would be disposed to form and pursue a scheme of tyranny or treachery"; nor
"that the state legislatures which must feel so many motives to watch, and
which possess so many means of counteracting the federal legislature,
would fail either to detect or to defeat a conspiracy of the latter against the
liberties of their common constituents." The separation of powers and
checks and balances at the National level will also be a safeguard for popular
government, Madison notes. "The improbability of such a mercenary and
perfidious combination of the several members of government standing on
as different foundations as republican principles will well admit, and at the
same time accountable to the society over which they are placed, ought alone
to quiet this apprehension," he asserts. It is possible to carry political
suspicion too far. "As there is a degree of depravity in mankind which
requires a certain degree of circumspection and distrust," Madison says, "so
there are other qualities in human nature, which justify a certain portion of
esteem and confidence." Were the people completely corrupt, "chains of
despotism" would be necessary to "restrain them from destroying and
devouring one another," he observes.

During this discussion, Madison affirms his belief in a more pervasive
sense of American patriotism than, according to Gerald Stourzh, Hamilton
tends to presume.[15] Madison does not think the House will be particularly
vulnerable to the bribes of foreigners: "If foreign gold could so easily

corrupt our federal rulers, and enable them to ensnare and betray their constituents, how has it happened that we are at this time a free and independent nation?" The Continental Congress of the Revolutionary War period was much smaller than the proposed House and more removed from the people. "Yet we know by happy experience that the public trust was not betrayed; nor has the purity of our public councils in this particular ever suffered even from the whispers of calumny," he remarks. Nor will the president and the Senate be able to pervert the House; their "emoluments of office" will be insufficient for that purpose, and "their private fortunes, as they must all be American citizens, cannot possibly be sources of danger." Madison apparently assumes that a propertied American will naturally identify with the nation and will rarely, if ever, betray its interests.

Federalist No. 56 considers whether the House "will be too small to possess a due knowledge of the interests of its constituents" (378-83). Madison acknowledges that the representatives may not be conversant with certain minor matters, but he maintains that the "ignorance of a variety of minute and particular objects, which do not lie within the compass of legislation, is consistent with every attribute necessary to a due performance of the legislative trust." The chief objects of federal attention—commerce, taxation, and the militia—are such that the requisite information about a state's interests may be possessed "by a very few intelligent men diffusively elected within the state." The representatives will be able to inform each other about the situation in their respective parts of the country, Madison notes. He also repeats his previous observation that future years will see the various sections of the United Staes becoming more alike. "The changes of time, as was formerly remarked, on the comparative situation of the different states," he says, "will have an assimilating effect." To be sure, economic development will cause the states to become internally more heterogeneous, but they will increasingly be alike in their diversity.

This passage constitutes Madison's clearest reconciliation of the nationalism that underlies Publius's argument in general with the pluralism that is featured in No. 10 and elsewhere. The social differentiation resulting from the growth of industry will persist and increase, he believes, whereas regional variations will tend to disappear. We will become more tightly bound together as a nation even as our society becomes more complex. This complexity obviously does not necessarily denote an antagonism of interests, in Madison's view. He thinks that our various concerns can be harmonized from a national pespective. He observes that in Britain, "a nation whose affairs are in the highest degree diversified and complicated," a relatively small number of "representatives of the nation" are a serviceable "depository of the safety, interest and happiness of eight millions." Madison implies that the United States under the proposed Constitution will enjoy a similar felicity.

The next essay, No. 57, argues against the charge that the House of Representatives will lack "sympathy with the mass of the people" (384-90). Avers Madison, "the aim of every political Constitution is or ought to be first to obtain for rulers, men who possess most wisdom to discern, and most virtue to pursue the common good of the society; and in the next place, to take the most effectual precautions for keeping them virtuous, whilst they continue to hold their public trust." In a republic, the rulers are chosen by popular election and are kept faithful by "numerous and various" means, the "most effectual" of which are terms short enough to "maintain a proper responsibility to the people." Nothing about the proposed House is contrary to these "principles of republican government," Madison maintains. "The electors are to be the great body of the people of the United States." Furthermore, "No qualification of wealth, of birth, of religious faith, or of civil profession, is permitted to fetter the judgement or disappoint the inclinations of the people," he somewhat grandiloquently proclaims.

The fidelity of the representatives will be secured in several ways, Madison declares. "In the first place," he observes, the people will tend to elect candidates who, "as they will have been distinguished by the preference of their fellow citizens . . . will be somewhat distinguished also, by those qualities which entitle them to it, and which promise a sincere and scrupulous regard to the nature of their engagements." Also, "motives of a . . . selfish nature will operate: the "pride and vanity" of the representative will "attach him to a form of government which favors his pretentions, and gives him a share in its honors and distinctions." All this "would be found very insufficient," Madison concedes, "without the restraint of frequent elections," but these are required for members of the House. And finally, he points out, "they can make no law which will not have its full operation on themselves and their friends, as well as on the great mass of society." What will stop the representatives from passing laws that exempt themselves? "I answer," says Madison, "the genius of the whole system, the nature of just and constitutional laws, and above all the vigilant and manly spirit which actuates the people of America." Thus, Madison concludes: "Duty, gratitude, interest, ambition itself, are the chords by which" the House "will be bound to fidelity and sympathy with the great mass of the people."

Madison scores the excessive suspicions of the Anti-Federalists. "What," he pertinently asks, "are we to say to the men who profess the most flaming zeal for Republican Government, yet boldly impeach the fundamental principle of it; who pretend to be champions for the right and the capacity of the people to chuse their own rulers, yet maintain that they will prefer those only who will immediately and infallibly betray the trust committed to them?" Madison may not be entirely certain of the wisdom of the future representatives, but he does not doubt their essential trustworthiness.

In No. 58, Madison asserts that the number of representatives will in fact be increased from time to time, as population growth demands. It is the House that will desire such an augmentation, he points out, and the Senate that possibly might not. The House will be able to make its wishes prevail. "Notwithstanding the equal authority which will subsist between the two houses, it cannot be doubted that the house composed of the greater number of members, when supported by the more powerful states, and speaking the known and determined sense of a majority of the people, will have no small advantage in a question depending on the comparative firmness of the two houses" (391-97). Moreover, he contends, since to omit the measure would be to defy the Constitution, this "advantage must be increased by the consciousness felt by the same side, of being supported in its demands, by right, by reason, and by the constitution; and the consciousness on the opposite side, of contending against the force of all these solemn considerations." A majority "coalition" that "on ordinary occasions" might be prevented "would not fail to take place, when not merely prompted by common interest, but justified by equity and the principles of the constitution." Once again we see Madison affirming that national majorities are more likely to have good motivations than bad ones.

Madison repeats his previous argument that increasing the number of representatives beyond the point required for "safety, . . . local information, and . . . diffusive sympathy with the whole society" would not be a good idea. "In the antient republics," he declares, "where the whole body of the people assembled in person, a single orator, or an artful statesman, was generally seen to rule with as compleat a sway, as if a sceptre had been placed in his single hands. On the same principle the more multitudinous a representative assembly may be rendered, the more it will partake of the infirmities incident to collective meetings of the people." In that case, Madison notes: "The countenance of the government may become more democratic, but the soul that animates it will be more oligarchic."

He concludes this essay with an attack on the idea of requiring more than a majority vote to pass legislation in the House. "That some advantages might have resulted from such a precaution, cannot be denied," he admits. "It might have been an additional shield to some particular interests, and another obstacle generally to hasty and partial measures." However, he adds, "these considerations are outweighed by the inconveniencies in the opposite scale. In all cases where justice or the general good might require new laws to be passed, or active measures to be pursued, the fundamental principle of free government would be reversed. It would be no longer the majority that would rule; the power would be transferred to the minority." This passage casts grave doubt on the proposition that Madison was primarily an opponent of majoritarianism and positive government; the greater number is here presumed to be right more often than not, and the harm of preventing good laws is assumed to outweigh the benefit of stopping bad ones. Hamilton made the same argument in No. 22 (140-42).

This is the end of Madison's consideration of the proposed House of Representatives. He portrays that body as a true reflection of the American people as a whole, but one that will possess at least a certain degree of wisdom and virtue. At this point, Publius proceeds to examine the institutions that are designed to supply whatever sagacity the representatives may lack.

After an absence of six weeks, Hamilton reentered the fray with three papers on the regulation of federal elections. They are analyzed in the next chapter. Following these, Madison's last two papers appeared, No. 62 and No. 63, which begin the discussion of the proposed United States Senate.

Madison portrays the Senate as an embodiment of elite virtue; he expects this council to contribute needed stability and wisdom to the affairs of America. It is, in the first place, intended to be a check on the House of Representatives. That body, with its short term and its comparatively numerous membership, is designed to be a reasonably close approximation of the people at large; but what it thereby attains in faithfulness to the general will, it loses in consistency, farsightedness, and discretion, Madison feels; the senators should compensate for the failings of the representatives with regard to the passage of legislation. This argument marks a change in Madison's view of checks and balances. That idea has previously been presented only as a protection for the whole people against traitorous rulers; now it is seen as a device for restraining the people themselves.

Besides counteracting the House, the Senate has a certain role peculiar to itself; it deals with the legislative aspect of foreign affairs. Madison shows why this council is the proper institution for that purpose, and thereby entirely shifts his focus from the idea of checks and balances to that of separation of powers for the purpose of efficiency. He says that the qualities of a Senate are needed in our relations with foreign powers, and he does not seem to want the House involved in such matters at all.

In No. 62, Madison first provides a brief justification for the qualifications of the senators, which, "as distinguished from those of representatives, consist in a more advanced age, and a longer period of citizenship" (415-22). Senators must be thirty years old and nine years a citizen, whereas the requirements for representatives are twenty-five and seven. "The propriety of these distinctions," Madison points out, "is explained by the nature of the senatorial trust; which requiring greater extent of information and stability of character, requires at the same time that the senator should have reached a period of life most likely to supply these advantages; and which participating immediately in transactions with foreign nations, ought to be exercised by none who are not thoroughly weaned from the prepossessions and habits incident to foreign birth and education." This last statement shows that Madison believed the American people to possess distinctive national traits, not present in the inhabitants of other lands. But he clearly did not regard these characteristics as deep-seated aspects of the individual's personality, because just nine years will "thoroughly" convert a foreigner into a reliable citizen.

Madison proceeds to briefly and rather perfunctorily contend for two aspects of the new Senate that he, in fact, abominated and had vigorously opposed in Philadelphia: the election of senators by the state legislatures and the equal representation of the states. The former of these, he says, "is probably the most congenial with the public opinion," will "secure the authority" of the states and "form a convenient link between the two systems," and will "favor a select appointment." Madison had argued quite otherwise at the Convention, noting that since the state legislatures were largely responsible for the country's problems, they could hardly be expected to solve them.[16] The abbreviated nature of his comments here suggest that he has not really changed his mind.

The provision for state equality in the Senate gave Madison much heartburn. Virginia had the largest population of any state and stood to be greatly disadvantaged by that method. Thus his words on this point are not particularly convincing. Indeed, his first remarks sound quite apologetic: "Equality of representation in the senate," he says, "being evidently the result of compromise between the opposite pretentions of the large and the small states, does not call for much discussion." Madison adds that "it is superfluous to try by the standards of theory, a part of the constitution which is allowed on all hands to be the result not of theory, but 'of a spirit of amity, and that mutual deference and concession which the peculiarity of our political situation rendered indispensable.' " It is a "lesser evil" than disunion, he says. This was Madison's true view of the matter, and it is not a ringing endorsement.

Madison now points out "that in a compound republic partaking both of the national and the federal character, the government ought to be founded on a mixture of the principles of proportional and equal representation." Yet he had rejected this very argument at the Convention. The new government, he had then observed, would never act on the states as states, but only on individuals. Thus, he felt, the people should be proportionately represented in the Senate and House alike.[17] He now declares that state equality is both "a constitutional recognition of the portion of sovereignty remaining in the individual states, and an instrument for preserving that residuary sovereignty," and that it should on this account be as "acceptable to the large" as it is "to the small states." But he does not quite say it is good in itself.

Madison does contend that equality in the Senate will serve as an "additional impediment . . . against improper acts of legislation." This is because all laws must be enacted by both "a majority of the people" and "a majority of the states." But, having said this, he proceeds to argue against his own point: "It must be acknowledged that this complicated check on legislation may in some instances be injurious as well as beneficial; and that the peculiar defense which it involves in favour of the smaller states would be more rational, if any interests common to them, and distinct from those of the other states, would otherwise be exposed to peculiar danger." Yet, he decides, since the larger states will on their side control the other body, and "as the facility and excess of law-making seem to be the diseases to which our government are most liable, it is not impossible that this part of the constitution may be more convenient in practice than it appears to many in contemplation." In other words, state equality is a good idea because it may not be as bad as it seems. Approval could hardly be more tepid.

Madison has so far been unconvincingly and rather disingenuously presenting arguments that he himself at most half believes. But having reached the stage in the argument at which his actual priorities can be expressed, his discussion suddenly becomes more pointed and full. He turns to the topic of the "number of senators and the duration of their appointment" and for the first time bothers, in a general way, "to enquire into the purposes which are to be answered by a senate." He presents a profound analysis of the typical flaws in a popular regime, which render an elite lawmaking body desirable for a republican constitution.

First, Madison says, the Senate may forestall the other branches of the government should they "prove unfaithful to their important trust." This, of course, is an argument that we have heard before: checks and balances are a protection for the whole people against the usurpations of their rulers. Madison admits that such official treachery is less likely to happen in a republic than in other polities, presumably because of the representative system. But the need for checking exists nevertheless, he observes, and the Senate will do it. For this purpose, it will be appropriate for the two legislative houses to be distinguished "from each other by every circumstance which will consist with a due harmony in all proper measures, and with the genuine principles of republican government." It is worth remembering that Madison expects the House and Senate to harmonize on "proper measures." Governmental stalemate as such is not his objective.

Second, Madison notes, there is a "propensity of all single and numerous assemblies," such as the proposed House of Representatives, "to yield to the impulse of sudden and violent passions." In order to counter such excesses, the senators are relatively few in number and possess lengthy appointments. Third, the members of the more popular body, due to their short terms and frequent turnover, will lack experience and knowledge concerning public affairs and will thus make errors due to ignorance Declares Madison, "no small share of the present embarrassments of America is to be charged on the blunders of our governments." The new Senate will help correct this situation. These latter two arguments are different from the first. They suggest that the House is being checked for positive reasons of wise governance, rather than just on negative grounds of preventing tyranny—and they imply that the representatives are dangerous not because they will flout popular opinion, but because they will reflect it all too well.

Fourth, he contends, "The mutability in the public councils, arising from a rapid succession of new members, however qualified they may be, points out in the strongest manner, the necessity of some stable institution in the government." Wisdom is needed in the ruling institutions of society, but so is mere steadiness. This is especially the case with regard to foreign affairs, says Madison. He paints a rather grim picture of international rivalries. "One nation is to another what one individual is to another; with this melancholy distinction perhaps, that the former with few of the benevolent emotions than the latter, are under fewer restraints also from taking undue advantage of the indiscretions of each other. Every nation consequently whose affairs betray a want of wisdom and stability, may calculate on every loss which can be sustained from the more systematic policy of its wiser neighbours." Also, he adds, the "internal effects of a mutable policy are still more calamitous. It poisons the blessings of liberty itself." Legislation becomes "voluminous" and "incoherent," and the "attachment and reverence" of the people towards the government is diminished.

A major disadvantage of an unstable regime is the discouragement it gives to "every useful undertaking; the success and profit of which may depend on a continuance of existing arrangements." No worthy capitalistic investments can be made under such conditions, Madison declares: "What prudent merchant will hazard his fortunes in any new branch of commerce, when he knows not but that his plans may be rendered unlawful before they can be executed? What farmer or manufacturer will lay himself out for the encouragement given to any particular cultivation or establishment, when he can have no assurance that his preparatory labors and advances will not render him a victim to an inconstant government?" This passage is worth notice because it is the only one in *The Federalist* that comes close to suggesting that the Senate serves as a special protection for property, a duty that critics such as Beard have seen as the main reason for that body, but that is otherwise unmentioned by Publius.[18] It seems significant that Madison presents this function not as the safeguard of an absolute right, but as a security for socially beneficial private enterprises.

According to No. 63, a "fifth desideratum illustrating the utility of a Senate, is the want of a due sense of national character" (422-31). By this, Madison means an appreciation for the American people as a corporate body with a collective identity—and therefore having a proper image to maintain in the eyes of other countries. He notes that a concern for national character can be expected only from "an assembly so durably invested with public trust, that the pride and consequence of its members may be sensibly incorporated with the reputation and prosperity of the community." Applied to the Senate, this comment constitutes a republican version of the argument for a hereditary aristocracy—the idea that a socially privileged elite will identify with the community in which it has such a valuable stake, and will therefore offer disinterested leadership. Hamilton had expressed that notion at Philadelphia: the British House of Lords, he declared, "is a most noble institution. Having nothing to hope for by a change, and a sufficient interest by means of their property, in being faithful to the national interest, they form a permanent barrier agst. every pernicious innovation."[19] Hamilton doubted whether such a council was possible in a republic: "No temporary Senate will have firmness eno' to answer the purpose," he said. Madison, however, feels that these qualities will be found in the proposed Senate, at least to some extent.

There are obviously major differences between the British Lords lauded by Hamilton and the senatorial elite described by Madison. The aristocracy is linked to the nation by their property and their social rank, whereas Madison sees the senators as similarly bound through their six-year terms. We may sympathize with Hamilton's contention that the connective force of a temporary office is hardly comparable to that of a landed estate and a permanent title. Yet Madison's concept is most interesting as a sign of his relatively modern cast of mind. The senators, he says, are valuable because of their national perspective. He does not envision them as a separate caste, but as a relatively enlightened segment of the people with an enlarged understanding of the communal bond between all Americans. Hamilton's notion, expressed at the Convention, is the traditional argument for a nobility. Madison, however, portrays the Senate strictly as a national elite of the present-day variety. In both cases, we are reminded of the early affinity of nationalism for the aristocratic conception of society. Madison has, in this instance, left archaic presumptions more completely behind.

Madison feels that the semiaristocratic identification of the senators with the nation will be most useful in foreign affairs, where it will render our government more responsible in its dealings with the rest of the globe. The "half-yearly representatives of Rhode-Island," he points out, could hardly be expected to pay much attention to "the light in which" their "iniquitous measures . . . would be viewed by foreign nations, or even by the sister states." The more permanent and steadier Senate will show greater concern for our national reputation. Whatever we do, Madison somewhat cynically suggests, we should at least try to seem competent. "Independently of the merits of any particular plan or measure, it is desirable on various accounts, that it should appear to other nations as the offspring of a wise and honorable policy." Less cynically, he notes that world opinion may serve to correct our own prejudices. "In doubtful cases, particularly where the national councils may be warped by some strong passion, or momentary interest, the presumed or known opinion of the impartial world, may be the best guide that can be followed." We know from the previous essay that Madison regarded international relations as rather a dog-eat-dog affair; yet he also recognizes limits to acceptable national behavior. He, like Jay, is a polycentric nationalist.

As his sixth point, Madison introduces a "new" and "paradoxical" idea: frequent elections will actually operate in some respects to weaken, rather than to strengthen, the responsibility of officials to their constituents. "The objects of government may be divided into two classes," he says, "the one depending on measures which have singly an immediate and sensible operation; the other depending on a succession of well chosen and well connected measures, which have a gradual and perhaps unobserved operation." Frequent elections will enforce responsibility as to the first of these, but will actually obscure any responsibility for the latter. "An assembly elected for so short a term as to be unable to provide more than one or two links in a chain of measures, . . . ought not to be answerable for the final result," Madison observes. "Nor is it possible for the people to estimate the share of influence which their annual assemblies may respectively have on events resulting from the mixed transactions of several years," he adds. The senators, with their long terms, may be held "justly and effectually answerable" for the attainment of long-range public objectives.

Finally, Madison forthrightly tells his readers that a Senate is necessary to counteract their own political limitations. "As the cool and deliberate sense of the community ought in all governments, and actually will in all free governments ultimately prevail over the views of its rulers; so there are particular moments in public affairs, when the people stimulated by some irregular passion, or some illicit advantage, or misled by the artful misrepresentations of interested men, may call for measures which they themselves will afterwards be the most ready to lament and condemn." The Senate can "suspend the blow meditated by the people against themselves, until reason, justice and truth, can regain their authority over the public mind." Thus checks and balances are not only a safeguard for the citizenry against usurpers, as indicated in No. 51, but also a protection against the political blunders of those very citizens. Madison diplomatically prefaces this argument with a kind word for his fellow Americans, who are declared to be "little blinded by prejudice, or corrupted by flattery," and who therefore can stand to hear of their own shortcomings.

He now makes his final reference to the argument of No. 10. It is true, he admits, "that a people spread over an extensive region, cannot like the crouded inhabitants of a small district, be subject to the infection of violent passions; or to the danger of combining in the pursuit of unjust measures." This is, indeed, "one of the principal recommendations" of the American union. Yet this does not obviate the need for "auxiliary precautions" like the Senate, he contends. It appears that the division of power in the new central regime may, after all, serve the same purpose as the multiplicity of interest groups found in the whole nation: the taming of factious majorities. No. 51, we recall, implied otherwise. It seems that Madison has now decided that protection of minority rights is a purpose of the Senate—although hardly the main one, judging by his relatively brief mention of this function.

Finally, Madison engages in a lengthy historical dissertation featuring various references to Sparta, Rome, Carthage, Athens, the Ephori, the Archons, and the Cosmi of Crete. He notes that "history informs us of no long lived republic which had not a senate." He clearly envisions the proposed American upper house primarily as a strong body that will offer guidance and direction to the nation. But he denies that the new Senate will ever manage to transform itself into "a tyrannical aristocracy." He points out that before "such a revolution can be effected, the senate . . . must in the first place corrupt itself; must next corrupt the state legislatures, must then corrupt the house of representatives, and must finally corrupt the people at large." Experience indeed "proves the irresistable force possessed by that branch of a free government, which has the people on its side." He concludes: "Against the force of the immediate representatives of the people, nothing will be able to maintain even the constitutional authority of the senate, but such a display of enlightened policy, and attachment to the public good, as will divide with that branch of the legislature, the affections and support of the entire body of the people themselves." With that happy thought, Madison retires as Publius.

It is true that Madison's essays may give, at least on first reading, a somewhat different impression than is conveyed by the contributions of his colleagues. The Virginia statesman appears less vehement than Hamilton, less serenely confident than Jay, more inclined to balance and weigh competing considerations. Yet, as already observed, the contrast is really a matter of style, not substance. Madison may seem more equivocal than he actually is. He makes more reference to the diversities of the American people than the other authors are inclined to do—but he also regards his fellow citizens as unified in many respects. He thinks they have a common interest that their leaders can perceive and promote. He predicts that the House of Representatives will be the most powerful branch of the proposed government because it can speak for a determined national majority, and he believes that the Senate is necessary to provide a corporate national perspective. He says that the American nation will develop in the future through a process of assimilation—which is also the opinion of Hamilton and Jay. There is no real contradiction between these three.

Madison does not call for a generally passive regime. To be sure, he regards the separation of powers and checks and balances as useful for the prevention of impulsive popular mistakes, yet he presents his case in more of a positive than a negative vein. He envisions the Senate frustrating the foolish actions of the more plebeian chamber, and of the people in general, but he also sees the elite council as providing steady leadership, particularly with respect to foreign affairs. His aim seems more constructive than negative. This Senate does not, on the whole, appear calculated to weaken the authority of the government. Madison mentions property-related issues only briefly, and then in such a way as to suggest that his real concern is intelligent economic management, not the safeguarding of an absolute individual right. It is hinted that the Senate may on occasion protect minorities, but this function is not presented as that body's principal duty, by any means. The Senate is, in Madison's opinion, a champion of the larger national good, not a stronghold for special interests. The Virginian writes as a political chief who wishes to strengthen the ruling institutions of the country, not as a servant of the wealthy class, desiring merely to avoid public regulation.

Federalist No. 63 appeared March 1, 1788. Within days, Madison was on his way home. Hamilton again took up the pen of Publius. This literary project had far outgrown its initial conception, but there remained a great deal to be said.

8
Hamilton
Provides Leadership

Federalist No. 59, which marks Hamilton's return, was published on February 22, 1788. From this point, except for a pair of essays by Madison and one by Jay, Hamilton wrote all of the remaining papers. The last number to appear in the daily newspapers was No. 77, on April 2. Hamilton was then called away to his legal briefs and to more pressing political concerns and left the argument of Publius for the time being uncompleted. Brutus—who had been gamely continuing, although at only about one-eighth of Hamilton's output—immediately ceased publication. The first volume of the M'Lean edition of *The Federalist*, containing the papers through No. 36, had already been brought out in March. On May 28, the second volume came off the presses. This tome featured the first appearance of the final eight essays. Hamilton hurriedly sent off a copy to Madison in Virginia, where he was engaged in his celebrated oratorical duel with Patrick Henry.[1] On June 17, Hamilton and Jay met with the other New York delegates at Poughkeepsie, where they proceeded to make some notable speeches of their own over the next few weeks. The authors of *The Federalist* laid down their pens only to plunge even deeper into the swirl of public controversy.

The remaining *Federalist* papers discuss the institutions of the proposed government that can be regarded as somewhat remote from the people: the Senate, the presidency, and the federal judiciary. The themes of previous essays reappear here. Hamilton is constantly stressing the utility of national centralization and the concomitant necessity for vigorous, farsighted, upright political leadership. The division of powers is presented as a device against despotism, but as with Madison's view, it frequently seems to achieve a concentration rather than a dispersion of authority.

Hamilton's first three papers upon his return—Nos. 59, 60, and 61—deal with Congress's power under the Constitution to alter any state regulations concerning the "times, places, and manner" of electing members of the national House and Senate, "except as to the places of choosing Senators."[2] This is both a necessary and an unexceptionable authority, he argues.

In No. 59, Hamilton declares that the "propriety" of a national oversight of these elections "rests upon the evidence of this plain proposition, that every government ought to contain in itself the means of its own preservation" (397-403). This rule has not been invariably observed in the design of the Constitution, he admits, but the "just reasoner will . . . disapprove every deviation from it, which may not appear to have been dictated by . . . necessity." And even in such a case, "though he may acquiesce in the necessity; yet he will not cease to regard a departure from so fundamental a principle, as a portion of imperfection in the system which may prove the seed of future weakness and perhaps anarchy." Hamilton points out that putting "an exclusive power of regulating elections for the National Government, in the hands of the State Legislatures, would leave the existence of the Union entirely at their mercy. They could at any moment annihilate it, by neglecting to provide for the choice of persons to administer its affairs."

Hamilton now gives an example of one of those deviations from the proper rule, dictated by necessity and presaging future weakness and anarchy, that has unfortunately been included in the proposed Constitution. "It is certainly true," he admits, "that the State Legislatures, by forbearing the appointment of Senators, may destroy the National Government." But this "evil . . . could not have been avoided without excluding the States, in their political capacities, wholly from a place in the organization of the National Government." Had this been done, "it would doubtless have been interpreted into an entire dereliction of the fœderal principle; and would certainly have deprived the State governments of that absolute safe-guard, which they will have under this provision." Thus, Hamilton notes, "however wise it may have been, to have submitted in this instance to an inconvenience, for the attainment of a necessary advantage, or a greater good, no inference can be drawn from thence to favor an accumulation of the evil, where no necessity urges, nor any greater good invites." The states can disrupt the election of the senators, and that will be problem enough without allowing them any further authority of the sort.

Thus Hamilton here speaks equivocally of one of the foremost federal features of the Constitution. To be sure, since only one-third of the senators will be elected at any one time, state control over this process is relatively tolerable, he admits. Still, it is an "inconvenience" and even an "evil" that could lead to debility and chaos. True, it achieves a "necessary advantage" and "greater good"—the "absolute" safeguarding of the states. But Hamilton actually sounds rather lukewarm concerning the benefits of this course. To have denied the states the right to participate in the national regime would have been "interpreted" as a disregarding of federalism, he asserts; it "may" have been wise to allow them that prerogative. Thus he gives lip service to this provision, but he shows no real enthusiasm for it. His own suggestion, which he presented at Philadelphia, was for senators to be named by "electors chosen for that purpose by the people."[3]

Hamilton concludes this essay with a discussion of the dangers of allowing the states too much power. He notes that occasions may arise in which the "people of America" are "warmly attached to the government of the Union," while at the same time "the particular rulers of particular States, stimulated by the natural rivalship of power and by the hopes of personal aggrandizement, and supported by a strong faction in each of these States, may be in a very opposite temper." He mentions the "scheme of separate confederacies, which will . . . be a never failing bait to all such influential characters in the State administrations as are capable of preferring their own emolument and advancement to the public weal." These disaffected provincial leaders will not refrain from "seizing the opportunity of some casual dissatisfaction among the people . . . which perhaps they may themselves have excited," and their nefarious plots of disunion will always be "patronised and abetted" by "the intrigues of foreign powers." Therefore, the states must not be given "guardianship" over the "preservation" of the union, Hamilton warns.

Federalist No. 60 considers the possibility that the federal power to regulate elections might "be employed . . . to promote the election of some favourite class of men in exclusion of others; by confining the places of election to particular districts, and rendering it impracticable to the citizens at large to partake in the choice" (403-10). Snorts Hamilton, "of all chimerical suppositions, this seems to be the most chimerical." Should the national rulers attempt such a "violent" and "improper" course, they would undoubtedly be faced with "an immediate revolt of the great body of the people—headed and directed by the state governments." And Hamilton expects that the "diversity in the state of property, in the genius, manners, and habits of the people of the different parts of the union" will bar any agreement among "their representatives" concerning which of the "ranks and conditions in society" to favor. He seemingly recalls that he has expressed some less pluralistic sentiments in previous papers and tries to harmonize his words: The Americans will indeed tend towards "a gradual assimilation," he admits; but he claims that certain differences may still remain "permanently." Finally, "the circumstance, which will be likely to have the greatest influence in the matter, will be the dissimilar modes of constituting the several component parts of the government." The three branches will never concur "in a predilection for any particular" group.

Hamilton observes that agriculturalists and merchants are the two classes that plausibly might aim at an undue prominence in the new federal government, and he reassuringly maintains "that it is infinitely less likely, that either of them should gain an ascendant in the national councils, than that the one or the other of them should predominate in all the local councils." The sentiment of the nation will tend to be more moderate than that of any particular state: "the national representation . . . will be an emanation from a greater variety of interests, and in much more various proportions, than are to be found in a single state," says Hamilton, adding that "it will be much less apt to espouse" agriculture or commerce "with a decided partiality, than the representation of any single state." Here is the argument of No. 10 in all its glory. If either of the two classes does tend to prevail, it will be the farmers: "In a country consisting chiefly of the cultivators of land where the rulers of an equal representation obtain the landed interest must upon the whole preponderate in the government." But Hamilton, the spokesman for the merchants, is not worried on that account. He declares himself to be confident that "men accustomed to investigate the sources of public prosperity, upon a large scale, must be . . . well convinced of the utility of commerce." A nationwide perspective will give each partial interest its due, he presumes.

The next essay, No. 61, argues that the New York State Constitution contains no better protection of the people's right to vote than is found in the plan of the Philadelphia Convention. Yet that charter has "never been thought chargeable with inattention to the security of liberty" (410-14). Therefore, Hamilton declares, the antagonists of the new national government "ought at least to prove to us, that it is easier to subvert the liberties of three millions of people, with the advantage of local governments to head their opposition, than of two hundred thousand people, who are destitute of that advantage." He proceeds to sound Madison's theme: the danger of a "predominant faction" within a state and the moderating effect of a multiplicity of interest groups across the nation. Also, he notes a "positive advantage which will result" from national regulation of elections: "the circumstance of uniformity in the time of elections for the Fœderal House of Representatives." Hamilton asserts that if "each State may choose its own time of election, it is possible there may be at least as many different periods as there are months in the year," and that "uniformity may be found by experience to be . . . both . . . a security against the perpetuation of the same spirit in the body; and . . . a cure for the diseases of faction."

The following two papers are Madison's last, already discussed, on the Senate. The next three consider further aspects of this elite body. Jay makes his final appearance in *Federalist* No. 64. He argues that the proposed Constitution is right to entrust the whole treaty-making power to the president and the Senate.

Jay begins with praise of the procedures for choosing senators and the president—by the state legislatures and "select bodies of electors," respectively. Such methods, says Jay, have "vastly the advantage of elections by the people in their collective capacity, where the activity of party zeal taking advantage of the supineness, the ignorance, and the hopes and fears of the unwary and interested, often places men in office by the votes of a small proportion of the electors" (432-38). Having paid this compliment to the voters he is trying to woo, Jay proceeds to infer that "the president and senators so chosen will always be of the number of those who best understand our national interests, whether considered in relation to the several states or to foreign nations, who are best able to promote those interests, and whose reputation for integrity inspires and merits confidence. With such men," he confidently affirms, "the power of making treaties may be safely lodged."

This passage is the strongest endorsement in *The Federalist* of the system of indirect election. Publius shows little love for the state legislatures in general, but Jay predicts here that they will at least choose capable senators. His sentiments contrast with the remarks of his two colleagues on the subject; Hamilton and Madison supported the state appointment of senators for reasons of expediency, not conviction, and their words on behalf of the method in *The Federalist* are not especially enthusiastic. Jay sounds more heartfelt in his espousal. Of course, since he praises the state legislatures simply as collections of well-informed individuals, his comments suggest no advantage from the involvement of the states as corporate entities in this process.

Jay notes "the absolute necessity of system in the conduct of . . . national affairs," and he emphasizes the unsuitability of the House of Representatives on this account. "They who wish to commit the power under consideration to a popular assembly, composed of members constantly coming and going in quick succession," he declares, "seem not to recollect that such a body must necessarily be inadequate to the attainment of those great objects, which require to be steadily contemplated in all their relations and circumstances, and which can only be approached and achieved by measures, which not only talents, but also exact information and often much time are necessary to concert and to execute." In addition to being "able and honest," the senators will "continue in place a sufficient time to become perfectly acquainted with our national concerns, and to form and introduce a system for the management of them." Also, the fact that only a portion of the Senate will be subject to removal at any one time, "by leaving a considerable residue of the old ones in place," preserves "uniformity and order, as well as a constant succession of official information," Jay points out.

Jay asserts that the promotion of commerce especially requires a coordinated governmental plan. "There are few," he says, "who will not admit that the affairs of trade and navigation should be pursued by a system cautiously formed and steadily pursued; and that both our treaties and our laws should correspond with, and be made to promote it." The Senate is the body to maintain "conformity" to any such scheme, Jay conends.

But even the Senate may be a little too open for some purposes, Jay confesses. Treaty negotiations will frequently require "perfect *secrecy* and immediate *dispatch*," and sometimes the chief executive is essential in that regard. "There are cases where the most useful intelligence may be obtained, if the persons possessing it can be relieved from apprehensions of discovery. Those apprehensions will operate on those persons whether they are actuated by mercenary or friendly motives, and there doubtless are many of both descriptions, who would rely on the secrecy of the president, but who would not confide in that of the senate, and still less in that of a large popular assembly," Jay realistically observes. Also, the president can act on the spur of the moment, which is often necessary: "there frequently are occasions when days, nay even hours, are precious," he notes. "As in the field, so in the cabinet, there are moments to be seized as they pass, and they who preside in either, should be left in capacity to improve them." Thus, in the field of foreign policy, the Senate will supply "talents, information, integrity, and deliberate investigations on the one hand," whereas the president will provide "secrecy and dispatch on the other."

These comments by Jay will appear congenial to modern advocates of strong executive leadership in foreign policy, although critics of the imperial presidency will respond that he at least takes the oversight role of the Senate seriously. Jay clearly believes the *conduct* of foreign policy should be left entirely to the executive branch, with the Senate limited to the role of judging the results—and with the Senate alone playing that role. He would not be very pleased to find the House involved with these matters and would regard any wider public meddling with them as unthinkable.

Jay notes that some opponents of the new Constitution object to treaties being deemed "the supreme laws of the land" and feel that such agreements, "like acts of assembly, should be repealable at pleasure." He very sensibly observes "that a treaty is only another name for a bargain; and that it would be impossible to find a nation who would make any bargain with us, which should be binding on them *absolutely*, but on us only so long and so far as we may think proper to be bound by it." Two nations are necessary to make treaties, Jay declares, and it follows that "as the consent of both was essential to their formation at first, so must it ever afterwards be to alter or cancel them." Such agreements are inherently "beyond the lawful reach of legislative acts" and will remain so "at any future period or under any form of government," he says. Thus, under the proposed Constitution, the Senate and the president—institutions somewhat insulated from the vagaries of the masses—will possess the power to commit the country to obligations that the direct representatives of the people will be unable to repeal, consistent with the laws of nations. Jay obviously does not think this is a problem; he regards it as a wise procedure.

Thus, the separation of powers, usually regarded as a method of dispersing power and of slowing down the government, can serve the values of centralization and speed. The president and the Senate are presented by Publius as checks on the encroachments of the House of Representatives. Yet these two bodies together have been given the authority to conclude certain important matters by themselves, with no interference from the popular branch. The prerogative of treaty making exists in a highly concentrated form in the proposed Constitution.

Jay believes there is little danger that the authority entrusted to this elite group will be misused. These sagacious officials will act on behalf of the entire nation: "In proportion as the United States assume a national form, and a national character, so will the good of the whole be more and more an object of attention; and the government must be a weak one indeed, if it should forget that the good of the whole can only be promoted by advancing the good of each of the parts or members which compose the whole." It is evident that Jay, like his colleagues, sees American nationhood as something that will grow stronger in the future, rather than something that is already fully formed. Yet the interests of individuals are even now connected with that of their country, Jay asserts. "It will not be in the power of the president and senate to make any treaties, by which they and their families and estates will not be equally bound and affected with the rest of the community; and having no private interest distinct from that of the nation, they will be under no temptations to neglect the latter," he contends.

Finally, Jay summarily dismisses the possibility of corruption: "He must either have been very unfortunate in his intercourse with the world, or possess a heart very susceptible of such impressions, who can think it probable that the president and two-thirds of the senate will ever be capable of such unworthy conduct," he says. Jay thus exits on the same note he came in on. As in *Federalist* No. 2, he here celebrates the communal ties of the American people and the wisdom and honesty of their most prominent leaders. The idea of a national elite underlies the whole argument of Publius, but it is undoubtedly most clearly expressed by Jay.

In *Federalist* No. 65, Hamilton defends the Senate's designation as the court for impeachment trials. Charges concerning "misconduct of public men" will "seldom fail to agitate the passions of the whole community, and to divide it into parties," he notes (439-45). The House of Representatives, the direct voice of the people, will rightfully present the indictment. But the Senate should decide the case. "What other body would be likely to feel confidence enough in its own situation, to preserve unawed and uninfluenced the necessary impartiality between an individual accused, and the representatives of the people, his accusers?" The Supreme Court would not have been as proper because, among other considerations, the judges may not "possess the degree of credit and authority, which might, on certain occasions, be indispensable, towards reconciling the people to a decision, that should happen to clash with an accusation brought by their immediate representatives." Hamilton manifests sympathy for the situation "of men, whose firm and faithful execution of their duty might have exposed them to the persecution of an intemperate or designing majority in the House of Representatives." He observes bluntly that "the demon of faction will at certain seasons extend his sceptre over all numerous bodies of men."

Federalist No. 66 answers several miscellaneous objections to the impeachment role of the Senate, the most substantial of which is "that it contributes to an undue accumulation of power in that body, tending to give to the government a countenance too aristocratic" (445-51). Hamilton first points out that every power allotted to the Senate has been given to it for good reasons. Moreover, he adds, there is no actual danger that the Senate will ever outweigh the House of Representatives: "the most popular branch of every government, partaking of the republican genius, by being generally the favorite of the people, will be as generally a full match, if not an overmatch, for every other member of the government." He lists the various particular authorities of the House, such as the "exclusive privilege of originating money bills" and "the sole right of instituting impeachments." He dwells most on the fact that the House of Representatives "will be the umpire in all elections of the president, which do not unite the suffrages of a majority of the whole number of electors." This, thinks Hamilton, is a momentous power: "It would not perhaps be rash to predict, that as a means of influence it will be found to outweigh all the peculiar attributes of the Senate." His crystal ball goes awry here.

Hamilton proceeds to make some more prescient remarks on the probable presidential dominance of the federal appointment process. The executive, he observes, will make the real choice of officials. Indeed, the senators "might even entertain a preference to some other person, at the very moment they were assenting to the one proposed; because . . . they could not be sure, if they withheld their assent, that the subsequent nomination would fall upon their own favorite." In Hamilton's opinion, as we shall see, this is probably a good thing, because one person is a better judge of character than any collectivity can possibly be (510-11).

The next eleven essays consider the office of president of the United States. Hamilton believes the most important attribute of this functionary will be vigor and decisiveness in the execution of the laws. Secondarily, the chief executive will serve as a check on attempted usurpations or unwise actions by the legislature. The presidency is a mixture of both popular and elite elements, Hamilton feels. The electoral college provides both for taking the public pulse and for refining the signal, whereas the four-year term gives duration, but not too much. Indefinite reeligibility is said to be a crucial provision. It is envisioned that the chief executive may on occasion need to withstand the clamors of the multitude, but Hamilton seemingly finds this official less aristocratic than the Senate. The presidency is the supreme instance of centralization of political power in the proposed government, and the argument for the concentration of governmental authority is strongly made by Publius in the course of this discussion.

Federalist No. 67 consists basically of a refutation of the fourth letter of Cato, which had been published three and a half months earlier.[4] Publius charges that, "calculating on the aversion of the people to monarchy," the opponents of the new Constitution have grossly exaggerated the puissance of the president (452-57). "He has been seated on a throne surrounded with minions and mistresses," Hamilton sarcastically observes, "giving audience to the envoys of foreign potentates, in all the supercilious pomp of majesty." The author devotes considerable space to denouncing a mistaken remark by Cato that the president is empowered to make temporary appointments of senators. He unmercifully castigates this error as a "deliberate imposture and deception," a "false and unfounded suggestion," and a "shameful outrage . . . offered to the dictates of truth and to the rules of fair dealing." This essay is little more than a diatribe over what probably was an honest misapprehension of Cato's. Hamilton himself finally acknowledges that No. 67 features "a severity of animadversion little congenial to the general spirit of these papers." But since Cato was rumored to be his enemy Clinton, he apparently could not resist the cheap shot.

The next essay, No. 68, begins on a far more congenial note. "The mode of appointment of the chief magistrate" has met with general approval, observes Hamilton, even from those who oppose the plan as a whole (457-62). He instances the Federal Farmer, whom he calls the "most plausible" of his party "who has appeared in print." Hamilton's discussion of the electoral college system reveals much about his view of the presidency.

"It was desirable," Hamilton says, "that the sense of the people should operate in the choice of the person to whom so important a trust was to be confided. This end will be answered by committing the right of making it, not to any pre-established body, but to men, chosen by the people for the special purpose, and at the particular conjuncture." Thus the popular mood of the moment will be a major factor in the selection process. But that mood will be subject to some elite guidance and interpretation. "It was equally desirable," Hamilton continues, "that the immediate election should be made by men most capable of analizing the qualities adapted to the station, and acting under the circumstances favourable to deliberation and to a judicious combination of all the reasons and inducements, which were proper to govern their choice. A small number of persons, selected by their fellow citizens from the general mass, will be most likely to possess the information and discernment requisite to so complicated an investigation," he contends. The electors, it seems, through their knowledge of the characters of our leaders, will select the chief best able to translate the inchoate desires of the public into effective action. It should be noted that Hamilton here speaks of "the people" as a single entity. His words have a pronounced nationalistic tinge in this passage.

It is interesting to observe that Hamilton does not at any point characterize the electoral college as a mechanism to counteract or frustrate the popular will. Rather, he seems to envision this body as an expression of public opinion. He stresses the fact that the electors are chosen for the single specific duty of selecting a president, and he is evidently suggesting that the voters will have thoroughly canvassed their intentions in that regard. The electors will provide intelligent direction for the popular will, but it is not particularly anticipated that they will try to stand against it. Since Publius does not hesitate to identify other political bodies that are expected to thwart the masses on occasion, this omission is undoubtedly significant. It should also be noted that Hamilton always presumes the electors will be chosen by the people, ignoring the fact that the state legislatures technically have the right, under the Constitution, to determine that selection—a detail that Madison has not forgotten (311). Hamilton is the more prophetic on this point, Madison the more pendantically correct.

Hamilton does, however, appear to see some virtue to state-level action in the presidential contest: "As the electors, chosen in each state, are to assemble and vote in the state, in which they are chosen, this detached and divided situation will expose them much less to heats and ferments, which might be communicated from them to the people, than if they were all to be convened at one time, in one place." This passage constitutes the greatest praise that Publius ever gives to a decentralized procedure. Hamilton probably has in mind such precedents as the tumultuous assemblies of nobles who elected the kings of Poland amid scenes of violence and foreign bribery.[5] It will not "be found easy," he points out, to inveigle electors "dispersed as they would be over thirteen states" into improper "combinations."

This passage is not, of course, strictly speaking an argument for federalism, since Hamilton does not envision the states per se playing a role in the presidential election process. Still, these comments appear disharmonious with the usual nationalism of Publius. Perhaps Hamilton felt that the unusual perils of a presidential race dictated a departure from his ordinary principles. Or perhaps he merely wished to praise the Constitution's provisions and did not care about consistency. In any case, he does perceive the problem with a decentralized election: The electors may be scattered not only geographically, but also in their votes. In that event, a national body must choose. "But as a majority of the votes might not always happen to centre on one man and as it might be unsafe to permit less than a majority to be conclusive, it is provided, that in such a contingency, the house of representatives shall select." Indeed, we know from No. 66 that Hamilton must have thought that the House would exercise this power rather often, since he finds it one of that council's most impressive prerogatives (448).

Hamilton is also concerned about the danger of corruption, which he thinks will arise "chiefly from the desire in foreign powers to gain an improper ascendant in our councils." His remedy for this evil is not dispersion, however, but democracy. He notes that the choosing of the electors will be "an immediate act of the people of America," and that it will be "for the temporary and sole purpose of making the appointment." The officials of the national government "who from situation might be suspected of too great devotion to the president in office" are not eligible to be made electors. "Thus," Hamilton observes, "without corrupting the body of the people, the immediate agents in the election will at least enter upon the task, free from any sinister byass." To pervert them after they have been chosen will be impossibly difficult: "The business of corruption, when it is to embrace so considerable a number of men, requires time, as well as means," and the electors' "transient existence" will not allow this. Here, incidentally, is yet another passage that refers to the American people as a single entity.

As Hamilton now points out, an "important desideratum was, that the executive should be independent for his continuance in office on all, but the people themselves." For this reason, he notes, the Constitution has made "his re-election to depend on a special body of representatives, deputed by the society for the single purpose of making this important choice." Once again, the popular side of the presidency is emphasized. Hamilton predicts that the position will generally be occupied by sagacious statesmen. "Talents for low intrigue and the little arts of popularity may alone suffice to elevate a man to the first honors in a single state; but it will require other talents and a different kind of merit to establish him in the esteem and confidence of the whole union." This is no doubt a dig at Clinton. Hamilton loosely quotes Alexander Pope: "That which is best administered is best."[6] And although he declares that he "cannot acquiesce" in the poet's "political heresy," he does not entirely disagree either: "the true test of a good government is its aptitude and tendency to produce a good administration," he says. He concludes with a brief discussion of the vice-presidency, the only mention of this office in *The Federalist.*

In No. 69, Hamilton undertakes to contrast the authorities of the proposed president of the United States with those of the king of Great Britain and the governor of New York (462-70). His comparison is on the basis of a number of factors: tenure, liability to criminal prosecution, military prerogatives, strength of the legislative veto, right to conclude treaties, power over appointments, and many others. Hamilton decides that the potency of the president is less than that of the English monarch and about the same as that of his state's chief executive. Thus he tries to put his enemy, Governor Clinton, on the defensive. It is no doubt true that the powers of the British king were, on paper, far greater than the president's. Yet the New York governor was the strongest state executive in the nation at that time,[7] so the rough equivalence of the president to that official has quite a different significance than Hamilton implies. The proposed national executive was not a forceful chief by his standards, but in the context of eighteenth-century America, this was a relatively vigorous functionary.

Federalist No. 70 begins by noticing the "idea . . . that a vigorous executive is inconsistent with the genius of republican government" (471-80). Hamilton dismisses this notion without really bothering to refute it, on the grounds that a strong executive is in any case necessary for an adequate regime. Americans, it seems, must "hope" that their suspicions of executive power are "destitute of foundation." Hamilton lists the reasons for an energetic executive: "protection of the community against foreign attacks . . . steady administration of the laws . . . protection of property against those irregular and high handed combinations which sometimes interrupt the ordinary course of justice . . . security of liberty against the enterprises and assaults of ambition, of faction, and of anarchy." He also enumerates the constituent elements of this essential institution: "first unity, secondly duration, thirdly an adequate provision for its support, fourthly competent powers." And he notes the proper guards against executive abuse: "1st. a due dependence on the people, secondly a due responsibility." The need for unity is brilliantly argued in the present essay.

Hamilton, like Montesquieu, finds different qualities suitable for the executive and legislative branches. A community should not make laws lightly and should consider legislative proposals most carefully, he says. Once made, however, the laws should have firm and swift enforcement. Thus, he observes, political thinkers "have declared in favor of a single executive and a numerous legislature. They have . . . considered energy as the most necessary qualification of the former, and have regarded this as most applicable to power in a single hand." But they have called for a numerous membership of the lawmaking body: it is "adapted to deliberation and wisdom, and best calculated to conciliate the confidence of the people and to secure their privileges and interests." Then comes a passage congenial to pluralists: "In the legislature, promptitude of decision is oftener an evil than a benefit. The differences of opinion, and the jarring of parties in that department of the government, though they may sometimes obstruct salutary plans, yet often promote deliberation and circumspection; and serve to check excesses in the majority," Hamilton points out.

The latter part of this passage appears to place an overriding value on the safeguarding of minority interests in the legislative process. We shall recall, however, that Publius has expressed himself rather differently in earlier papers: both Hamilton and Madison have previously criticized requirements for extraordinary majorities in the lawmaking arena, on the grounds that these will tend to prevent necessary government actions and exalt the lesser over the greater number (140-41, 396-97). Indeed, the present essay does not say that legislative majorities are dangerous, but implies rather that such majorities, when they form under pluralistic conditions, are to be trusted. Also, this statement on behalf of a multitudinous legislative branch appears in the course of an argument demonstrating why the executive should be unified and decisive. It is obvious that Hamilton here is really concerned not with celebrating diversity and slowness as such, but with reminding his readers that these attributes are sufficiently supplied by other parts of the government and so do not need to be featured as qualities of the president.

Hamilton certainly shows an appreciation for the advantages of a concentration of political authority. "That unity is conducive to energy will not be disputed," he declares. "Decision, activity, secrecy, and dispatch will generally characterize the proceedings of one man, in a much more eminent degree, than the proceedings of any greater number; and in the proportion as the number is increased, these qualities will be diminished." He notes that the unity of the executive "may be destroyed in two ways; either by vesting the power in two or more magistrates of equal dignity and authority; or by vesting it ostensibly in one man, subject in whole or in part to the controul and co-operation of others, in the capacity of counsellors to him." These methods are not equally bad, for the first is worse than the second, but they are both undesirable and for the same reasons, Hamilton contends.

Disagreement, he points out, is endemic to human affairs and is especially common among political chieftains: "Whenever two or more persons are engaged in any common enterprize or pursuit, there is always danger of difference of opinion. If it be a public trust or office in which they are cloathed with equal dignity and authority, there is peculiar danger of personal emulation and even animosity." Hamilton notes that should such "dissentions" occur among members of the "supreme executive magistracy, . . . they might impede or frustrate the most important measures of the government, in the most critical emergencies of the state," besides promoting "factions" among the people. He considers at length the propensity of politicians to discordance: "Men often oppose a thing merely because they have had no agency in planning it, or because it may have been planned by those they dislike. But if they have been consulted and have happened to disapprove, opposition then becomes in their estimation an indispensable duty of self-love." Hamilton suggests that the opponents of the Constitution are motivated by "this despicable frailty, or rather detestable vice."

Plurality in the executive "tends to conceal faults, and destroy responsibility," he observes. Each member will condemn the others for whatever has gone wrong. "It often becomes impossible, amidst mutual accusations, to determine on whom the blame or the punishment ought really to fall." Hamilton instances the behavior of Clinton and his associates. Many "scandalous appointments to important offices" have been made in New York, but "the blame has been laid by the governor on the members of the council; who on their part have charged it upon his nomination," and the general public remains in ignorance. "In tenderness to individuals, I forbear to descend to particulars," Hamilton piously declares.

Hamilton points out that because the "person" of a monarch is "sacred," an executive council is necessary in a kingdom to provide responsibility. But an executive council in a republic is superflous—because a president is accountable for his actions—and actually tends to destroy responsibility. He notes that the concept of such a body stems from "that maxim of republican jealousy, which considers power as safer in the hands of a number of men than of a single man." Hamilton, of course, denies the truth of the idea, at least with regard to the executive power. But he adds that even "if the maxim should be admitted to be applicable to the case, I should contend that the advantage on that side would not counterballance the numerous disadvantages on the opposite side." This is a notable assertion. Hamilton is affirming that it is worthwhile to run some risk with regard to liberty in order to attain the advantages of strong executive power. If nothing else, this remark is admirable for its candor. But Hamilton never admits any actual contradiction between safety and executive unity.

The next two papers, No. 71 and No. 72, consider the duration of the term of the chief executive. In the first of these, Hamilton states that a term of some considerable length is necessary to motivate the president to use his powers with firmness. The writer's quasi-monarchical leanings are quite evident here.

Hamilton's reasonings are based on "a general principle of human nature, that a man will be interested in whatever he possesses, in proportion to the firmness or precariousness of the tenure, by which he holds it; will be less attached to what he holds by a momentary or uncertain title, than to what he enjoys by a durable or certain title; and of course will be willing to risk more for the sake of the one, than for the sake of the other" (481-86). This was the standard argument for monarchy: the permanence of the kingly office creates an identity of interest between ruler and nation. It is true that a lengthy term will allow the executive to act against the popular wishes, yet it will also motivate him to act for the welfare of the whole. A "Chief Magistrate" holding by a temporary tenure, however, "will be apt to feel himself too little interested in" his office "to hazard any material censure or perplexity, from the independent exertion of his powers, or from encountering the ill-humors, however transient, which may happen to prevail either in a considerable part of the society itself, or even in a predominant faction in the legislative body." This is essentially the same argument that Madison used in support of the quasi-aristocratic Senate: that a prolonged period of official service engenders an appreciation for "national character" that is not possessed by the fickle and shortsighted multitude.

Hamilton forthrightly states his conviction that the masses must often be opposed for their own good, even under a generally popular regime: "the republican principle demands, that the deliberate sense of the community should govern the conduct of those to whom they entrust the management of their affairs; but it does not require an unqualified complaisance to every sudden breese of passion, or to every transient impulse which the people may receive from the arts of men, who flatter their prejudices to betray their interests." He admits that, even in their mistakes, "the people commonly intend the public good." But he denies "that they always reason right about the means of promoting it." He expresses an ideal of public service that is both patronizing and rather noble: "When occasions present themselves in which the interests of the people are at variance with their inclinations, it is the duty of the persons whom they have appointed to be the guardians of those interests, to withstand the temporary delusions, in order to give them time and opportunity for more cool and sedate reflection." And he optimistically notes that the people have often raised "lasting monuments of their gratitude to the men, who had courage and magnanimity enough to serve them at the peril of their displeasure." Eventually, he seems to hope, they might even set up a statue of Alexander Hamilton.

The principle of separation of powers also necessitates an extended term for the new chief executive. Hamilton refers to the "tendency of the legislative authority to swallow every other" and additionally remarks that the "representatives of the people, in a popular assembly, seem sometimes to fancy that they are the people themselves." He admits that it may not be immediately obvious what the length of the term has to do with the president's independence from Congress, since that official is to be selected by a process entirely separate from the legislative body. "One answer to this inquiry," he says, "may be drawn from the principle already remarked, that is from the slender interest a man is apt to take in a short lived advantage, and the little inducement it affords him to expose himself on account of it to any considerable inconvenience or hazard." This is the monarchical argument again.

Hamilton now considers "whether a duration of four years would answer the end proposed." He had grave doubts of his own on this score. In his notorious speech at the Constitutional Convention he recommended a national "Governour," to be chosen by electors much in the way eventually provided, but to serve for life. He had observed with regard to the executive power that "the English model was the only good one on the subject. The Hereditary interest of the King was so interwoven with that of the Nation . . . that he was placed above the danger of being corrupted from abroad."[8] In Hamilton's view a limited term—and one of seven years was under discussion when he spoke—would never suffice for the new executive. Yet as Publius he sounds rather positive concerning the four-year presidency.

Hamilton admits that "it cannot be affirmed, that a duration of four years or any other limited duration would completely answer the end proposed; but it would contribute towards it in a degree which would have a material influence upon the spirit and the character of the government." Four years is enough to bolster the courage of a president who is "endued with a tolerable portion of fortitude," by allowing him "time . . . to make the community sensible of the propriety of the measures he might incline to pursue." It is true, Hamilton notes, that as the president's term of office draws to an end, "his confidence and with it, his firmness would decline; yet both the one and the other would derive support from the opportunities, which his previous continuance in the station had afforded him of establishing himself in the esteem and good will of his constituents." The term chosen appears to him reasonable. "As on the one hand, a duration of four years will contribute to the firmness of the executive in a sufficient degree to render it a very valuable ingredient in the composition; so on the other, it is not long enough to justify any alarm for the public liberty," he claims.

Hamilton may have had more doubts concerning the real strength of this executive than he admits as Publius. Notwithstanding his use of quasi-monarchical arguments, he does not appear to regard the presidency as a particularly aristocratic aspect of the proposed Constitution. He observes that the chief executive will be able to stand for a while against ignorant clamor, but this official must ultimately submit to the verdict of the electors chosen by the people. It seems clear that he expects the president to be a more popular official than he really thinks best. He concludes No. 71 in this way: "What would be to be feared from an elective magistrate of four years duration, with the confined authorities of a President of the United States? What but that he might be unequal to the task which the Constitution assigns him?"

Hamilton begins No. 72 with a wholehearted plea for stability in the "administration of government" (486-92). By this phrase, Hamilton means "executive details" such as these: "The actual conduct of foreign negotiations, the preparatory plans of finance, the application and disbursement of the public monies, in conformity to the general appropriations of the legislature, the arrangement of the army and navy, the direction of the operations of war . . . and other matters of a like nature." In other words, he is speaking of the ministerial responsibilities that would generally be assigned to bureaucrats in twentieth-century regimes. Hamilton regards constancy as of the highest importance in managing such matters; the hands to which they are committed should not be changed too often, he contends. Because the president must appoint and supervise these officials, "this view of the subject will at once suggest to us the intimate connection between the duration of the executive magistrate in office, and the stability of the system of administration." A lengthy presidential term is necessary. Hamilton lived before the days of the modern civil service, but he clearly would have applauded that development in the techniques of government.

Hamilton now turns to the consideration that, not improbably, more than anything else reconciled him to the executive branch as outlined by the Constitution: the indefinite reeligibility of the president. The seven-year term that he rejected at Philadelphia was one which forbade reelection of the chief executive,[9] whereas the four-year term that he praised as Publius allowed an unlimited number of reelections. The point was obviously of great importance to Hamilton, because the rest of No. 72 is devoted to a comprehensive and convincing analysis of the topic. "Nothing appears more plausible at first sight, nor more ill founded upon close inspection, than a scheme . . . of continuing the chief magistrate in office for a certain time, and then excluding him from it, either for a limited period, or for ever after," he says.

His first argument is the familiar monarchical one, modified to fit the circumstances of a republican polity. Hamilton contends that a possibly indefinite presidential tenure is needed to elicit disinterested and farsighted leadership from the incumbent. "There are few men," he judges, "who would not feel much less zeal for the discharge of a duty, when they were conscious that the advantages of the station, with which it was connected, must be relinquished at a determinate period, than when they were permitted to entertain a hope of obtaining by meriting a continuance of them." "The desire of reward is one of the strongest incentives to human conduct," he notes, adding that indefinite reelection will render the "interest" of the president coincident with his "duty." He maintains that "even the love of fame, the ruling passion of the noblest minds, which would prompt a man to plan and undertake extensive and arduous enterprises for the public bene-fit," would be stultified if the president "foresaw that he must quit the scene, before he could accomplish the task, and must commit that, together with his own reputation, to hands which might be unequal or unfriendly to the task." Under such conditions, "the most to be expected from the generality of men . . . is the negative merit of not doing harm instead of the positive merit of doing good," he declares.

This passage, incidentally, is not a bad summary of Hamilton's political viewpoint. We are informed here that the human race is generally motivated by self-interest; that the "noblest minds," from "love of fame," are nev-ertheless above such petty considerations; that the nation needs strong, positive leadership; and that "the negative merit of not doing harm" is, after all, not the sum total of political wisdom. Hamilton's preference for a strong, activist, regulating government is plainly displayed here.

He now adduces several additional arguments for the indefinite re-eligibility of the chief executive. "Another ill effect of the exclusion," he says, "would be the temptation to sordid views, to peculation, and in some instances, to usurpation." An "avaricious" president "might not scruple to have recourse to the most corrupt expedients to make the harvest as abun-dant as it was transitory." But "the same man probably, with a different prospect before him, might content himself with the regular perquisites of his station, and might even be unwilling to risk the consequences of an abuse of his opportunities. His avarice might be a guard upon his avarice." Moreover, an "ambitious" president might stage a coup rather than descend from his exalted post. "Would it promote the peace of the community, or the stability of the government," Hamilton pertinentaly inquires, "to have half a dozen men who had had credit enough to be raised to the seat of the supreme magistracy, wandering among the people like discontented ghosts, and sighing for a place which they were destined never more to possess?"

There are positive reasons, also, for indefinite reeligibility. The valuable experience gained by incumbent presidents is thereby secured for the nation. "Can it be wise to put this desirable and essential quality under the ban of the constitution," Hamilton asks, "and to declare that the moment it is acquired, its possessor shall be compelled to abandon the station in which it was acquired, and to which it is adapted?" There will be times when certain individuals will be essential to the country's salvation, he maintains. "There is no nation which has not at one period or another experienced an absolute necessity of the services of particular men, in particular situations . . . to the preservation of its political existence." No doubt Hamilton was thinking of George Washington; twentieth-century observers might also suggest the example of Franklin D. Roosevelt. "How unwise," Hamilton cogently argues, "must be every such self-denying ordinance, as serves to prohibit a nation from making use of its own citizens, in the manner best suited to its exigencies and circumstances!" To force a presidential change would guarantee a mutability of government. It is senseless to "prohibit the people from continuing their confidence, where they think it may be safely placed, and where by constancy on their part they may obviate the fatal inconveniences of fluctuating councils and a variable policy," Hamilton convincingly contends.

This essay contains some of the most persuasive reasoning in all the *Federalist* papers. It only remains to be noted that Hamilton's willingness to see the chief executive subjected to periodic reviews by the public does not seem to indicate that he had an especially elitist conception of that office.

In *Federalist* No. 73, Hamilton commences by praising the provision of the Consitution that the chief executive's compensation "shall neither be increased nor diminished during the period for which he shall have been elected" (492-99). To have assigned Congress the authority to modify the salary of the president would have wholly undermined the independence of that officer, he feels. "There are men who could neither be distressed nor won into a sacrifice of their duty; but this stern virtue is the growth of few soils: And in the main it will be found, that a power over a man's support is a power over his will," Hamilton characteristically declares.

Hamilton now considers the executive veto power. Once again, he draws our attention to the "propensity of the legislative department to intrude upon the rights and to absorb the powers of the other departments." The "primary" purpose of the presidential veto is to guard against this: It is a "shield to the executive." Without it, he declares, the president "might gradually be stripped of his authorities by successive resolutions, or annihilated by a single vote." Additionally, says Hamilton, the veto power serves a useful "secondary" function. "It establishes a salutary check upon the legislative body calculated to guard the community against the effects of faction, precipitancy, or of any impulse unfriendly to the public good, which may happen to influence a majority of that body." Hamilton leaves no doubt concerning his view of the relative weight of these two purposes. His main concern is the protection of the chief executive's prerogatives as warlord, administrator, and head of state. He does, however, foresee a legislative role for the president, and he welcomes it. "The oftener a measure is brought under examination, the greater the diversity in the situations of those who are to examine it," Hamilton maintains, "the less must be the danger of those errors which flow from want of due deliberation, or of those missteps which proceed from the contagion of some common passion or interest."

Hamilton seemingly conceives the president's legislative role in purely preventive terms. The chief executive, he says, will block unwise measures by Congress. He acknowledges that "the power of preventing bad laws includes that of preventing good ones," but he contends in this essay that the trade-off will be favorable. He points out that "inconstancy and mutability in the laws . . . form the greatest blemish in the character and genius of our governments," and he characterizes "every institution calculated to restrain the excess of law-making, and to keep things in the same state, in which they may happen to be at any given period, as much more likely to do good than harm; because it is favorable to greater stability in the system of legislation." The loss of "a few good laws will be amply compensated" by the prevention of "a number of bad ones." Hamilton thus lauds a divided and passive legislative power.

Publius has, of course, spoken out of both sides of his mouth on this question of whether it is on the whole better to prevent bad laws or to enact good ones. Thus, in No. 22 and No. 58 he favors majority rule, deprecates special interests, and points out "how much good may be prevented, and how much ill may be produced, by the power of hindering the doing what may be necessary (141, 397). But in No. 70 and the present essay he seemingly takes the opposite tack and values the prevention of error above the passage of possibly beneficial legislation (475). Yet there is a pattern to this apparent contrariety. In No. 22 and No. 58 Publius prefers action by a legislative majority to the delays of a minority faction. In the present essay, however, he is willing for a legislative majority to be overridden by the chief executive, who is answerable to the whole nation. He evidently chooses the majority over narrow special-interest groups, but he prefers a comprehensive community perspective to that of a mere majority. His praise of legislative slowness in No. 70 seems to have been motivated mainly by tactical considerations, as we noted; he desires to uphold presidential vigor and dispatch, so he contends that Congress is the preferred point for delay.

In general, therefore, we find that Publius wishes to restrain the majority in order to further the overall welfare of the nation—not just to benefit small groups, which ordinarily he regards as factious. Not every critic has observed this distinction, however. Thus Beard quotes the passage in the present essay as proof of his assertion that the Constitution was deliberately "so constructed as to break the force of majority rule and prevent invasions of the property rights of minorities."[10] He blithely ignores the fact that Publius makes numerous statements of a contrary tenor to the one cited and that the present essay does not, in truth, deal with minority rights at all, but with the long-term, comprehensive vision of the president. As we have seen, when Publius considers the ability of minorities to frustrate the predominant opinion of the country, he usually favors the general will.

Hamilton denies that the president will use his veto power too often. Quite the contrary: "The superior weight and influence of the legislative body in a free government, and the hazard to the executive in a trial of strength with that body," Hamilton contends, "afford a satisfactory security, that the negative would generally be employed with great caution, and that there would oftener be room for a charge of timidity than of rashness, in the exercise of it." He does not, however, consider the veto authority futile by any means; future presidents could use it, he thinks, in instances that involve "an immediate attack upon the constitutional rights of the executive, or . . . in which the public good [is] evidently and palpably sacrificed." In the first of these cases, "his fortitude would be stimulated by his immediate interest in the power of his office"; in the second, "by the probability of the sanction of his constituents; who though they would naturally incline to the legislative body, would," Hamilton thinks, "hardly suffer their partiality to delude them in a very plain case." Thus he envisions that the president might be on the popular side in a dispute with Congress.

In *Federalist* No. 74, Hamilton remarks on the obvious "propriety" of investing "military authority" solely in the president (500-503). "Of all the cares or concerns of government," he says, "the direction of war most peculiarly demands those qualities which distinguish the exercise of power by a single hand." He also contends that "the benign prerogative of pardoning" is best entrusted to one person; "the sense of responsibility is always strongest in proportion as it is undivided," he points out. "The reflection, that the fate of a fellow creature depended on his sole fiat, would naturally inspire scrupulousness and caution," Hamilton feels. "The dread of being accused of weakness or connivance would beget equal circumspection, though of a different kind." On the other hand, "as men generally derive confidence from their numbers," members of the legislature "might often encourage each other in an act of obduracy, and might be less sensible to the apprehension of suspicion or censure for an injudicious or affected clemency."

Finally, he observes, if an uprising occurs, "a well timed offer of pardon to the insurgents or rebels may restore the tranquility of the common-wealth." However, "the dilatory process of convening the Legislature" could let slip "the golden opportunity." "The loss of a week, a day, an hour may sometimes be fatal," he says. It was, incidentally, this passage of *The Federalist* that was quoted by a federal court judge in affirmation of President Ford's authority to pardon former president Nixon. "Evidence now available suggests a strong probability that the Nixon Administration was conducting a covert assault on American liberty and an insurrection and rebellion against constitutional government itself," declared Judge Fox. "By pardoning Richard Nixon . . . President Ford was taking steps, in the words of Alexander Hamilton in the Federalist, to 'restore the tranquility of the commonwealth' by a 'well-timed offer of pardon' to the putative rebel leader."[11]

The next essay, No. 75, discusses the president's power to make treaties, "provided two-thirds of the senators present concur" (503-9). Jay has al-ready dealt with this topic in No. 64, and Hamilton offers, he says, "only some supplementary remarks." The provision in question has been "as-sailed" on the grounds of "the trite topic of the intermixture of powers," he notes. He approvingly refers to Madison's explanation of why the partition-ing of the various functions of government neither can nor should be absolute (332); and he also contends that "the particular nature of the power of making treaties indicates a particular propriety" in "the union of the executive with the senate." The president alone should not possess this authority: "However proper or safe it may be in governments where the executive magistrate is an hereditary monarch, to commit to him the entire power of making treaties, it would be utterly unsafe and improper to entrust that power to an elective magistrate of four years duration." Hamilton once again displays his quasi-royalist opinions. He points out "that an hereditary monarch, though often the oppressor of his people, has personally too much at stake in the government to be in any material danger of being corrupted by foreign powers." A temporary official will not be entirely trustworthy: "An avaricious man might be tempted to betray the interests of the state to the acquisitions of wealth. An ambitious man might make his own aggrandize-ment, by the aid of a foreign power, the price of his treachery."

However, Hamilton maintains, "to have entrusted the power of making treaties to the senate alone, would have been to relinquish the benefits of the constitutional agency of the president, in the conduct of foreign negotiations." These benefits, of course, are no doubt the ones emphasized by Jay in No. 64, "secrecy and dispatch." Moreover, Hamilton observes that the president and Senate will be watchdogs on each other: "The joint possession of the power in question by the president and senate would afford a greater prospect of security, than the separate possession of it by either of them." And the president's sage leadership will contribute to success in America's foreign dealings, says Hamilton: "whoever has maturely weighed the circumstances, which must concur in the appointment of a president, will be satisfied that the office will always bid fair to be filled by men of such characters as to render their concurrence in the formation of treaties peculiarly desirable, as well on the score of wisdom as on that of integrity." At one point Hamilton refers to the president as "the constitutional representative of the nation," which surely seems a momentous phrase.

Like Jay, Hamilton argues against the participation of the House of Representatives in the treaty-making process. His contentions are familiar. The House will be "fluctuating" and "multitudinous," and therefore will not be competent for that purpose. "Accurate and comprehensive knowledge of foreign politics; a steady and systematic adherence to the same views; a nice and uniform sensibility to national character, decision, secrecy and dispatch; are incompatible with the genius of a body so variable and so numerous," he declares. He also criticizes a suggestion that two-thirds of the whole Senate be required for a treaty ratification, rather than two-thirds of those present. Hamilton points out that "it has been shewn . . . that all provisions which require more than the majority of any body to its resolutions have a direct tendency to embarrass the operations of the government and an indirect one to subject the sense of the majority to that of the minority." Here we have another statement of the majoritarian and activist Publius.

The next two essays, the last on the presidency, consider the power of the chief executive to nominate officials of the national government, subject to the consent of the Senate. "It is not easy," Hamilton asserts in No. 76, "to conceive a plan better calculated than this, to produce a judicious choice of men for filling the offices of the Union" (509-15).

He points out that the people in general cannot possibly make these appointments, "as, waving every other consideration it would leave them little time to do any thing else." Yet, surprisingly, the elitist Hamilton does not find the masses otherwise incapable of this task. "The people collectively from their number and from their dispersed situation cannot be regulated in their movements by that systematic spirit of cabal and intrigue, which will be urged as the chief objections to reposing the power in question in a body of men," he says. The commonality are at least not naturally factious, which is more than can be said for the legislature, it seems. These words do not comport well with the Constitution's provision for state legislative election of the U.S. senators—a feature praised by Jay in No. 64. Hamilton, we recall, did not really want the states to be involved in that process.

Given that the president is likely to possess "abilities, at least respectable," Hamilton holds that "one man of discernment is better fitted to analise and estimate the peculiar qualities adapted to particular offices, than a body of men of equal, or perhaps even of superior discernment." He reasons here along similar lines as in previous essays. "The sole and undivided responsibility of one man will naturally beget a livlier sense of duty and a more exact regard to reputation." Moreover: "A single well directed man by a single understanding, cannot be distracted and warped by that diversity of views, feelings and interests, which frequently distract and warp the resolutions of a collective body." Indeed, Hamilton observes that "there is nothing so apt to agitate the passions of mankind as personal considerations." Any decison on appointments made wholly by a legislature "will of course be the result either of a victory gained by one party over the other, or of a compromise between the parties. In either case, the intrinsic merit of the candidate will be too often out of sight." Hamilton expresses his disdain for the compromises dictated by legislative divisions: "In the last, the coalition will commonly turn upon some interested equivalent—'Give us the man we wish for this office, and you shall have the one you wish for that.' " He strongly preferred a single bold leader to a multifarious, pettifogging committee.

However, Hamilton does not believe that the president should exercise the authority of appointment on his own. The Senate's participation is "an excellent check upon a spirit of favoritism in the President, and would tend greatly to preventing the appointment of unfit characters from State prejudice, from family connection, from personal attachment, or from a view to popularity." Hamilton points out that the executive will retain the major voice concerning appointments. The president's "nomination" for an office may indeed "be overruled" on occasion, Hamilton acknowledges, but "this could only be to make place for another nomination by himself. The person ultimately appointed must be the object of his preference, though perhaps not in the first degree." The senators cannot challenge his primacy. "They could not even be certain that a future nomination would present a candidate in any degree more acceptable to them: And as their dissent might cast a kind of stigma upon the individual rejected; and might have the appearance of a reflection upon the judgement of the chief magistrate," Hamilton contends, "it is not likely that their sanction would often be refused, where there were not special and strong reasons for the refusal." This is, in fact, a rather accurate preview of how the federal appointment process has functioned under the Constitution.

Hamilton rejects the idea that the president will be able to corrupt the Senate with his power over appointments. He clarifies his opinion of human nature. "The supposition of universal venality in human nature is little less an error in political reasoning than the supposition of universal rectitude," he says, adding that the "institution of delegated power implies that there is a portion of virtue and honor among mankind, which may be a reasonable foundation of confidence." Even the British Parliament contains many honest statesmen, Hamilton declares. He concludes that "a man disposed to view human nature as it is, without either flattering its virtues or exaggerating its vices, will see sufficient ground of confidence in the probity of the Senate, to rest satisfied not only that it will be impracticable to the Executive to corrupt or seduce a majority of its members; but that the necessity of its co-operation . . . will be a considerable and salutary restraint upon . . . that magistrate." At least some people are honest, Hamilton believes.

Federalist No. 77 commences with perhaps Publius's most noteworthy blunder concerning the future workings of the proposed Constitution. Hamilton says the Senate's participation in the appointment process will help ensure the stability of government, because the "consent of that body would be necessary to displace as well as to appoint" (515-21). This is, of course, not correct. The arrangement that Hamilton describes was the idea behind the notorious "Tenure of Office Act," by which the congressional Republicans attempted to wrest control of the national administration from Pres. Andrew Johnson in 1867, but it has never been orthodox constitutional doctrine. Hamilton evidently expects national executive officers to be as dependent on the Senate for their continuance in office as on the president: "Where a man in any station had given satisfactory evidence of his fitness for it, a new president would be restrained from attempting a change . . . by the apprehension that the discountenance of the senate might frustrate the attempt, and bring some degree of discredit upon himself." These words come oddly from the man who has just noted at great length the superiority of a single individual over a numerous council for the purpose of deciding on appointments. He appears to regard the elite Senate as a check on a new and popular president attempting to install his minions in office.

Hamilton proceeds to contrast the appointment procedure of the proposed Constitution with that existing in New York State. Under the former, responsibility is clear; but by meeting in secret and leaving the extent of the governor's involvement uncertain, New York's council of appointment enables all parties to escape the "censure of a bad appointment," and also presents "an unbounded field for cabal and intrigue." Hamilton follows this analysis with one of his standard assaults on Clinton. And he points out the unsuitability of the House of Representatives for any role in the appointment process: "A body so fluctuating, and at the same time so numerous, can never be deemed proper for the exercise of that power," he says. "Its unfitness will appear manifest to all, when it is recollected that in half a century it may consist of three or four hundred persons."

Hamilton then briefly considers whether the presidency has "the requisites to safety in a republican sense—a due dependence on the people—a due responsibility?" He deduces his answer "from these circumstances, the election of the president once in four years by persons immediately chosen by the people for that purpose; and from his being at all times liable to impeachment . . . and to . . . subsequent prosecution in the common course of law." Last, he notes, this official will be checked by the Senate in the appointment process. It is significant that the first factor Hamilton mentions is the election by the people. With this affirmation of the fundamentally popular nature of the proposed chief executive, Publius ends his discussion of the subject.

The last eleven papers by Hamilton provide a fascinating mixture of semiobsolete monarchical concepts with an essentially accurate preview of the character of the American president. This official is presented as a force for unity and as a source of firm and decisive action. Presidential predominance in foreign affairs and in the choosing of national administrators is predicted and defended. The legislative role of the president is regarded only as a restraining one, but this function is certainly perceived as significant. In one respect, with regard to the discharging of officials, the future power of the president is underestimated, but Hamilton's vision is on the whole quite correct. Perhaps the most important point is that he foresees the chief executive as a popular leader. The electoral college is not portrayed as a bridle on the citizen body, but as an expression of the general will. Hamilton emphatically rejects the sort of president most suitable as a check on the populace—one with a lengthy term and no reelection—in favor of an executive with a shorter term and indefinite reeligibility. He probably would have preferred something closer to a king, but he recognizes that the new president must be a purely republican official and he seems fairly satisfied with what the Convention has wrought.

There is one major irony here. An unattractive feature of these papers is Hamilton's compulsive urge to denigrate Governor Clinton at every turn. The election was nigh, and Publius's philosophical calm was yielding to the passions of the political struggle. Yet Clinton was actually a vigorous and capable official. Indeed, he and Hamilton had cooperated very well during the Revolutionary War—when New York City was occupied by the British and the office of governor of that state was of great military significance. Clinton was an archetypal "courthouse" politician and notably cautious, but he was by no means a weak character. He was, in fact, an excellent prototype of the sort of energetic, yet popular executive foreseen by Hamilton in *The Federalist*.

The next six papers discuss the judicial branch of the proposed federal government. Of all the institutions established under the Constitution, only the Supreme Court was accorded the tenure that Hamilton felt was appropriate for the president and the Senate as well: "good behavior"—meaning for life, barring the commission of some definite misdeed. Hamilton was naturally quite partial to this authoritative agency. It is in these essays that Publius shows his greatest concern for the protection of the rights of minorities and individuals; yet he appears to be at least equally interested in the judiciary as an instrument of national unity.

Federalist No. 78 begins by discussing the provision for lifetime judicial tenure. This is justified, Hamilton says, because that branch "is beyond comparison the weakest of the three departments of power" and therefore requires this augmentation of its strength (521-30). "The judiciary, has no influence over either the sword or the purse, no direction either of the strength or of the wealth of the society, and can take no active resolution whatever," he observes. Hence, "though individual oppression may now and then proceed from the courts of justice, the general liberty of the people can never be endangered from that quarter: I mean, so long as the judiciary remains truly distinct from both the legislative and executive." Unfortunately, Hamilton notes, "from the natural feebleness of the judiciary, it is in continual jeopardy of being overpowered, awed or influenced by its coordinate branches." "Nothing," he asserts, "can contribute so much to its firmness and independence, as permanency in office," and "this quality may therefore be justly regarded as an indispensable ingredient in its constitution."

An independent judiciary is especially important "in a limited constitution," Hamilton contends. By this he means a charter "which contains certain specified exceptions to the legislative authority; such for instance as that it shall pass no bills of attainder, no *ex post facto* laws, and the like." He argues that "limitations of this kind can be preserved in practice no other way than through the medium of the courts of justice; whose duty it must be to declare all acts contrary to the manifest tenor of the constitution void." He explicitly rejects the viewpoint that "the legislative body are themselves the constitutional judges of their own powers, and that the construction they put upon them is conclusive upon the other departments." Not all of the Founders believed in the wisdom of judicial review, but Hamilton certainly did.

It is true that he does not say in so many words that the other branches of the government are bound to abide by the decisions of the Supreme Court on constitutional questions. But what he does say amounts to practically the same thing. He affirms the right of the judiciary to make its own rulings on matters falling within its purview. Thus, if Congress and the president persist in policies that the Supreme Court regards as unacceptable, these policies will be undone whenever they come before the judicial arm. Hamilton clearly expects this circumstance to influence the behavior of the other departments. Should "unjust and partial laws" be passed, injurious to "the private rights of particular classes of citizens," the "judicial magistracy is of vast importance in mitigating the severity, and confining the operation of such laws," he observes. The judges operate "as a check upon the legislative body . . . who, perceiving that obstacles to the success of an iniquitous intention are to be expected from the scruples of the courts, are . . . compelled by the very motives of the injustice they meditate, to qualify their attempts." The lawmakers will conform to the judgements of the federal judiciary simply because it would be futile to adopt policies that cannot be sustained in the courts.

Hamilton looks for the judiciary to intervene on behalf of the rights of individuals even in cases when the rights in question are not specifically mentioned in the fundamental charter. "It is not with a view to infractions of the constitution only that the independence of the judges may be an essential safeguard against the effects of occasional ill humors in the society," he says. It appears that the courts will ascertain and protect the natural rights of the citizenry. We already know that Publius believes in natural rights (8), but clear-cut references to them are not especially common in *The Federalist*. Their defense seems to be primarily a judicial responsibility.

Hamilton denies that his expansive view of the courts' function implies "a superiority of the judiciary to the legislative power." In fact, he says, it suggests only "that the power of the people is superior to both." Hamilton asserts that "the Courts were designed to be an intermediate body between the people and the legislature, in order, among other things, to keep the latter within the limits assigned to their authority." Our fundamental compact will be the result of direct popular action, and the will of the community as "declared in the constitution" is rightly above "the will of the legislature declared in its statutes." In spite of their indirect appointment and lifetime tenure, the judges are representatives of the people, Hamilton contends.

The courts' constituency is not, however, the majority of the moment with its possible vagaries, but the nation considered as a legally constituted body whose features are outlined in the basic charter. Hamilton maintains that not even the people are entitled to disregard the fundamental law. "Until the people have by some solemn and authoritative act annulled or changed the established form, it is binding upon themselves . . . and no presumption, or even knowledge of their sentiments, can warrant their representatives in a departure from it, prior to such an act." Thus the courts are not only meant to protect the populace against the usurpations of the rulers, but also to prevent the masses from committing oppressive acts of their own. The "integrity and moderation of the judiciary," he declares, should be equally prized by all, "as no man can be sure that he may not be tomorrow the victim of a spirit of injustice, by which he may be a gainer to-day." Of all the institutions of the national regime, the judiciary is most clearly designed to protect minorities from the tyranny of the greater number.

Yet Hamilton does not believe judges should exercise unchecked power. He asserts that the courts possess no "will, but merely judgement," which plainly suggests that he does not see jurists as having much room to maneuver. He shows one way their authority is to be limited: "To avoid an arbitrary discretion in the courts, it is indispensable that they should be bound down by strict rules and precedents, which serve to define and point out their duty in every particular case which comes before them." Hamilton mentions this restriction, however, only to call attention to the need for special wisdom and learning in the judiciary. Judges must undertake a "long and laborious study" of the law, and given "the ordinary depravity of mankind," only a few will "unite the requisite integrity with the requisite knowledge," he observes. The national judiciary will be an elite body, indeed.

The next essay, No. 79, commences with praise of the constitutional provision that judges' salaries shall not be decreased during their term of service. Hamilton points out that "a power over a man's subsistence amounts to a power over his will" (531-34). He then goes on to identify the main safeguard against arbitrary rulings by the courts. Judges "are liable to be impeached for mal-conduct by the house of representatives, and tried by the senate, and if convicted, may be dismissed from office and disqualified for holding any other." But Hamilton acknowledges that no mechanism for dismissing judges on grounds of "inability" has been included in the proposed charter. He is against the idea. "Such a provision," he says, "would either not be acted upon, or would be more liable to abuse than calculated to answer any good purpose."

Federalist No. 80 investigates "the proper extent of the federal judicature" and the constitutional provisions on that subject (534- 41). The nationalist theme immediately appears. Hamilton declares that the federal judicial power must extend to "causes . . . which arise out of the laws of the United States" or "which concern the execution of the provisions expressly contained in the articles of union." He seems mainly to desire to control the states: "What for instance," he asks, "would avail restrictions on the authority of the state legislatures, without some constitutional mode of enforcing the observance of them?" Hamilton here expresses probably the principal reason for the Founders' emphasis on judicial review. He says that limits on the prerogatives of the states will never "be scrupulously regarded, without some effectual power in the government to restrain or correct the infractions of them. This power," he declares, "must either be a direct negative on the state laws, or an authority in the federal courts, to over-rule such as might be in manifest contravention of the articles of union." He adds that he can imagine "no third course." Gouverneur Morris and Roger Sherman had similarly noted, at the Constitutional Convention, that a congressional authority to veto state acts was "unnecessary," since "a law that ought to be negatived would be set aside in the Judiciary department."[12] The federal courts were clearly meant to be a cement of the national union.

Hamilton also argues for the supremacy of the federal judiciary, based on the "necessity of uniformity in the interpretation of the national laws." He observes that "thirteen independent courts of final jurisdiction over the same causes, arising upon the same laws, is a hydra in government, from which nothing but contradiction and confusion can proceed." Also, says Hamilton, the federal courts should have cognizance of all cases "in which the United States are a party." He contends that "any other plan would be contrary to reason, to precedent, and to decorum."

Further, the national judicial power should extend to all cases "which involve the peace of the confederacy, whether they relate to the intercourse between the United States and foreign nations, or to that between the states themselves." Hamilton notes "that the peace of the whole ought not to be left at the disposal of a part" and warns of the possible grim consequences of capricious state actions. "As a denial or perversion of justice by the sentences of courts . . . is with reason classed among the just causes of war, it will follow that the federal judiciary ought to have cognizance of all causes in which the citizens of other countries are concerned." And Hamilton observes that the authority to intervene in interstate disputes "is perhaps not less essential to the peace of the union." He alludes to the need to "control" such iniquitous measures as "the fraudulent laws which have been passed in many of the states," and he stresses that only "the national judiciary," with "no local attachments," can ensure the "inviolable maintenance of that equality of privileges and immunities to which the citizens of the union will be entitled." Finally, the federal courts should decide "maritime causes," which "commonly affect the rights of foreigners" and so relate "to the public peace." The nationalistic arguments of this essay are quite reminiscent of the first half of *The Federalist*.

Federalist No. 81 begins with the comment: "That there ought to be one court of supreme and final jurisdiction is a proposition which has not been, and is not likely to be, contested" (541-52). Yet Hamilton notes that the question remains "whether it ought to be a distinct body, or a branch of the legislature." He rejects the latter idea on the grounds of separation of powers and checks and balances. It could not "be expected, that men who had infringed the constitution, in the character of legislators, would be disposed to repair the breach, in the character of judges." And he admits that judicial review—"the power of construing the laws according to the spirit of the constitution"—is not specifically mentioned in the proposed charter, but is rather "deducible . . . from the general theory of a limited constitution." Thus, remarks Hamilton, any objections to this authority as it will exist in the new government, will equally "serve to condemn every constitution that attempts to set bounds to the legislative discretion."

He declares "that the supposed danger of judiciary encroachments on the legislative authority . . . is in reality a phantom. Particular misconstructions and contraventions of the will of the legislature may now and then happen; but they can never be so extensive as to amount to an inconvenience, or in any sensible degree to affect the order of the political system." He observes in this connection the "comparative weakness" of the judicial authority, particularly its inability to support its usurpations by force." But the main check on the courts is the possibility of impeachment. "There never can be danger that the judges, by a series of deliberate usurpations on the authority of the legislature, would hazard the united resentment of the body entrusted with it, while this body was possessed of the means of punishing their presumptions by degrading them from their stations." Thus Hamilton does not regard the courts as absolutely sacrosanct. It is possible for the judges to abuse their position by purposely intruding on the rightful sphere of Congress—and this, he thinks, is grounds for removal from office.

Hamilton now argues for the constitutional provision allowing the establishment of inferior federal courts. State courts will not be adequate, he says. "The most discerning cannot foresee how far the prevalency of a local spirit may be found to disqualify the local tribunals for the jurisdiction of national causes. . . . State judges, holding their offices during pleasure, or from year to year, will be too little independent to be relied upon for an inflexible execution of the national laws." He dismisses a suggestion that the proposed charter will allow the states, as corporate entities, to be sued by individuals in the federal courts. "It is inherent in the nature of sovereignty, not to be amenable to the suit of an individual without its consent," he notes. The states retain partial sovereignty and so are not suable, Hamilton concludes. Of course, just a few years after these words were written, the United States Supreme Court, Chief Justice John Jay presiding, in the case of *Chisolm v. Georgia*, took exactly the same position that Hamilton here calls "mistaken" and "without foundation."[13] The Eleventh Amendment overturned Jay's ruling and retrospectively validated Publius's logic.

In No. 82, Hamilton considers the relationship between the federal courts set up by the Constitution and the state courts. He admits that "time only . . . can mature and perfect so compound a system, can liquidate the meaning of all the parts, and can adjust them to each other in a harmonious and consistent whole" (553-57). But he nevertheless contends that national and state judiciaries will enjoy "concurrent jurisdiction" over federal causes of action, with an appeal lying from the latter to the former. He says that "the national and state systems are to be regarded as one whole. The courts of the latter will of course be natural auxiliaries to the execution of the laws of the union, and an appeal from them will as naturally lie to that tribunal, which is destined to unite and assimilate the principles of national justice and the rules of national decisons."

Federalist No. 83 lengthily discusses the constitutional provision on trial by jury that would be required for criminal trials in the federal courts, but not for civil. The Anti-Federalists criticized the latter ommission. Hamilton reassuringly observes that Congress can legislatively make jury trials mandatory in civil cases, if they wish to do so. He doubts, however, that all cases are suitable. He says trial by jury is "a valuable safeguard to liberty," but hints that it is more important "as a defense against the oppressions of an hereditary monarch, than as a barrier to the tyranny of popular magistrates in a popular government" (558-74). Trial by jury will not be appropriate "in cases which concern the public peace with foreign nations," Hamilton observes. "Juries cannot be supposed competent to investigations, that require a thorough knowledge of the laws and usages of nations, and they will sometimes be under the influence of impressions which will not suffer them to pay sufficient regard to those considerations of public policy which ought to guide their inquiries." Nor can they grasp equity causes with "a long train of minute and independent particulars," he adds.

Hamilton's attitude toward trial by jury mirrors his feelings on popular government in general. He thinks it is a good system on the whole, although not well adapted to cases of unusual complexity or importance. The best procedure is one in which popular and elite elements are mixed. "As matters now stand, it would be necessary to corrupt both court and jury; for where the jury have gone evidently wrong, the court will generally grant a new trial, and it would be in most cases of little use to practice upon the jury, unless the court could be likewise gained. Here then is a double security; and it will readily be perceived that this complicated agency tends to preserve the purity of both institutions." On the other hand, he disapproves of allowing the various state provisions on trial by jury to obtain in federal courts within their limits. He strongly deprecates the "capricious operation of so dissimilar a method of trial in the same cases, under the same government." Finally, he notes that trial by jury, commendable though it is, is not really indispensable to the preservation of liberty. "The truth is that the general genius of a government is all that can be substantially relied upon for permanent effects. Particular provisions, though not altogether useless, have far less virtue and efficacy than are commonly ascribed to them."

This concludes Hamilton's discussion of the judicial branch. It remains to be noted only that Madison was markedly less enthusiastic about the benefits of authoritative courts than his colleague was. True, Madison always acknowledged the existence of judicial review under the Constitution. Indeed, in *Federalist* No. 44 he specifically states that the courts will "expound," and thereby correct, acts of Congress (305). He did not, however, especially approve of this way of settling constitutional questions, and he wished that another had been devised. He suggested at the Convention that Supreme Court decisions be explicitly limited to "cases of a Judiciary Nature," an obvious sign he feared they might overstep their proper bounds.[14] Yet he never expresses his doubts in *The Federalist* and so does not give Publius a split personality on the issue.

In his last two papers, Hamilton ties up a few loose ends, one of which is highly important. The Constitution originally did not include a bill of rights, and this lack was a favorite antifederal objection. Brutus and the Federal Farmer, among many others, had made reference to it.[15] Hamilton argues that a bill of rights is not necessary. His reasoning will win few plaudits from modern critics, but it is nonetheless interesting.

The question is discussed in No. 84. Hamilton notes that the Constitution does in fact contain some provisions for the protection of individual rights—a guarantee of *habeas corpus*, a prohibition of bills of attainder and *ex post facto* laws, the forbidding of titles of nobility, the requiring of jury trials in criminal cases, and various other safeguards. He stresses the importance of *habeas corpus* and the debarring of noble titles—saying of the latter, that "this may truly be denominated the corner stone of republican government; for so long as they are excluded, there can never be serious danger that the government will be any other than that of the people"

(575-87). Yet Hamilton goes on to indicate that these safeguards are not really necessary.

Bills of rights, he says, "are in their origin, stipulations between kings and their subjects, abridgements of prerogative in favor of privilege, reservations of rights not surrendered to the prince." They are out of place in a republic: "According to their primitive signification, they have no application to constitutions professedly founded upon the power of the people, and executed by their immediate representatives and servants. Here, in strictness, the people surrender nothing, and as they retain every thing, they have no need of particular reservations." Moreover, he adds, such provisions are not only unnecessary, they are dangerous—because they seem to imply that whatever has not been explicitly forbidden is permitted. A bill of rights "would contain various exceptions to powers which are not granted; and on this very account, would afford a colourable pretext to claim more than were granted," maintains Hamilton. "Why for instance, should it be said, that the liberty of the press shall not be restrained, when no power is given by which restrictions may be imposed?"

In the final analysis, Hamilton asserts, the defense of liberty must rest more with the overall temper of the populace than with legalistic prohibitions "which would sound much better in a treatise of ethics than in a constitution of government." Thus, he argues: "What is liberty of the press? Who can give it any definition which would not leave the utmost latitude for evasion? I hold it to be impractical; and from this I infer that its security, whatever fine declarations may be inserted in any constitution respecting it, must altogether depend on public opinion, and on the general spirit of the people and of the government. And here, after all, as intimated upon another occasion, must we seek for the only solid basis of all our rights." By establishing a popular regime, the plan of the Convention has done all that could rationally be expected to protect the rights of individuals, he declares.

This argument is interesting, and not without a certain force. Of course, it is not entirely congruent with what Hamilton himself maintains in the essays concerning the judiciary, or even with other sentiments of this very paper. He has just spent some time showing that popular majorities may sometimes adopt measures oppressive of individuals, and that "limitations" on government can be enforced by an independent judiciary (524). Moreover, if bills of rights are really superfluous, even dangerous, under a popular system, why have certain protections nevertheless been put into the body of the Constitution? One suspects that Hamilton, lawyerlike, is using all the arguments he can devise, regardless of consistency, in order to counter one of the more effective Anti-Federalist criticisms.

Yet Hamilton does have a point here. An observer of the present day might reflect that the fundamental charter of the Soviet Union contains as many fine words concerning individual rights as does the American Constitution; the difference between the two systems lies wholly in the underlying expectations and values of their societies. "Parchment barriers," as Madison has previously pointed out, are of themselves meaningless (333). The assertion that individual liberties are, realistically speaking, dependent on the "general spirit of the people" has clear nationalist implications. Far from disbelieving, Publius quite plainly assumes that human beings possess natural rights; yet he declares that these rights will become effectual only insofar as they are congruent with the attitudes of the population concerned. Indeed, Publius generally portrays American freedom as the outgrowth of a characteristic national "genius"—that is, a product of our local social mores—rather than a manifestation of universal political truths. He thus offers what seems to be a blend of Lockean liberal and nationalistic perspectives, with the latter as strongly represented as the former.

In the remainder of No. 84, Hamilton denies that federal officials will be too far removed from their constituents to be properly supervised by them. He notes that the state governments will be vigilant, "if it were only from rivalship of power," and will surely warn the people of any dangerous tendencies at the national center. Furthermore, "the citizens who inhabit the country at and near the seat of government, will in all questions that affect the general liberty and prosperity, have the same interest with those who are at a distance; and . . . will stand ready to sound the alarm." He rejects the charge that a stronger national regime will require an increase in public expenditures. "What difference can it make in point of expense," he asks, "to pay officers of the customs appointed by the state, or those appointed by the United States?" In many ways, he declares, the new government will be cheaper than the old. First, "a great part of the business, which now keeps congress sitting through the year, will be transacted by the president." Also, the state legislatures will not have to meet as often, because they will no longer be involved in national affairs.

He begins No. 85 with an apology to the reader that he will not be discussing two points that, in *Federalist* No. 1, he said he intended to cover. They are: "the analogy of the proposed government to your own state constitution" and "the additional security, which its adoption will afford to republican government, to liberty and to property" (587-95). Hamilton rightly notes that "these heads have been . . . anticipated and exhausted in the progress of the work." Concerning the second topic he briefly lists a few familiar items: "restraints . . . on local factions"; "diminution of . . . foreign intrigue"; "absolute . . . exclusion of titles of nobility"; and "precautions against . . . those practices on the part of the state governments, which have undermined . . . property and credit"; among others. There is little need to rehash these topics, he admits.

Hamilton now reveals something of the strong emotions to which he was prone. "The charge of a conspiracy against the liberties of the people . . . indiscriminately brought against the advocates of the plan, has something in it too wanton and too malignant not to excite the indignation of every man who feels in his own bosom a refutation of the calumny," he contends. He apologizes for any "intemperances of expression" into which he may have fallen. "It is certain that I have frequently felt a struggle between sensibility and moderation," he confesses. He appeals to his reader to "beware of an obstinate adherence to party," and to "reflect that the object he is to decide is not a particular interest of the community, but the very existence of the nation." The Constitution, "though it may not be perfect in every part, is upon the whole a good one," Hamilton maintains. He sounds a realistic note. "I never expect to see a perfect work from imperfect man. The result of the deliberations of all collective bodies must necessarily be a compound as well of the errors and prejudices, as of the good sense and wisdom of the individuals of whom they are composed." Furthermore, "the compacts which are to embrace thirteeen distinct states, in a common bond of amity and union, must as necessarily be a compromise of as many dissimilar interests and inclinations." He rhetorically inquires: "How can perfection spring from such materials?"

Moreover, Hamilton observes, if alterations to the charter are desired, they will be far easier to obtain after it is adopted, than before. He denies that the national regime will attempt to obstruct amendments or in general to rule in an oppressive or unpopular way. "The intrinsic difficulty of governing thirteen states at any rate, independent of calculations upon an ordinary degree of public spirit and integrity, will," he declares, "in my opinion, constantly impose on the national rulers the necessity of a spirit of accommodation to the reasonable expectations of their constituents." He points out the necessity for a prompt decision: "A nation without a national government is, in my view, an awful spectacle. The establishment of a constitution, in time of profound peace, by the voluntary consent of a whole people, is a prodigy, to the completion of which I look forward with trembling anxiety." On this nationalistic note and with a final parting shot at the "powerful individuals, in this and in other states," who "are enemies to a general national government, in every possible shape," Publius concludes.

The later essays of Hamilton fully conform to the nationalistic orientation of his earlier offerings. His remarks on the president, with their emphasis on the need for unity and vigor, are a powerful argument for the concentration of political power, reminiscent of Hobbes. His image of the proposed chief executive retains distinct monarchical touches; yet this officer has been transmuted into the "constitutional representative of the nation." Hamilton's comments on the federal judiciary also have a nationalistic tenor: he points out the necessity for a single final authority on judicial questions and the inexpedience of allowing the thirteen separate state court systems to take the lead in such matters. Finally, he suggests the practical subordination of the abstract rights of the individual to the values of the community. Publius sustains the national theme from the beginning to the end of *The Federalist*.

9

Publius the Nationalist

The exposition of the argument of Publius is now complete, and it is time to stand back from the canvas to take an overall look. The foregoing analysis has shown that *The Federalist* exhibits a clearly nationalist outlook and that the other prominent themes of the essays—federalism, separation of powers, checks and balances, and the interest-group theory of No. 10—are less central to Publius's purpose. Without difficulty, we can ascertain from the text of this treatise, what we know anyway from other sources, that Hamilton, Madison, and Jay wished above all else to coordinate the resources of the American nation and in reality had no love for the federal features of the new Constitution.

The present study has identified four key propositions that can be considered to comprise the nationalist point of view. All are present in *The Federalist*, which maintains that (1) the American people constitute a nation; (2) their domestic affairs should be free from foreign interference; (3) they should be governed by a centralized authority; and (4) this regime should represent the political will of the population as a whole.

The clearest affirmation of American nationhood is found at the very beginning of *The Federalist*, in the strking description of No. 2 (9-10). Jay's notable statement exhibits a clear comprehension of what a nation is, it expressly asserts that governments should be founded on national ties, and it comes at the very outset of the argument of Publius, where we expect to find the fundamental premises of the entire case. Hamilton in No. 12 and Madison in No. 14 also portray America as a community bound together by geography, "blended and interwoven" interests, "affinity of language and manners," "kindred blood," and other typical aspects of nationality (74-78, 88). *The Federalist* always presumes that, in general, national affinities readily serve as the foundation for a political bond: No. 13 observes that regimes coalesce around "the links of national sympathy and connection"; No. 18 identifies a uniformity of language and custom as the main reason for the success of the Achaean league; No. 19 advances "homogeneous manners" as an explanation for the ability of the Swiss to stay together; No. 49 points out the advantage to the rulers of having "the prejudices of the community" on their side; and No. 85 proclaims that "a nation without a national government is, in my view, an awful spectacle" (81-82, 114, 122-23, 340, 594). Undoubtedly, a nationalistic vision is behind this argument for the Constitution.

It is true that Publius seems to regard two components of the national connection, geography and material interest, as especially relevant to the American situation. The American provinces are geographically near to each other and distant from Europe. Thus their respective residents will frequently interact, which requires that their concerns somehow be harmonized, lest conflict and even war result (40). On the other hand, Americans need not become involved in the quarrels of far-off parts of the world. Therefore, as long as we are united, we need not risk the presence of those "engines of despotism," large standing armies (46). Publius considers the practical concerns of the American people to be naturally congruent: our national leaders, he says, will "regard the interest of the whole, and the particular interests of the parts as connected with that of the whole" (21). He condemns factions because they seek advantages "adverse to the rights of other citizens, or to the permanent and aggregate interests of the community" (57). And he constantly makes reference to "the public good," or "justice and the general good," or "the general welfare," or other phrases denoting our country's overall well-being (5, 60, 482, 353, 424). He emphatically believes that all Americans may jointly flourish and should act together.

Publius constantly refers to the residents of the United States as a single collective mass, using such phrases as "the people of this country," "one united people," "the great body of the people," "the people of America," "the great body of the community," "the great bulk of the citizens of America," "the majority of America," or simply, "the people" (3, 9, 309, 375, 573, 584, 590). He believes that we are largely shaped by our communal attachments. The militia is harmless to liberty because "what shadow of danger can there be from men who are daily mingling with the rest of their countrymen; and who participate with them in the same feelings, sentiments, habits and interests?" (185). Senators must be American citizens, and hence they will not use their "private fortunes" in a way contrary to the national interest (377). A certain amount of time is needed to assimilate immigrants into the nation (415). Americans feel for each other "the affection of friends"; we are "a band of brethren" who "speak with one voice"; and we are imbued with a unique "spirit" or "genius" that "nourishes freedom, and in turn is nourished by it" (294, 9-10, 387). Publius sees this united social body as the foundation of the Constitution. Hamilton maintains that "the fabric of American Empire ought to rest on the solid basis of the consent of the people" (146), and Madison avows that "the Fœderal and

State Governments" are rightfully "dependent on the great body of the citizens of the United States" (315).

The Federalist not only perceives America as a nation in the fullest sense, but also expresses prominent concern for our national self-determination. Publius repeatedly contends that preservation of the union is essential to forestall foreign interference in our internal affairs. He shudders at the prospect of "three or four independent and probably discordant republics and confederacies, one inclining to Britain, another to France, and a third to Spain, and perhaps played off against each other by the three." He warns of "foreign corruption"; he notes that domestic factions may receive "secret succors from foreign powers"; and he calls "the diminution of the opportunities to foreign intrigue" a principal benefit of the Constitution (23, 27, 142, 294, 588). Publius believes in the irrespressible antagonism of nations: Jay shows how our welfare will inevitably clash with that of several European powers; Hamilton mintains that "the causes of hostility among nations are innumerable"; and Madison observes the utter lack of "benevolent feelings" of nations for each other (19-20, 28, 420). Thus, we must keep other countries at arms' length.

The need for centralized government is Publius's favorite topic. From the beginning to the end of *The Federalist*, he is most emphatic on the virtues of coordinated planning, uniformity, and a comprehensive perspective. Decisions of importance to the whole country, the authors say, must be made at the center by leaders who can take a broad view. The Continental Congress exemplifies this kind of chieftainship, notes Jay: "being convened from different parts of the country, they brought with them and communicated to each other a variety of useful information" (11). A national regime, Jay observes, "can move on uniform principles of policy—It can harmonize, assimilate, and protect the several parts and members, and extend the benefit of its foresight and precautions to each" (20-21). And Madison declares that "the public affairs of the union . . . can with difficulty be correctly learnt in any other place, than in the central councils, to which a knowledge of them will be brought by the representatives of every part" (363).

Let Publius consider any problem of the day, and his remedy is likely to involve an all-embracing, coherent program by the central government. Does America need a navy? The federal authorities must put "Southern wood" together with "seamen . . . drawn from the Northern hive." Is a more efficient revenue system required? A national regime motivated "to provide against violations every where," is the answer. Is a better national defense necessary? "Who so likely to make suitable provisions . . . as that body . . . which, as the center of information, will best understand . . . the dangers

that threaten—as the representative of the whole will feel itself . . . interested in the preservation of every part . . . and which . . . can . . . establish
uniformity and concert in the plans and measures, by which the common
safety is to be secured?" Should "the organization and discipline of the
militia" be improved? The solution is "uniformity," to be achieved "by
confiding the regulation of the militia to the direction of the national
authority." Is the foreign policy of the Confederation confused? We want the
"certainty and uniformity" of one national line of conduct. What is to be
gained by national regulation of elections for the House? We will attain the
"positive advantage" of "uniformity," of course (70-71, 77, 149, 181, 281,
413).

The necessity for comprehensive management of America's economic
affairs is emphasized by Publius, particularly in No. 11. "Under a vigorous
national government, the natural strength and resources of the country,
directed to a common interest, would baffle all the combinations of European jealousy to restrain our growth," he says. We can defeat our foreign
competitors with "prohibitory regulations, extending at the same time
throughout the States," which will force other nations "to bid against each
other, for the privileges of our markets." Any internal trade barriers should,
however, be lowered: "unrestrained intercourse between the States themselves will advance the trade of each," he asserts. Thus a potent national
government is needed both to control America's foreign commerce and to
ensure the absence of domestic impediments (65-73). This is obviously pure
neomercantilism, or economic nationalism. No. 22 presents the reverse of
this desirable policy—the defective practices of the confederation. The
Articles have assigned the national government no power over trade, so
foreign countries may enter our domestic market without hindrance, and
"the interfering and unneighbourly regulations of some States" against each
other threaten to turn fellow Americans into "foreigners and aliens," Publius
contends (137).

Besides the simple absence of certain powers, such as that over commerce, Publius feels that "the great and radical vice in the . . . existing
Confederation is in the principle of legislation for States or governments, in
their corporate or collective capacities." As a result, he notes, decisions of
the national rulers are "in practice . . . mere recommendations, which the
States observe or disregard at their option." But the provincial leaders do not
possess the wide-ranging perspective of the central representatives. The
subordinate members will evaluate national policies "without that knowledge of national circumstances and reasons of state, which is essential to a
right judgement, and with that strong predilection in favor of local objects,
which can hardly fail to mislead the decision." The only answer is for the

federal regime to act directly on individuals, Publius asserts. National enactments should "pass into immediate operation upon the citizens themselves" (93, 103).

And the public power of America should not only be centralized, but strong and active as well. Publius observes that "the vigour of government is essential to the security of liberty," that "energetic government" is needed to "preserve the Union of so large an empire" as America; that the national regime must be allowed "an unconfined authority, as to all those objects . . . entrusted to its management"; that "a weak constitution must necessarily terminate in dissolution . . . or . . . usurpation"; and that "tyranny has perhaps oftener grown out of the assumptions of power, called for, on pressing exigencies, by a defective constitution, than by the full exercise of the largest constitutional authorities" (5, 127, 191). Publius devotes seven essays to the need for an unlimited power of taxation at the federal level, and five to the necessity for a national standing army to suppress rebellions among the people. He endorses the concept of implied powers (303-4). He obviously does not favor a passive regime. In short, Publius is above all else concerned to make the case for a forceful centralized government. Although Hobbes's name is not mentioned in this work, his presence can be felt.

Publius is certain that the system of free elections will ensure popular control of the new regime, and he manifests this faith throughout *The Federalist*. Thus, he says, the standing army under the Constitution will be no real threat to American freedom because "the whole power of the proposed government is in the hands of the representatives of the people." He calls representation the "great mechanical power in government, by . . . which, the will of the largest political body may be concentred, and its force directed to any object, which the public good requires." Our rulers will respect the popular will because they are "dependent on the suffrages of . . . fellow-citizens for the continuance of public honors." Indeed, the proposed House of Representatives may be *too* close to the masses (178, 84, 221, 424-25). Even in No. 51, the notable discussion of checks and balances, Publius admits that these contrivances are only "auxiliary precautions" against despotism and that the best safeguard against tyranny is the government's "dependence on the people" (349). True, Publius uses two different concepts of representation, but both equally assert the government's ability to personate the nation.

Thus it is plain that the argument of Publius conforms in all important respects to the political theory of the nation-state. Yet it is possible to be more specific than this: Publius is a nation-builder. He is dealing with a population whose national sentiments cannot be taken for granted. He thinks that the common people will ordinarily feel more attached to their states than to the nation as a whole: "Upon the same principle that a man is more attached to his family than to his neighbourhood, to his neighbourhood than to the community at large, the people of each state would be apt to feel a stronger byass towards their local governments, than towards the government of the Union" (107). Stourzh, in his notable study of Hamilton's political philosophy, labels that statesman's project "Nation-Building without Patriotism," and although the phrase is somewhat overdrawn, it is true that not only Hamilton, but also Publius, usually presumes strong national feelings to be rare among the people.[1] *The Federalist* relies on sagacious political leaders to provide a comprehensive perspective: "the public voice pronounced by the representatives of the people, will be more consonant to the public good, than if pronounced by the people themselves convened for the purpose," it is said (62).

These comments on the weakness of national sentiments and the need for elite leadership do not reflect any lack of nationalistic vision on Publius's part, but simply the conditions of the day. A nation, we have noted, does not really exist from time immemorial, although that may be the official myth. Those entities are created out of populations that, while they may have numerous objective characteristics such as language or religion in common, do not originally think of themselves as belonging together. Initially, the bearers of the national idea are members of the social elite. The peasants of the rural hinterland tend to be localistic and familistic in their orientation and generally identify with the more inclusive community only after the national state has been in existence for some time. *The Federalist* was written before the full popularization of the idea of American nationhood.

That Publius is a genuine modern nationalist—rather than merely a paternalistic elitist—will further appear from two additional considerations. First, the authors reject aristocratic social distinctions. The "most decisive" mark of the republicanism of the new regime, Publius says, is the "absolute prohibition of titles of nobility." This provision, indeed,is "the corner stone of republican government" (253, 577-78). Publius always assumes that the members of the American governing class will see themselves not as a privileged caste, but as part of a larger community. Our future wise rulers will be representatives of the nation, not an aristocracy set above the great majority. Second, Publius feels that the American commonalty will develop a broadened perspective after the establishment of a strong central regime. "The more . . . the national authority . . . is familiarized to their sight and to their feelings," Publius says, "the greater will be the probability that it will conciliate the respect and attachment of the community." Internal improvements, including post roads built by the national government, will help to bring our people closer together, and this "will contribute to a general assimilation of their manners and laws" (173, 363-64). In No. 60 Publius asserts that some diversity will always remain, but even in that essay he anticipates "a gradual assimilation" of our population (405).

And Publius shows in another way his appreciation of the fact that nationalistic feelings frequently follow, rather than precede, the exercise of governmental power. He points out that just as the American nation can be solidified by the operations of a centralized regime, so partial confederacies or the continuance of undiluted state sovereignty can irrevocably divide it (26-27). His recognition that communal sentiments grow up around existing political boundaries does not make Publius any less a nationalist. It only proves that he is a realistic adherent of that view.

Thus we find all significant aspects of the political theory of nationalism present somewhere in the argument of *The Federalist*. Our analysis of the text of the great work allows us to make an even stronger statement, however. Not only is Publius—the composite personality formed by the blending of Hamilton, Madison, and Jay—a nationalist, but each of the three authors individually is, as well. Separate scrutiny has, in fact, shown no substantive variance between the writers. True, there are certain discrepancies: Hamilton and Madison do not agree on the definition of a federal government, for example; and Hamilton is far more concerned about the dangers of foreign bribery than Madison and Jay appear to be. There are other inconsistencies. Yet none of these is crucially important. On the whole, the Publii display a uniform outlook. These men did not really concur on everything, as future events would reveal. But their disagreements were not very evident when they composed their notable justification for the Constitution.

There surely can be no doubt concerning Jay's nationalism. He wrote but a handful of essays, and his principal themes are strongly marked: American nationhood, threats from abroad, and the wisdom of a centralized elite. Indeed, so unequivocal and so strategically located are his comments that if we thought *The Federalist* were the work of one individual, we would unhesitatingly pronounce this person to be a nationalist, based largely on Jay's contributions. The national vision of No. 2 would be assumed to underlie all of Publius's subsequent remarks. But we know that this paper was the work of a writer who produced a few of the later numbers, so a resistant critic could conceivably question whether this clear-cut nationalistic perspective is characteristic of the rest of the work.

Yet will anyone really deny that Hamilton is also of this mind? His constant refrain in *The Federalist* is the imperative need for national centralization, as this was the polestar of his political career. Although he does not enumerate the elements of nationality as precisely as his colleague does in No. 2, his observations in No. 12 and No. 13 show that he shares Jay's conception of the American nation. He repeatedly praises the sagacity of the national elite. The two New Yorkers are clearly compatible in outlook. And although Jay's *Federalst* papers are few, Hamilton's are numerous. When we add them together we discover that fifty-six of the eighty-five essays, or two-thirds of the total, present the opinions of unadulterated nationalists. Indeed, past doubts about Publius's attitude have always centered on Madison.

Our careful review of the Virginian's contributions has shown that, contrary to what is often asserted, he expresses the same kind of nationalistic sentiments as his associates. The famous No. 10 is a criticism of small-scale government and a statement on behalf of a territorially extensive republic. Similarly, No. 14 is a plea for a large nation-state. No. 18 and No. 19 acknowledge the significance of national ties. No. 41 through No. 46 reiterate the Hamiltonian arguments for centralization. The discussion of the House of Representatives exhibits complete confidence that these delegates can accurately embody the will of the American people. And the discussion of the upper house likens this branch to the senates of ancient Carthage and Rome—strong councils that provided elite leadership for their communities. The idea of nationalism underlies Madison's essays as surely as it does the rest of *The Federalist*.

If there is any variance between Madison and his collagues, it is purely one of nuance. Hamilton and Jay are quite forceful and uncompromising in their call for national unification. Madison, who has a bit more of the philosopher in him, takes a less vehement approach, admits uncertainties, and affects an objective attitude. It is possibly fair to say that the Virginian is not so single-mindedly nationalistic as the other two. He gives an appreciable amount of attention and space to themes that seem only indirectly tied to the national concept: the multiplicity of interest groups envisioned in No. 10 and the checks and balances lauded in No. 51, for example. Hamilton and Jay rarely stray from a straight nationalist course, whereas Madison more frequently wanders in the byways of the argument. But we must not overrate the extent of the divergence. There is no major contradiction and no split personality. Madison asserts nothing inconsistent with the nationalistic point of view that he and his partners all uphold.

Moreover, just as Madison mixes his nationalism with a regard for counterveiling powers, so Hamilton also now and then pauses in his praise of centralization to remark on the advantages of interest-group pluralism and to call for a division of the governmental authorities. Madison expatiates more lengthily on these topics, but Hamilton obviously does not disagree. This is at most a difference in emphasis. The large principles that unite the

Publii appear far more significant than the fine points by which they may be distinguished.

When Publius turns his attention to the internal structure of the new regime, he stresses the concepts of separation of powers and checks and balances. Therefore, we must decide whether those ideas are compatible with the nationalist viewpoint.

Three purposes are said to be served by these principles of organization. First, the public is protected from efforts by the rulers to usurp domestic power, since questionable actions on the part of one branch can be blocked by the others. This justification is emphasized in No. 51. Second, the community is secured from unwise or oppressive actions by the majority. In a sense this could be regarded as a protection for the people—from themselves. Yet this object clearly has an elitist tinge that is absent from the first. Third, the separation of powers is designed to allot governmental functions to those agencies able to carry them out most effectively. For example, the president and the Senate, which are seen as wiser and more stable than the populistic House, are envisioned as the sole actors with regard to American foreign policy. Contrary to the common presumption, none of these purposes necessarily implies a wish for a weak or passive national government.

Thus the first objective, restraint of the rulers, appears desirable to Publius precisely because he contemplates a potent central government: the feeble confederation authorities could be concentrated in one body without danger, Publius observes, but not the "additional powers" provided in the Constitution (145). Publius thinks that the federal regime should possess extensive prerogatives and should energetically employ them for the common good, yet he also understands the need to prevent abuse of these prerogatives. The authors of *The Federalist* were not simplistic thinkers; they were capable of arguing for a certain idea—national vigor—while at the same time recognizing the possible pitfalls of their favored course and trying to guard against them. Their wish to check the federal regime by means of an internal division is not a sign that they intended, in general, to prevent activity at the national level, but is only a qualification—or even a logical concomitant—of their dominant impulse toward energy and centralization. They anticipate that the separate branches will maintain "due harmony in all proper measures" (418).

Publius's second justification for governmental partition—the restraint of the majority—appears in two guises in *The Federalist*: it is sometimes said to be merely a means of blocking the foolish impulses of the direct representatives of the people, which can be taken as a call for passivity. But it is also frequently presented as a mechanism whereby wisdom may be injected into the policy-making process, and this latter formulation evidently envisions not that the authorities will ultimately be paralyzed, but rather that their actions will be rendered more judicous if at least some of them are sheltered from the whims of the commonalty. To a great extent, the less populistic agencies of the new central regime have been insulated from public clamor precisely to make them stronger, so that they can implement farsighted positive programs tending to the overall national benefit.

This point shades into the third argument for the division of government: that different segments of it will be relatively more effective for different purposes. Under this heading, some very important powers have been entirely concentrated in the president and the Senate. This arrangement certainly does not seem calculated to promote a diffusion and weakening of authority.

Which of these three reasons is most important to Publius? The first is featured in No. 51, the general discussion of separation of powers, whereas the second is actually disclaimed in that essay and the third is not mentioned. It is hardly surprising that the most populistic of the reasons—the one that speaks to the readers' possible feelings of distrust for the rulers—is stressed in the overall theoretical statement. The subsequent analysis of the various national branches emphasizes other factors, however. The House is not perceived as a checking body, but as an expression of the general will. The Senate and the president are envisioned as checking the majority—but usually in a positive way, by providing steady and wise leadership for the nation. On the whole, these agencies evidently are meant to be strong and vigorous. The courts, however, are prominently intended to safeguard the natural rights of the citizens by restraining the other branches—and, if necessary, the multitude. The judiciary, at least, does seem largely devoted to the protection of minority groups and individuals.

Thus the prevention of official despotism is one of the reasons for the separation of powers found in the Constitution, but not the only one, and governmental passivity as such is not the goal. We should remember that Publius always regards the system of popular representation as in itself sufficient to ensure the faithfulness of the national rulers to the democratic process. The authors of The Federalist were themselves among the popularly chosen governing elite of the nation, and they do not really believe that persons of their type are likely to be dangerous to the liberties of America. Madison specifically says that the division of public authority is only an "auxiliary" safeguard against tyranny, in the event the representative system breaks down.

Nationalistic presumptions underlie Publius's whole discussion of the structure of the new regime. It is true that one can detect in The Federalist a certain tension between two different concepts of the nation, the populist and the corporate—neither of which can be considered the only correct interpretation of the national idea. The blending of the two found in this work seems as appropriate a way as any to express the complexities of nationalism.

The House of Representatives is the incarnation of the populist concept. This body will "have an immediate dependence on, & an intimate sympathy with the people," and members will "dwell among the people at large," will possess "connections of blood, of friendship, and of acquaintance" with the "influential part of the society," and will be regarded as "confidential guardians of the rights and liberties of the people." In short, the House will speak "the sense of a majority (355, 341-42, 393). Publius also thinks the House will tend to partake of the infirmities of the masses and, therefore, will need to be checked by cooler and wiser heads, but he never doubts that the House can stand for the nation in a majoritarian sense. Rousseau's skepticism concerning representation—"the moment a people allows itself to be represented, it is no longer free"[2]—has no echo in the argument of *The Federalist*. Publius does once or twice hint that the House may act against the people, but he more often suggests that any fears of its possible infidelity are groundless.

The Senate has certain federalistic features, but Publius pays little attention to them. The chief recommendation of this body, he maintains, is that it will identify with the nation as a corporate entity. The senators will have a "due sense of national character"; they will comprise "an assembly so durably invested with public trust, that the pride and consequence of its members may be sensibly incorporated with the reputation and prosperity of the community"; they will seek "the good of the whole"; and they will be trustworthy because they cannot "make any treaties, by which they and their families and estates will not be equally bound and affected with the rest of the community; and having no private interest distinct from that of the nation, they will be under no temptations to neglect the latter" (423, 437-38). This elite council will bring stability and discretion to our national affairs, Publius contends.

The president will combine elements of centralization, populism, and elitism. The executive power has been allotted to one official because "unity is conducive to energy," Publius points out. The presidential election procedure has been given a popular flavor in that it will depend on "men, chosen by the people for the special purpose, and at the particular conjuncture." But the electors are an elite group who will "possess the information and discernment requisite to so complicated an investigation." The president will be "the constitutional representative of the nation" with regard to foreign affairs. "If we are to be one nation in any respect, it clearly ought to be in respect to other nations," Publius asserts (472, 458, 460, 506, 279). Like the Senate, the chief executive will tend to identify with the nation in a long-term sense, less perhaps on account of the four-year term per se, than because of the possibility of indefinite reelection. It is hoped therefore, that the president will not shrink from "extensive and arduous enterprises for the public benefit, requiring considerable time to mature and perfect them" (481-92, 488). If this is not an "imperial" president, it is at least a vigorous one.

The independent judiciary will "declare all acts contrary to the manifest tenor of the constitution void," Publius asserts. He seems principally interested in this power as a means of controlling the states: it is the only feasible alternative to a direct national government veto of state actions. But the federal courts are also meant to restrain the other branches of the central regime, and the people themselves when temporary infatuation causes them to stray from their rational character. Because the fundamental charter is the legal expression of the permanent will of the community, Publius clearly regards the judiciary as a voice for the nation in its corporate aspect. And it is a force for centralization. There is a need for a single final authority to provide "uniformity in the interpretation of the national laws," he says (524, 535).

Thus the argument of Publius features a complete version of the political theory of the nation-state and a governmental plan that has been structured in accord with the imperatives of that theory. Centralization, populism, and a sense of corporate nationality have been blended in the institutions of the new regime.

Having presented his readers with an analysis of the American situation clearly implying the necessity for a centralized national government, Publius proceeds to recommend a rather different kind of regime, a federal union of partially sovereign states. He gives reasons for this choice, but they are weak ones and contrary to his general stance. Were we to judge strictly from the text of *The Federalist*, this proposal would not be easy for us to understand. There is a serious disjunction between the nationalistic principles of Publius and the federal nature of the plan.

Publius repeatedly maintains that the scheme of the Convention involves a division of sovereignty between the national government and the states. Indeed, Hamilton insists that the new charter will create a true confederation (55). Madison more accurately says that "the proposed Constitution . . . is in strictness neither a national nor a federal constitution, but a composition of both" (257). The two authors agree, however, that the states will retain very great powers under the sugggested compact. Publius notes that the ratification process is on a state-by-state basis; that senators are allotted according to state equality and chosen by the state legislatures; that the powers of the national government are enumerated, with the rest by implication left to the states; and that the presidential election and constitutional amendment procedures have federal aspects. Also, Publius points out how, under the recommended design, "the State Legislatures, by forbearing the appointment of Senators, may destroy the National Government." This is an "absolute safe-guard" of the state governments, Publius believes (253-57, 400-401). Our authors may have overstated the federal aspects of the proposed arrangement (55-56, 254, 256, 351)—may, indeed, have misappropriated the term *federal* as it was then understood. But they genuinely saw the Constitution as allowing the state governments considerable authority, even so.

So far, the anticonsolidationist school of critics might feel to a degree vindicated. It is true that in No. 39 Publius labels our Constitution as something more than a mere federal union, but he also regard it as rather less than a centralized nation-state. The real problem for the anticonsolidationist interpretation arises when we ask why Publius considers this arrangement to be necessary. Given the clear nationalistic predilections of *The Federalist*, why does Publius not simply recommend a unitary national government? Hamilton, Madison, and Jay have provided us with a partially federal government, but with no particularly good rationale for one.

Publius portrays the states as shortsighted, uncooperative, erratic, factious, and badly led, noting that these entities are often tempted by "local . . . interests" and "the prospect of present loss or advantage" into actions contrary to the general good. "The rulers of the respective members, whether they have a constitutional right to do it or not, will undertake to judge of the propriety" of national policies and will do this "in a spirit of interested and suspicious scrutiny," without the information that is available at the federal level. America's sad experience with the Articles of Confederation shows that the states will not spontaneously work together (15, 97). Besides their awkward tendency to scamper off in thirteen different directions, they are prone to the domination of selfish special-interest groups. Also, they are "too unstable," and their "fluctuating" measures often include "sudden changes and legislative interference in cases affecting personal rights." Finally, they have been saddled with unimpressive chiefs, like Governor Clinton, "who possess not qualifications to extend their influence beyond the narrow circles of personal intrigue" (57, 301, 53).

The baleful weight of the states is, of course, accentuated under the confederation, because of the feebleness of the national regime. But Publius admits that these entities will continue their harmful ways under the Constitution and that the federal structure of the new government will contribute to the mischief. "There is in the nature of sovereign power an impatience of controul," he points out. Thus it is precisely the fact that the states in our federal system retain some sovereignty that encourages divisive courses. The states will tend to "encroach on the national authorities." Their jurisdiction over "criminal and civil justice" will "render them . . . dangerous rivals to the power of the Union." Publius discovers "an inherent and intrinsic weakness in all Fœderal Constitutions." He maintains that "the State Governments will too naturally be prone to a rivalship with that of the Union, the foundation of which will be the love of power." He flatly asserts that "the danger which most threatens our political welfare, is, that the State Governments will finally sap the foundations of the Union." He feels that under the proposed charter "a local spirit will infallibly prevail . . . in the members of Congress." And he spells out the possible problems with "concurrent jurisdiction." The suggested Constitution may be an improvement over the Articles of Confederation, but it will hardly be free from provincial troublemaking (96-97, 106, 117, 159, 205-6, 311, 318, 199-208).

Yet if the states are so potentially harmful, why have they been allowed to retain a large degree of sovereignty? Publius gives two reasons to justify the federal aspect of the proposed Constitution, neither of which appears sufficient to outweigh the dangers which have been enumerated at length.

First, Publius contends that the states are useful for purposes of local administration. The best statement of this point is in No. 10, where he declares that national officials may be "too little acquainted" with the "local circumstances and lesser interests" of the American population and that "the Federal Constitution forms a happy combination in this respect; the great and aggregate interests being referred to the national, the local and particular to the state legislatures" (63). State sovereignty will protect the provinces against attempts by the central government to interfere in their rightful sphere. Yet this rationale for federalism is less than conclusive, because Publius consistently denies that the national rulers will ever attempt to meddle with those matters appropriate for state action (105-7, 199, 317). Indeed, in No. 14 he asserts that even were the states to be "abolished," the general government would willingly, even necessarily, "reinstate them in their proper jurisdiction" (86). Such statements, far from justifying the federal system, tend to show that it is superfluous. A unitary national regime could set up subordinate bodies for local purposes, as states establish counties, and according to Publius undoubtedly would do so. To invest the states with a perilous degree of sovereign power in order to counter a nonexistent threat to their internal autonomy appears a quixotic procedure, contrary to our authors' usual style.

Moreover, Publius explicitly approves a future expansion of the central regime's area of responsibility, if this is truly desired by the American people (173-74, 308-9, 315-16). National encroachments are not in this view necessarily an evil—a consideration that further diminishes the importance of federalism, from this perspective. Indeed, certain passages in *The Federalist* imply that the general government might not be wholly incompetent for local administration, after all (225, 300, 546-48). These statements should not be overstressed, because Publius more often indicates that there is some advantage to state management of minor matters, but his comments show that he is not a fanatic on the question. In fact, there are but a handful of references to the need for local governance in the whole treatise. This was not a priority concern of Hamilton, Madison and Jay.

The second, and intrinsically more important, justification for the federal system is the usefulness of the states for purposes of resistance to despotism. The provinces "will always be not only vigilant but suspicious and jealous guardians of the rights of the citizens, against incroachments from the Fœderal government . . . and will be ready enough, if any thing improper appears, to sound the alarm to the people and not only to be the voice but if necessary the arm of their resistance" (168-69). Several additional passages also cast the states in that role (179, 317-23, 412-13, 582-83). Thus although the Constitution allows these subordinate polities no direct role in the devising or implementing of national policy, they can nevertheless serve as organs of "that original right of self-defense which is paramount to all positive forms of government" (178-79). And it is specifically the status of the states as partially sovereign entities that will render them formidable at the head of a necessary popular rebellion, Publius believes. He points out that the states, possessing "all the organs of civil power and the confidence of the people, . . . can at once adopt a regular plan of opposition, in which they can combine all the resources of the community" (107-8, 180). If corporate state action is indeed essential for the preservation of American freedom, we have an argument for federalism, it would appear.

Unfortunately for the anticonsolidationist interpretation of *The Federalist*, however, Publius plainly does *not* believe this. He unequivocally and at length contend that the danger of a national military despotism is so remote as to be unthinkable, even without considering the possible role of the states. He quite ridicules the idea that "every man, the instant he took his seat in the national senate or house of representatives, would commence a traitor to his constituents," or that a conspiracy against popular liberties "would be persevered in and transmitted along, through all the successive variations in the representative body, which biennial elections would naturally produce." Again, he scornfully dismisses the fears of a military coup by the officials of the national government as "more like the incoherent dreams of a delirious jealousy, or the misjudged exaggerations of a counterfeit zeal, than like the sober apprehensions of genuine patriotism" (169, 321). Publius is confident that the federal House of Representatives will embody the popular will. Should the system of representation break down, the separation of powers will provide an additional line of defense. The actual need for state insurrections appears most problematical.

In summary, therefore, according to Publius's own statement of the case, the federal system will provide a pointless defense against two unlikely perils as the meager return for a real, concrete risk of the disruption of the union by the states. As a justification for federalism, this is remarkably unpersuasive. Nor is it plausible to suggest that Publius simply values this small increment of protection against national tyranny more than he does the practical inconvenience involved. Of all political writers, few have been less willing than Publius to endure actual harm for the sake of a merely theoretical good. He scorns "refinements, which owe their origin to a zeal for liberty more ardent than enlightened" (164). He is definitely not one to hamper the national authorities for no good reason, yet that plainly seems to be the effect of federalism. His argument for this arrangement is not merely unconvincing, it is also decidedly out of character.

Indeed, Publius shows a marked lack of enthusiasm for the federal features of the proposed Constitution. For example, he never finds anything good to say about state equality in the Senate: his most positive comment is that in practice this provision may not be as harmful as it appears in theory, and he declares that state equality "contradicts that fundamental maxim of republican government, which requires that the sense of the majority should prevail" (417, 139). He is slightly more favorable concerning the election of senators by the state legislatures, since these bodies will at least be composed of relatively well-informed persons and so will probably make capable choices. But he mentions no advantage to involving the states in their corporate capacities in this process. In fact, he regards as an "inconvenience" and an "evil" the fact that "State Legislatures, by forbearing the appointment of Senators, may destroy the national Government" (433, 400-401). The only federal aspect of the new plan that he unequivocally approves is the state-by-state vote of the electoral college (458-59). And here the virtue acclaimed is rather dispersion than federalism. Publius never applauds the participation of the state government as such in the presidential election process.

It is a sign of Publius's lack of real interest in federalism that there is no paper devoted to a general theoretical statement of the notion. Critics who see pluralism as the principal conception of *The Federalist* point to No. 10, those who prefer to emphasize the separation of powers and checks and balances underscore No. 51, and the nationalists stress No. 2, but where is the great essay on federalism? No. 9 and No. 39 try to define federalism and show how it is a major feature of the Constitution, but their definitions are not consistent, and neither these nor any other of the *Federalist* papers presents the concept in a systematic and comprehensive fashion or states its advantages over a unitary system in an organized and complete way. The rationale for federalism can only be collected from scattered references in various essays. If this were really the main theme of the work, one suspects that the authors would have made it easier for us to grasp.

Finally, there is a significant omission in *The Federalist*. The most important argument for the American federal system is the one put forward by Morley in *Freedom and Federalism*: "the federal form was historically ordained, by the fact that the original thirteen colonies . . . had . . . developed widely differing political and social customs." Our federalism is a safeguard for these diverse regional mores.[3] Indeed, this is the only real justification for leaving sovereign power in the hands of subnational units— that they have some unique values and interests which only their own residents can appreciate and be trusted to defend. This argument, however, is not to be found in the *Federalist* papers. Although Publius recognizes the existence of much regional variation among our people, he never presents this variation as worthy of political expression. To Publius, our regional differences are to be brushed under the carpet for the present and hopefully reduced by assimilation in the future. They are not seen as positive goods to be preserved by the decentralization of power.

The argument based on diverse social custom has a superficial similarity to one of the arguments Publius does use, the advantage of local administration, but these are not really the same. Local administration is advocated in *The Federalist* not as a means of preserving distinctive provincial usages, but simply as a convenient way to dispose of trivial matters that do not affect the general good and that require a knowledge of petty circumstances beneath the attention of the national rulers. Thus the "supervision of agriculture" is declared by Publius to be a naturally local function because it has no bearing on the welfare of the country as a whole; Publius never suggests that the states possess intrinsically different ideals concerning agriculture, or anything else, that deserve to be upheld against the intrusion of uniform national values (106). With respect to the prevention of federal despotism, Publius only regards the states as instruments of the whole people, never as a protection for minorities against the majority.

The argument of *The Federalist*, therefore, can be described as a clashing mixture of nationalism and federalism, with the former much predominating. Publius's general outlook, his practical maxims of politics, and his analysis of the situation of America are basically nationalistic. The plan presented is partly federal, but these features are neither emphasized nor well justified. Thus the text of this treatise accurately mirrors the real political inclinations of Hamilton, Madison, and Jay in 1787-88. They were, in truth, men of nationalistic principles obliged to support a federal proposal that none of them liked wholeheartedly. All had suggested solutions to the American governmental crisis that were markedly less solicitous of the states than the design adopted at Philadelphia. The Publii would have preferred to deprive the provinces of all sovereignty. Because this could not be done, they supported the Constitution as better than nothing. Once they had accepted this federal scheme, of course, they rightly insisted on its harmlessness to the states. They genuinely believed—or rather feared—that under the proposed regime these entities would retain enough clout to disrupt the intentions, good or bad, of the country's rulers.

The federalistic suggestions of Publius are clearly intrusive elements in his overall philosophy. Indeed, it is remarkable that he pays as little lip service as he does to this aspect of the plan. His portrayal of the states is consistently unfavorable, and he is generally lukewarm or even critical concerning the federal features of the Constitution. He gives little evidence of believing that the superfluous protection the states offer against national despotism, under the Constitution, really outweighs their capacity for mischief. His vaunted theory of federalism is actually only the *ex post facto* rationalization of a political compromise. His true nationalistic bent seems evident.

Less need be said here about Madison's interest-group theory, because it is not especially contradictory to the nationalist outlook, superficial appearances notwithstanding. Madison does say that an extensive American polity will include a variety of special interests and that the multiplicity of these will tend to have a stabilizing effect on the system as a whole. Yet to elevate this insight, however striking it may be, into Publius's main point is a gross distortion, plausible only to those who have read No. 10 but none of the other papers. In general, Publius feels that the chief merit of the Constitution is that it will bind us together, not that it will multiply the number of our divisions. Since factions we must have, he thinks it best that they be numerous and weak, but this is hardly the leading idea of *The Federalist*.

Madison, it must be recalled, is not a pluralist in the present-day sense. He dislikes the activity of organized special-interest groups, and he believes that superficial contradictions among the people are reconcilable in terms of the welfare of the nation as a whole. The Publii do not perceive the legislative process as a matter of bargain and compromise between various partial interests, but as an affair of discussion and eventual agreement among wise and just statesmen on a comprehensive program to advance the common good. Balitzer's eccentric contention notwithstanding, Madison would not approve of PACs.[4]

Publius's recognition of American diversity does not clash with his nationalism, although this might seem to be the case at first glance. The authors, including Madison, clearly believe, and state on several occasions, that national commonalities—language, custom, territory, political values, and so forth—are the proper basis for a government. The renowned thesis of No. 10 simply amounts to the proposition that no population, however homogeneous, can possibly be alike in every respect and that it is better to have many minor divisions instead of a few great ones. Madison never says that it is intrinsically bad for people to agree as much as possible, only that it is "impracticable" for "every citizen" to have "the same opinions, the same passions, and the same interests." In fact, he points out certain disadvantages to pluralism. "This variety of interests . . . may have a salutary influence on the administration of the Government when formed; yet every one must be sensible of the contrary influence which must have been experienced in the task of forming it" (58, 237-38). Hamilton also notes the difficulty of drafting a Constitution for a rather pluralistic nation (591). If Publius thinks it is difficult to fashion a regime for a diversified people, then he must believe it is relatively easy to create one for a people not diversified. Thus Publius accepts the central insight of the political theory of the nation-state.

In connection with pluralism, we should note Beard's contention that the authors of *The Federalist* were really concerned with the safeguarding of propertied interests. This is also the opinion of Dietze, who says that "national power was for Hamilton by no means an end in itself, but was a mere means for securing the happiness of the individual, of which the protection of property constituted a prominent part."[5] It is true that Publius sees the proposed regime providing "additional security . . . to republican government, to liberty, and to property" (587). Yet the protection of private interests or property rights per se does not appear to be his main concern, as a matter of fact. Publius is far more solicitous to secure the vigorous administration of the public affairs of the American community than to enlarge the boundaries of individual autonomy. Publius is both a staunch nationalist and a classical liberal, and the former position seems at least as basic as the latter.

Publius's attitude is not that of the bourgeois individualist who merely wants to be left alone by the government. He is rather the semiaristocratic leader of society who seeks to order the affairs of the community for the common good. His concern for the rights of property seems to stem more from a belief that commerce serves the nation than from an ideological commitment to abstract individual freedom. Thus, to illustrate, Beard and other critics claim that Publius envisions the Senate as protecting property.[6] In fact, *The Federalist* mentions this consideration just once. No. 62 praises the stability of the proposed Senate and expatiates on the evils of "inconstant government." "What prudent merchant," Publius asks, "will hazard his fortunes in any new branch of commerce, when he knows not but that his plans may be rendered unlawful before they can be executed?" (421-22). It is evident that Publius writes here strictly from the standpoint of an intelligent economic manager; he asserts no general right of property owners to be free from public control. Publius expects that the Senate will uphold the long-term welfare of the nation and will consequently be appropriately solicitous of capitalists. But he does not mean to exempt propertied interests from social regulation.

Even Epstein, whose analysis is usually most perceptive, cannot quite rid himself of the presumption that Publius primarily intends to secure the rights of individuals. He notes that Madison, in No. 10 and elsewhere, distinguishes between "justice" and "the public good"—that is, between questions of right and questions of community interest. Of course, Epstein admits, Madison never observes any real conflict between these considerations. It appears that in Publius's view they are really intertwined—that justice can only be obtained if the community is prosperous and well defended, while violations of rights will produce civil discord and will therefore be contrary to the public good. Epstein acknowledges that "this mutual dependence suggests a large degree of harmony between the two objects when they are properly understood." Yet he still asserts that, at least in No. 10, "justice is given the most emphasis" and that for the Publii the securing of rights is "more fundamental" than practical concerns.[7] This conclusion, however, does not seem warranted by the text of *The Federalist*.

Publius always presumes that the welfare of the nation and the preservation of personal rights inevitably go hand in hand. At no point does he contemplate a choice of one over the other; he plainly thinks they will stand or fall together. A divided and weak polity will not be hospitable to freedom, in this view, whereas abridgements of liberty and justice will undermine the stability and well-being of the country. Were Publius forced to choose between community interest and abstract right, it is by no means obvious that he would select the latter. He observes in No. 2: "Nothing is more certain than the indispensable necessity of Government, and it is equally undeniable, that whenever and however it is instituted, the people must cede to it some of their natural rights, in order to vest it with requisite powers." In No. 8 he declares: "Safety from external danger is the most powerful director of national conduct. Even the ardent love of liberty will, after a time, give way to its dictates." He says in No. 51 that factional unrest may justify establishment of a regime "altogether independent of the people" (8, 45, 352). We are aware from other sources that Hamilton and Madison were even willing to see property rights violated for the general good, although they affirm this with apparent reluctance and numerous qualifications.[8] Of course, the Publii hold that liberty, safety, and prosperity will be perfectly reconcilable under the new Constitution.

Publius's highly pragmatic attitude towards these issues is most evident in his discussion of a bill of rights in No. 84. He does not deny that individuals possess natural rights, but declares that as a practical matter personal liberties are subordinate to "the general spirit of the people and of the government" (580). In a sense, this is his way of reconciling the liberal and nationalistic viewpoints. Rights exist in theory, he admits, but the will of the nation is controlling in fact.

In summary, Publius is not a federalist, nor a pluralist in the modern sense, nor all that much of a libertarian. It is true that he expects his project of national centralization to occur without prejudice to the right of individuals—indeed, he believes that nationalism and the protection of rights are naturally allied—but the former of these is the distinctive theme of *The Federalist*, not the latter. We appear to have returned more or less to the opinion of Chief Justice Marshall in *Cohens v. Virginia*: the argument of Publius is most credible when it calls for the establishment of a powerful central authority, and otherwise suspect. Above all else, Publius is a nationalist.

10

The Significance
of *The Federalist*

The foregoing is obviously no trivial conclusion. The essays of Publius are generally conceded to occupy an eminent place within the Western political tradition and to possess a particular relevance to the governmental affairs of the United States. Our discovery that *The Federalist* is truly an argument for nationalism is material in both of these contexts.

Western critics in general, like Americans, have interpreted *The Federalist* in various ways, but they appear to have most commonly perceived it as a justification for that peculiar Yankee invention, federalism. Dietze recounts that although the tract was at first favorably received in France, the Jacobins turned against it on the grounds that a federal government was not conducive to a united country. Brissot de Warville, one of the chief Girondist leaders, "was judged to be an advocate of the dismemberment of France, because he had borrowed a copy of that work." In Germany, Publius's treatise has often been cited by those desiring a *Bundesstaat*, that is a "federal union" of the German states, the most distinguished of these being probably Dr. Hugo Preuss, who was the author of the ill-fated Weimar constitution. Strongly nationalistic Germans have regarded *The Federalist* as less favorable to their pretensions. Post–World War II Italian decentralizers have deemed the work supportive of their cause.[1] And the British, too, seem to see federalism as the key to Publius's case, as indicated by John Stuart Mill's comment quoted in the first chapter of the present study.[2]

Thus the prevalent world opinion of the argument of Publius appears to be that it is an apologia for a federally divided, as opposed to a unitary national, government; and that, as such, it articulates a distinctive American view of politics. Because nation-states, not federations, are the dominant governmental form of the twentieth century, and nationalism has on the whole been far more influential in the world than federalism, this interpretation puts the treatise somewhat outside the mainstream of political thought in general. The nationalistic reading of Publius, however, tends to assimilate *The Federalist* to the Western tradition and, perhaps ironically, to lessen the importance of its distinctively American flavor. The real meaning of *The Federalist*, it seems, is not to be found in the equivocal and unimpressive rationale for partial state sovereignty that it contains, but instead in the clear and highly creative expression of the political theory of nationalism that Publius far more wholeheartedly pronounces.

As we observed in chapter 3, *The Federalist* was written at a time when the various elements of the nationalist conception had not yet coalesced. The notion of a self-governing political community, as handed down from the ancient Greeks, was still generally associated with the city-state. National differences were marked, but were not usually the object of intense popular feeling, and were not always regarded as politically relevant. The advantages of centralization were known, but were often deemed inseparable from despotism. And representative institutions were not admired by all critics, nor particularly seen as the mechanism by which a nation could exert power over itself. No existing regime wholly qualified as a modern nation-state as of 1787, and no previous political thinker had yet articulated the modern theory of nationalism. Hamilton, Madison, and Jay, however, put all the pieces together. Publius presumes that Americans are a distinct community of sentiment and interest; he presents the concept of a nation more systematically than anything attempted by Machiavelli or Montesquieu; he lauds the advantages of centralized management in terms reminiscent of Hobbes; and he voices a Lockean confidence in representative institutions as instruments of popular control. It is not unreasonable to consider Publius the world's first true nationalist.

Many peculiarities of the argument of *The Federalist* can be explained by reference to the undeveloped condition of nationalist thought at the time the work was written. We have seen that there was often something of an aristocratic tinge to what passed for nationalism in the eighteenth century. The literate and politically active classes were the only ones accustomed to thinking in national terms. Ordinary people tended to have more limited horizons. The relatively elitist viewpoint of Publius is something that we would logically expect from a nationalist writer of that day. Knowing of no example to the contrary, he feels that nationalism is a bit too abstract for the masses. This outlook may seem bloodless by comparison with the more populistic spirit engendered by the French Revolution. But the democratic impulse present at the rise of the French nation was an absolutely unprecedented phenomenon, which the Publii could hardly have taken into account.

Thus *The Federalist* is a product of its time. Yet we should not overstress this fact. The work is far more remarkable for the extent to which it achieves a modern national vision than for its superficial archaisms. It is wrong to think of Publius as in any important respect falling short of full nationalism.

His upper-class rulers comprise a national elite—the elected delegates of the people—not a titled aristocracy placed above the common run of society. True, he regards his fellow citizens as preoccupied with local concerns and in some ways rather diverse, but he looks forward to their eventual assimilation, furthered by the operations of a centralized government. He considers the American nation to be something that will develop over time, rather than something that immutably exists, but this fact makes him no less a nationalist. It does, however, point to another of his key aspects.

Not only is *The Federalist* the first great work of political science to amalgamate certain elements of the Western tradition into the full theory of nationalism, it also constitutes a description of the project of nation building, and as such speaks directly to our contemporary world. Myriads of nationalist revolutions have taken place, in all parts of the globe, in the last two centuries. The elites who have engineered these upheavals have in the aftermath of their struggles been required to construct new national regimes to reinforce the affinities of their people—or to create affinities where they did not exist before. The American Founders were the prototypical example of such an elite, and *The Federalist* examines the various considerations involved in the nation-building process in terms still applicable in the present day.

The affinity of Publius's outlook with that of later nationalist rulers is illustrated by a representative modern example of the type, Kwame Nkrumah, prolific author and former president of Ghana. As a socialist and something of an authoritarian, Nkrumah was hardly a consistent disciple of the American Founders, but the argument of his book, *Africa Must Unite*, reminds us of *The Federalist* on almost every page. Thus he recounts how he countered the machinations of "separatist groups" in Ghana by spearheading the establishment of a strong presidential system, explicitly modeled on the United States Constitution, and giving him authority to "exercise the positive leadership . . . so vital to a country seeking to pull itself up by its bootstraps." Also, he is a fervent pan-Africanist who argues that the "economic weakness" of that continent requires "integrated planning within an over-all policy decided by a continental authority." He calls for a "continent-wide system" of "roads and railways," for the elimination of "internal customs barriers," for the creation of a "common currency," and for the establishment of an African "central bank of issue." And he observes that "a Union of African States must strengthen our influence on the international scene, as all Africa will speak with one concerted voice."[3]

Nkrumah recommends that existing African governments form a federal union. He quotes extensively from the Constitution of the United States, and explicitly offers that charter as a model.[4] He suggests that it may be possible to unite and "yet preserve to some extent the sovereignty of each State." He proposes "a continental parliament" with "a lower and an upper house, the one to permit . . . discussion . . . by a representation based on population; the other, ensuring the equality of the associated States, regardless of size." If Africa does not manage to politically unite, the consequences will be grave, he maintains: "economic friction among us would certainly lead to bitter political rivalry." He warns above all against "neocolonialism and its major instrument, balkanization." The "imperialist powers" will "endeavour to create fissions in the national front," in order to maintain their former colonies in a dependent status—especially economically. War could result "if African states make . . . alliances with rival powers outside Africa," he contends. Also, disunity requires every state to have its own military force, which "imposes a heavy financial burden on even the most wealthy African states," he observes.[5]

It would be possible to go on, but the point is clear. These are essentially the arguments of Publius. Nkrumah acknowledges the relevance of the American experience to his own projects, perceives separation of powers as a device to provide a strong executive, and sees federalism as a device to unify the African nation. But careful analysis also shows important differences between these two; there is no question of an absolute identity of approach. Nor does Nkrumah reveal any trace of the specific influence of Publius. What we seem to have here is a case of convergent evolution— leaders of quite distinct peoples and centuries finding analogous solutions to comparable problems. *The Federalist* is a distinguished contribution to the literature on the construction of nations.

Nkrumah's book also helps us gain some perspective on certain elements of Publius's argument that have often been criticized: the dislike of political parties and the insistence upon insulating a major part of the government from popular pressures. The African statesman discusses at length the "violently destructive opposition" that he faced. "Their politics," he declares, "have been narrowly regional in concept, and often violent, abusive and terroristic in action." He contrasts the disruptive activities of his Ghanaian antagonists with the "responsibility and maturity" of the opposition parties of more politically developed nations. Criticism, Nkrumah says, "if it is to be of benefit . . . must be constructive. This is the strength of the opposition in the established democracies of the world. They recognize that they, together with the government of the day, proceed from the major premise that they have a joint aim, to advance the welfare of the people." These parties will have ideological differences, Nkrumah acknowledges. "There remain, however, broad areas of internal and foreign affairs where there is a community of view."[6] He notes that in the end he was obliged, reluctantly, of course, to forbid the opposition to organize along tribal or religious lines.[7] Ultimately, in fact, his regime simply suppressed the dissident elements and established a single-party dictatorship in Ghana.

It is perhaps not entirely safe to take the impressions of a harassed head of state as a balanced assessment of conditions, yet Nkrumah's point is worth considering. Political opposition may be harmless and even beneficial in a fully functioning nation-state, where all citizens, even those who happen to dislike the current party in power, feel a fundamental sense of identification with the community as a whole. But such opposition may take on a different character in a fledgling nation, where political ties are less well developed—particularly if the dissidence happens to coincide, as it frequently will, with the major fracture lines in the society. In such a context, the necessity for national unity must constantly be invoked to hold the social body together, and governments, even popular ones, will often take on a rather imperious character in order to control the clamor of divisive groups. Many of Publius's attitudes are explained when they are viewed in this context. The American Founders intended six-year Senate terms, an independent judiciary, and a small standing army to solve the problems that Nkrumah combated with police-state tactics. Rather than being pilloried for their unfashionable elitism, the Founders should be praised for the mildness of their methods. How many Third World revolutions have had so democratic a conclusion?

The Founders' distaste for political parties is usually taken to be a slight defect on their part, a sign of their relative naïveté, compared to the wisdom of the present day. Thus, Richard Hofstadter has pronounced: "I believe that the gradual acceptance of parties and of the system of a recognized partisan opposition . . . marked a net gain in the sophistication of political thought and practice over the anti-party thought . . . that had prevailed in the Anglo-American tradition in the eighteenth century and earlier."[8] Hofstadter's thesis may be salvageable, if it is taken to mean simply that the idea of the usefulness of parties is an advanced conception that can be widely accepted only after a population has reached a fair level of political maturity. But the historian also seems to think that the Founders were wrong to oppose political parties in the America of 1787, and that assumption is rather more doubtful. There is hardly a nation builder in the history of the world who has not found it necessary to discourage internal dissension to some extent, and there is no reason why the American Founders should have been exempt from this fact of political life. The party conflict that developed in the 1790s was ferocious and divisive. Even the Federalists resorted to separatism when they lost national power in the early nineteenth century. Political parties were probably more dangerous to the community then than now.

The issue of economic development deserves a brief comment at this point. Nkrumah is a socialist and as such is convinced of "the uncounted advantages which planning has in the first place over the *laissez faire* go-as-you-please policies of the early pioneers of industrialism." He identifies the United States as "the most vocal proponent of free enterprise, unfettered by central planning."9 Yet our examination of the argument of Publius suggests that the gap between Publius's approach to these matters and Nkrumah's is rather less than might be presumed. Publius regards the American economy as an ensemble of interests demanding centralized public regulation, and he desires national unity in order to extort economic advantages from other countries. Nkrumah's goals are pretty much the same. It is true that Hamilton planned for private enterprise to be the main engine of development, whereas Nkrumah gives the principal role to government. This certainly is no small difference. Yet insofar as they are economic nationalists, they are quite comparable. Hamilton was no great lover of laissez-faire.

So Publius was perhaps the world's first nationalist, and a most prophetic one. But what does his vision mean to Americans, who are the primary heirs to this wisdom?

It is hardly feasible to cover in a single chapter all the many ways in which *The Federalist* has affected the course of American political thought, but we may consider, in a brief and summary way, how Publius's nationalistic viewpoint relates to the characteristic political values of this country.

To summarize the distinctive political perspective of America in a few words is not easy, but a reasonable attempt to do so is found in Charles V. Hamilton's textbook, *American Government*. Professor Hamilton finds "three important assumptions" at the heart of the American attitude. First, "fragmented government is the best way to guard against tyranny and to protect individual liberty"; second, "the best way to ensure economic growth and development is to have the government involved as little as possible in the economy"; and third, "American government is a pluralist system" that is "best understood by examining the role of various interest groups in the policy-making process."10 It might be possible to add other points to Professor Hamilton's list, but these do appear to be typical of what we regard as the American tradition. Remarkably, *The Federalist* is basically negative toward all three of these notions.

Thus Publius is surely no patron of fragmented government: centralization is his first love and his incessant refrain. Nor is he notable as an advocate of the free market. He presumes that the government will regulate the economy, by tariffs if in no other way, and he simply desires that any such regulation occur on the national, rather than the state, level. And his opinion of pluralism is crucially different from that presented by Professor Hamilton as distinctively American. Our typical view is said to be that it is good for many interest groups to be directly involved in the policy-making process. This is not Publius's opinion, however. He thinks faction is inevitable but harmful, and he wants political issues to be settled by a representative elite answerable only to a broad public and intent upon the promotion of the general welfare. A paradigm less like the mere balancing of partial interests could hardly be devised. Publius is a nationalist who seeks unity, not a pluralist who enjoys diversity for its own sake.

In short, the argument of Publius is more a criticism than a celebration of ordinary American political values. The work is addressed to an audience in this country and so pays lip service to our prejudices. Nevertheless, it asserts an ideal of positive, strong, centralized government that is quite contrary to what is commonly thought to be the American preference. It appears that Publius is not a typical American—but, then, the Founders never regarded themselves as average. Yet it seems somewhat paradoxical to maintain that *The Federalist*, a foundation of American political thought, is not really in the mainstream of our tradition. It would probably be better to say that careful examination of the argument of Publius indicates that the American tradition is more complex and inclusive than it is frequently presumed to be. Decentralization, laissez-faire, and pluralism, although attractive ideas to many of us, are not the sum total of our political wisdom. The concept of a powerful central government regulating the economy and enforcing a degree of national uniformity is not un-American. Nor does Publius stand alone in the record of our political life.

Many nineteenth-century developments were directly, or at least closely, linked to the Publii themselves. Thus Hamilton's economic policy—the payment of the national debt, the assumption of state debts, and the establishment of a national bank, which he achieved, and the protective tariff system, which he did not achieve—was a practical expression of the nationalistic line of Publius. The chief justiceship of John Marshall bolstered national supremacy by means of judicial review. The "War Hawk" congressmen elected in 1810-11, led by Henry Clay and John C. Calhoun, were unequivocally nationalistic, although rather more belligerent than the calm and judicious Publius. After the War of 1812 they achieved enactment of protective tariffs, rechartered Hamilton's national bank, and pushed a great plan for extensive internal improvements. President Madison strongly supported their nationalistic program, except for internal improvements, and he vetoed that proposal with the comment that although internal improvements were certainly desirable, they were regrettably unconstitutional.[11] He suggested a constitutional amendment. Thus, as president Madison perfectly exemplified the outlook of Publius—a nationalistic view of affairs, combined with a more limited idea of the American charter. He saw the Constitution as less nationalistic than it ought to be.

Somewhat later, Daniel Webster's eloquent answer to Robert Hayne, with its famous peroration—"Liberty and Union, now and forever, one and inseparable"—is in the manner of Publius.[12] So is President Andrew Jackson's proclamation on the nullification crisis, in which he says that the United States "is a government in which all the people are represented, which operates directly on the people individually, not upon the States"; that "each State" has "parted with so many powers as to constitute, jointly with the other States, a single nation"; and that "the power to annul a law of the United States, assumed by one State," is "incompatible with the existence of the Union."[13] The same may also be said of President Lincoln's first inaugural, with its warning of the dire consequences of secession: "Physically speaking, we cannot separate. . . . A husband and wife may be divorced, and go out of the presence and beyond the reach of each other, but the different parts of our country cannot do this. They cannot but remain face to face, and intercourse, either amicable or hostile, must continue between them. . . . Can aliens make treaties easier than friends can make laws? Can treaties be more faithfully enforced between aliens, than laws can between friends?"[14] These are clearly the sentiments of Publius.

In the twentieth century, the clearest embodiment of the general outlook of *The Federalist* is to be found in the progressive Republican ideology associated with Theodore Roosevelt. Roosevelt greatly admired at least two of the Publii. He describes Hamilton as "the most brilliant American statesman who ever lived, possessing the loftiest and keenest intellect of his time." Jay, he says, "lacked Hamilton's brilliant audacity and genius; but he possessed an austere purity and poise of character which his greater companion did not."[15] Roosevelt unkindly dismisses Madison as a "ridiculously incompetent" war leader, who "was only fit to be President in a time of profound peace."[16] Yet seemingly the Virginian was at least a good publicist, for *The Federalist*, in Roosevelt's view, is "a book which ranks among the ablest and best which have ever been written on politics and government."[17] It was one of the works he included in the "pigskin library" that he carried with him on big game hunts and trips around the world.[18] As we know, an admiration for this treatise is no guarantee that the admirer actually understands its message. But in the case of Roosevelt, there appears to be a real resemblance; his nationalism and his trust in positive government are definitely reminiscent of Publius.

Roosevelt makes no bones about his nationalistic inclinations. "I am not for overcentralization; but I do ask that we work in a spirit of broad and far-reaching nationalism when we work for what concerns the people as a whole. We are all Americans. Our common interests are as broad as the continent. The National Government belongs to the whole American people, and, where the whole American people are interested, that interest can be guarded effectively only by the national government." He praises Marshall's Supreme Court for promoting "that spirit which made and kept us a nation, a great, free, united people, instead of permitting us to dissolve into a snarl of jangling and contemptible little independent commonwealths, with governments oscillating between the rule of a dictator, the rule of an oligarchy, and the rule of a mob." And he quotes with evident approval Publius's observation that "a government ought to contain in itself every power requisite to the full accomplishment of the objects committed to its care."[19]

Roosevelt admired Hamilton tremendously, but he was obliged to admit that this brilliant statesman was a rather poor politician and too aristocratic: "Lincoln, who . . . conscientiously carried out the Hamiltonian tradition, was superior to Hamilton just because he was a politician and was a genuine democrat, and therefore suited to lead a genuine democracy." Yet Roosevelt himself had more than a trace of noblesse oblige in his makeup. "A flatterer is not a good companion for any man," he notes, "and the public man who rises only by flattering his constituents is just as unsafe a companion for them." He observes that "our aim, the aim of those of us who stand for true progress, for true Nationalism, for true democracy, is not only to give the people power, but, ourselves as part of the people, to try to see that the power is used aright, that it is used with wisdom, with courage, with self-restraint, and in a spirit of the broadest kindliness and charity toward all men."[20] These comments do appear to be in the manner of Publius. Roosevelt once called himself "a radical who most earnestly desires to see the radical programme carried out by conservatives." "I want that movement to take place under sober responsible men, not under demagogues," he added.[21] This seems a neat expression of the fundamental attitude of Hamilton, Madison, and Jay.

Roosevelt compared his crusade against corporate malefactors to the intentions of the Founders. He observes that "any proposition to exercise the power of the State on behalf of the public against great corporations . . . is often spoken of as an innovation and even as an outrage upon the principles of the Constitution." But he denies the charge: "The prime reason for the founding of the Constitution was to enable the central government to take charge of all foreign trade and all interstate trade."[22] He notes that the giant economic entities of the modern world must be regulated: "The people will not permit these enormous corporations to be free from governmental control." For the states to do the regulating would "bring us back dangerously near the chaos of the days of the Confederation." Thus, "so far as the great trusts are concerned, only the National Government can deal with them";[23] and such supervision is "not an effort to do something new . . . but an effort to accomplish the purpose of the Constitution, by applying it to conditions which have arisen since the Constitution was adopted." Yet Roosevelt disclaims any wish to persecute business. The public authorities "should just as scrupulously remember the rights of the corporation as the rights of the people," he maintains.[24]

Roosevelt saw the American economy as an essentially harmonious assemblage of interests. "It is all-essential to the continuance of our healthy national life that we should recognize this community of interest among our people," he points out. "The welfare of each of us is dependent fundamentally upon the welfare of all of us, and therefore in public life that man is the best representative of each of us . . . whose endeavor it is, not to represent any special class and promote merely that class's selfish interests, but to represent all true and honest men of all sections and all classes and to work for their interests by working for our common country."[25] Consistent with such a perspective, he advocates "a protective tariff, with duties sufficiently high to equalize the cost of production at home and abroad, primarily for the purpose of keeping the wages of the wage-worker and, therefore, his standard of living, at a sufficient height, and also to allow a reasonable profit on the business."[26] The link with Hamilton seems evident enough.

All in all, it is among progressive Republicans of the Theodore Roosevelt variety that we find the closest modern analogues to the viewpoint of Publius. In such circles we see support for vigorous, positive action by the national government, combined with heartfelt loyalty to the economic system based on private property. America's problems must be energetically tackled, Roosevelt says, but this should be done in a way that does not excessively disturb existing business arrangements. Publius would undoubtedly agree with this general approach. It is true that *The Federalist* does not specifically deal with those social welfare issues that Roosevelt often discusses and that loom so large in the consciousness of the present era. But Publius's conception of the nation—that it is an interrelated whole that requires to be centrally managed in the overall interest—can very easily be used, given the conditions of contemporary America, to justify corporate regulation and, to some extent, the welfare state.

Indeed, not only progressive Republicans, but New Deal Democrats as well have gained inspiration from the authors of *The Federalist* and the words of Publius. The writings of Brant, already briefly discussed, are perhaps the most impressive attempt to associate twentieth-century American liberalism with the intentions of the Founders. Brant's acutely argued if partisan tract *Storm Over the Constitution* demonstrates that the authors of the American charter generally took a far more expansive view of their handiwork than subsequent advocates of limited government and states' rights have presumed. Surprisingly, however, Brant does not use *The Federalist* to bolster his case. He seems to suggest that, if anything, this treatise conceals the nationalistic truth: "Not even the *Federalist Papers* can be taken without reserve as an index to the views of the men who wrote them," he claims. Madison, for one, was "anxious . . . to conceal the extent to which he had advocated the destruction of state power" at the Convention, Brant says.[27]

By the time Brant came to write his great biography of Madison, however, he had somewhat modified his reading of *The Federalist*. Now he observes that Madison takes a generally nationalistic stance as Publius— that he calls for roads and canals to unify the country; affirms the Convention's authority to establish "a firm national government"; recommends a "national military power . . . indefinite in scope"; and endorses the concept of implied powers. Brant notes that some of these positions contradict certain of the Virginian's subsequent stands as a Jeffersonian Republican. "Many times, after he became a strict constructionist, Madison must have wished that this part of his paper had blown out of a window," remarks Brant, with regard to one of the Virginian's effusions as Publius.[28] And Brant does not merely stress Madison's evident nationalism; he also tries to claim him as an early New Dealer!

Brant notes that *Federalist* No. 10 presents a theory of economic determination similar to Marx's, but with a different conclusion. Madison, says Brant, was no socialist, nor a "property-defending conservative," but a precocious liberal: "a pioneer advocate of controlled capitalism." Brant observes that Madison emphasizes "the protection of different and unequal faculties of acquiring property" in No. 10. The historian comments: "Abstractly, that is equally a demand that the smallest acquisitive faculty be protected against the largest, and the largest against the smallest." In Brant's view, therefore, Madison wanted the government to hold the balance between the commonalty and the rich, not simply to favor the latter against the former. Indeed, Brant can show that Madison on other occasions explicitly advocated measures that were calculated to reduce disparities of wealth, and that he even contemplated the use of taxation for that purpose.[29] Our fourth president apparently drew the line at absolute leveling and inflation, since he inveighs in No. 10 against "a rage for paper money, for an abolition of debts, for an equal division of property, or for any other improper or wicked project." But he was quite willing to support more moderate policies to promote social equality.

The idea that one of the Framers was a precursor of Franklin D. Roosevelt may seem odd in this era when the American tradition is commonly identified with social conservatism. Yet Brant's argument has some validity. Modern liberalism may be loosely described as a mixture of Jefferson's ideals with Hamilton's methods, and Madison indeed appears to occupy a political position in between those two men. He was rather more nationalistic than his fellow Virginian, yet he was more democratically inclined than Hamilton. During the years of Federalist ascendancy, Madison somewhat gravitated toward a states' rights stance. After his party captured the presidency in 1800, however, he basically reverted to his earlier position. Even Jefferson became more favorable to national power when he had it. The Virginia Dynasty undid none of the Hamiltonian policies; indeed, President Madison completed his former colleague's program by signing into law the protective tariff of 1816. But Madison did not simply identify the good of the nation with the profits of business. As a political champion of the agricultural interest, he, like Jefferson, was by no means uncritically enamored of capitalists.

Thus Brant is correct to note the parallels between Madison's attitude and that of twentieth-century liberalism. The Father of the Constitution was a nationalist, at least most of the time, and could be critical of rampant capitalism, at least when Jefferson was around. The significance of Madison's protoliberalism should not be exaggerated, however. He did support Jefferson's attempt to forestall the concentration of property by means of certain changes in Virginia's inheritance laws, but that is about as radical as Madison ever got.[30] Also, perhaps influenced by his fellow authors, he shows few Jeffersonian tendencies in *The Federalist*: Publius considers inequality of wealth to be inevitable and not necessarily reprehensible. The propertied and the propertyless may conflict, he admits, but they need not; the national interest encompasses them both. A liberal might note that Publius does not display the kind of inflexible reverence for property rights that would absolutely rule out redistributive policies of a moderate sort, but neither does he give any sign of contemplating such measures.

Brant, a good liberal, tends to concentrate his attention on Madison, who, if no Jacobin, was still somewhat more populistic than the other Publii. But Brant also acknowledges the paradoxical fact that it is Hamilton, the staunch elitist, who most convincingly asserts the ideal of a strong national government, which the New Deal liberals embraced. Brant observes that "the modern Democrats" love to "make speeches eulogizing the glorious heritage of Jeffersonian principles, but the political system they proceed to build up is the system of Alexander Hamilton."[31] Indeed, no less a liberal light than Arthur Schlesinger, Jr., has pronounced that "the Federalist Party of Washington, Hamilton, and Adams had a high sense of national welfare and a capacity to think in terms other than those of immediate class interest"; and that "posterity should be grateful that men who believed in strong government created the precedents of the republic and not men, like Jefferson, who feared strong government." Schlesinger adds that "even the Jeffersonians . . . eventually concurred in the leading measures of Hamilton."[32] The rather ironic affinity of modern liberalism for the most hardheaded and aristocratic of the Publii is evident.

An observer at the time of Publius's bicentennial, however, finds few traces of this brand of positive nationalism in the America of the 1980s. The Reagan administration did spark a superficial rebirth of patriotism in this country. But mere flag-waving is not consistent nationalism, and the conservative movement of the present era deviates in many ways from Publius's viewpoint. Domestically, the Republicans have attempted, with some success, to eviscerate Democratic-sponsored federal social welfare programs and to hand these responsibilities back to the states—on the grounds that the Framers intended the role of the national regime in our system to be a stringently limited one. The Republicans have also attempted, through deregulation and tax cuts, to bring us as near as possible to the free market envisioned by Adam Smith, because they perceive government controls as intrinsically inefficient and contrary to the American way. One conservative guru has declared that "our Founding Fathers must have read *The Wealth of Nations* with great satisfaction."[33] But it is obvious how little this corresponds to the actual outlook of *The Federalist*.

Underlying Publius's case for the Constitution is the idea that the American people form a national community. We naturally belong together, he asserts; our interests are inextricably intertwined, and we share a common destiny. Yet the current Republican domestic policy is based on the denial of American community, in any but a purely formal sense. The national government declines to be accountable for ensuring the social welfare of the American people and hands this critical duty over to the states, with all their diversities and vagaries. A program more disintegrative of the nation would be hard to devise. Should this approach prevail, the states would undoubtedly attempt to foist their welfare populations onto each other, and the free movement of persons around the whole country would be hampered by competing regulations. It is easy to imagine what Hamilton would say about such proposals. True, social welfare was not seen as a national concern in 1787. Yet Publius never suggests that it would be wrong for the central regime to enlarge its scope of operations, should future conditions warrant such action. Indeed, he welcomes the extension of national power to issues of internal concern, because such exertions of authority will tend to assimilate our people, he says.

The laissez-faire ideology underlying Reaganomics is also quite contrary to the ideas of national community found in *The Federalist*. Publius presumes that the central government will be busily engaged in regulating the economy in order to harmonize the interests of all Americans. Indeed, he specifically says that the benefits of such regulation are a leading reason to adopt the new charter. And while some of the Founders no doubt were entranced by Adam Smith, Hamilton was certainly not among them. Those who would assimilate laissez-faire to the American tradition should recall that the greatest secretary of the treasury in our history—a man whose clearheaded realism and general acumen are universally acclaimed—was a neomercantilist and an ardent protectionist who would have had nothing but contempt for a government willing to stake the national welfare on the uncertainties of the unsupervised free market. Interestingly enough, the decade of the 1980s saw the rise of a protectionist "Hamiltonian" wing of the Democratic party.

This is not to say that Publius particularly resembles a 1980s domestic liberal, however, for he would wholly reject the cultural pluralism and interest-group style of politics fashionable on the American left during this period. *The Federalist* maintains that self-centered factions should, as far as possible, be excluded from involvement in the governmental process, to allow our rulers to act on the basis of a comprehensive national perspective. The practice of serially placating every imaginable segment of society would be considered by Publius an abdication of leadership.

With regard to foreign policy issues, *The Federalist* at no point suggests anything resembling an imperial role for America. Indeed, Publius is something of an isolationist. True, he anticipates that America will on occasion need to intervene abroad, but he expects that we will mostly keep to ourselves. The insulated geographical position of the United States is, in fact, one of the principal arguments for American unification, according to Publius: we are fortunate in being able to avoid the follies and wars of the rest of the world. Among other things, we can do without a large military establishment that could threaten our liberties. He does recommend that we combine with the rest of the Western Hemisphere to keep the Europeans away, but this preview of the Monroe Doctrine seems designed primarily to hold trouble at arm's length. It is strange that our modern neoisolationists have not made more of Publius.

Yet if Publius deviates from conservatism by declining to act as a global policeman, neither does he express much sympathy for the sort of idealistic humanitarianism that characterizes the modern liberal stance on foreign affairs. Liberals favor noble goals such as disarmament and the peaceful resolution of all international disputes, and they generally presume that nations, like individuals, should adhere to high moral principles. Publius, however, perceives nations as inherently motivated by self-interest and ruthless in their methods. The use of force, he maintains, is necessary to prevail or even survive in the global arena. The dream of perpetual peace is a delusion. The United States should not even rule out the possibility of an offensive war. It is, of course, conceivable that Publius might adjust his thinking somewhat today, in view of the dangers of the nuclear age. But he is certainly no pacifist. His world is essentially the world of Machiavelli. He does not foresee America as an imperial power, but neither does he propose altruism. He envisions the United States as simply promoting its own interest in the world, as other nations do.

Moreover, to the further discomfiture of contemporary liberals, Publius sees foreign policy as largely an executive prerogative. For reasons of "secrecy and dispatch," the president must be given great leeway in the conduct of our relations with other countries, he thinks; the stable Senate may be competent to advise the chief executive in this area, but not the tumultuous House or the ignorant masses. Publius adds—with particular reference to the subject of national security—that "wise politicians will be cautious about fettering the government with restrictions, that cannot be observed; because . . . every breach of the fundamental laws, though dictated by necessity, impairs that sacred reverence . . . in the breasts of the rulers towards the constitution of a country, and forms a precedent for other breaches" (163). In other words, if leaders must violate the rules in order to be effective, the system is in trouble. Necessary authorities should be granted in a constitutional manner, Publius argues. Thus he suggests a partial extenuation for the escapades of Col. Oliver North and warns of the grave danger should such behavior become widespread in our chiefs.

The Publii would not be especially pleased with either present-day conservative or liberal opinions concerning themselves. The Right is at least formally respectful of the wisdom of the Founders, although modern conservatives unfortunately have a tendency to distort the content of that wisdom to serve the purposes of their faction. Liberals are inclined to take an even more objectionable stance, by claiming that the Founders were reactionaries, and their opinions therefore suspect. On this point there is indeed a large difference between the American Left of previous years and that of the post–Vietnam War era. The New Dealers, as we have noted, identified with the American Framers, seeing them as nationalists and combing their works for intimations of a social conscience. Liberals and radicals of the present day, however—at least those in academe—are more prone to denigrate the Founders, in Beardean fashion, inaccurately, as merely the defenders of bourgeois property rights. It is highly unlikely that the interests of the Left have been served by this perverse tendency to spurn any positive connection with the main currents of the American past.

In short, neither the laissez-faire individualism of Reaganite conservatism nor the divisive pluralism of the liberal opposition has much to do with Publius's brand of nationalism. Yet either party could, it seems, approach the ideal: the Republicans by recalling the methods of Theodore Roosevelt, the Democrats by recapturing the New Deal's sense of participating in the American tradition. By so doing, each party would also draw closer to the preeminent source of political wisdom in our literature: *The Federalist*, the blueprint of the American nation.

Notes

1. Will the Real Publius Please Stand Up?

1. Niccolò Machiavelli, *The Chief Works and Others*, vol. 1, *The Discourses*, trans. Allan Gilbert (Durham, NC: Duke Univ. Press, 1965), p. 419.

2. George Washington, *The Writings of George Washington*, vol. 30, ed. J.C. Fitzpatrick, (Washington, DC, 1939), p. 66; Julian P. Boyd, ed., *The Papers of Thomas Jefferson*, vol. 14 (Princeton, NJ: Princeton Univ. Press, 1958), p. 118; Alexis de Tocqueville, *Democracy in America*, vol. 1 (New York: Random House, Vintage Books, 1945), p. 119; John Stuart Mill, *Utilitarianism, Liberty, and Representative Government* (New York: E.P. Dutton, 1951), p. 498.

3. See, for instance, Charles A. Beard, *Economic Origins of Jeffersonian Democracy* (New York: Macmillan, 1927), p. 5; Jacob Ernest Cooke, *Alexander Hamilton* (New York: Charles Scribner's Sons, 1982), p. 53; Clinton Rossiter, ed., "Introduction," *The Federalist* (New York: New American Library, 1961), p. vii; and Garry Wills, *Explaining America* (Garden City, NY: Doubleday, 1981), pp. xii-xiii.

4. Edward S. Corwin, *The Constitution and What It Means Today*, 14th ed. (Princeton, NJ: Princeton Univ. Press, 1978), p. 167.

5. Cohens v. Virginia, 6 Wheat., 418-419 (1821).

6. Irving Brant, *James Madison: The Virginia Revolutionist* (New York: Bobbs-Merrill, 1941), p. 11; idem, *James Madison and American Nationalism* (Princeton, NJ: Van Nostrand, [1968]), p. 15; idem, *James Madison: Father of the Constitution* (Indianapolis: Bobbs-Merrill, 1950), p. 18.

7. Cooke, *Alexander Hamilton*, pp. 56, 57.

8. Roy P. Fairfield, ed., "Bibliographical Appendix," *The Federalist Papers*, (Baltimore: Johns Hopkins Univ. Press, 1981), pp. 309-310.

9. Felix Morley, *Freedom and Federalism* (Indianapolis: Liberty Press, 1981), pp. 48, 10, xxii.

10. *Text of the Address by the President to the National Conference of State Legislatures, Atlanta, Georgia* (Washington, DC: The White House, Office of the Press Secretary, July 30, 1981), pp. 3, 6.

11. Charles A. Beard, *An Economic Interpretation of the Constitution of the United States* (New York: Macmillan, 1913), pp. v, 153.

12. James MacGregor Burns, *The Deadlock of Democracy* (Englewood Cliffs, NJ: Prentice-Hall, 1963), pp. 22, 7, 23.

13. Alfred Balitzer, *A Nation of Associations* (Washington, DC: American Society of Association Executives and the American Medical Political Action Committee, 1981), pp. 27, 40.

14. Douglas Adair, *Fame and the Founding Fathers*, ed. Trevor Colbourn. (New York: W.W. Norton, 1974), p. 53.

15. Rexford G. Tugwell, *The Compromising of the Constitution* (Notre Dame, IN: Univ. of Notre Dame Press, [1976]), p. 59. For a more balanced treatment of the "advocacy" issue see Richard B. Morris, "Explaining America: The Federalist. By Garry Wills," *Columbia Law Review* 82 no. 2 (March 1982): 406-09.

16. Wills, *Explaining America,* pp. ix, 267.

17. Martin Diamond, "The Federalist's View of Federalism," in *Essays in Federalism,* ed. George Benson (Claremont, CA: Institute for Studies in Federalism, 1962), pp. 21-64.

18. Albert Furtwangler, *The Authority of Publius* (Ithaca, NY: Cornell Univ. Press, 1984), pp. 65, 102, 23-32, 39-43.

19. Roy P. Fairfield, ed., "Introduction," *The Federalist Papers,* (Baltimore: John Hopkins Univ. Press, 1981), pp. xvii, xviii.

20. Gottfried Dietze, *The Federalist: A Classic on Federalism and Free Government* (Baltimore: John Hopkins Univ. Press, 1960).

21. Alexander Hamilton, James Madison, and John Jay, *The Federalist,* ed. Jacob E. Cooke (Middletown, CT: Wesleyan Univ. Press, 1961), pp. 9, 10. All subsequent citations are to this edition and are indicated by page references in the text.

22. J.W. Horrocks, *A Short History of Mercantilism* (New York: Brentano's Publishers, [1925]), pp. 3, 4.

23. Samuel H. Beer, "Federalism, Nationalism, and Democracy in America," *The American Political Science Review* 72, no. 1 (March 1978): 12.

24. Samuel H. Beer, "Liberalism and the National Idea," in *Left, Right and Center: Essays on Liberalism and Conservatism in the United States,* ed. Robert A. Goldwin (Chicago: Rand Mcnally, 1965), p. 154.

25. Samuel H. Beer, "The idea of the Nation," *The New Republic* 3522 (July 19 and 26, 1982): 23, 24, 29.

26. Richard B. Morris, ed., *John Jay: The Making of a Revolutionary 1745-1780* (New York: Harper and Row, 1975); idem, *John Jay: The Winning of the Peace* (New York: Harper and Row, 1980).

27. Richard B. Morris, *The American Revolution Reconsidered* (New York: Harper and Row, 1967), pp. 2-3, 162, 132.

28. Richard B. Morris, *The Emerging Nations and the American Revolution* (New York: Harper and Row, 1970).

29. Richard B. Morris, *Witnesses at the Creation* (New York: Holt, Rinehart and Winston, 1985), p. 260.

30. Jack N. Rakove, *The Beginnings of National Politics* (Baltimore: Johns Hoplins Univ. Press, 1979), p. xvi.

31. Bernard Bailyn, *The Ideological Origins of the American Revolution* (Cambridge, MA: Belknap Press, 1967); and Gordon Wood, *The Creation of the American Republic* (Chapel Hill: Univ. of North Carolina Press, 1969).

32. Wood, *Creation,* pp. 53, 612, 499-503, 505, 464, 467, 473, 409-13.

33. Ibid., pp. 503, 460-63, 530-47, 562.

34. Wills, *Explaining America,* pp. 20-21; 187 and 189; 47, 165, 169, and 172-73; 20-21, 30-31, and 202; 268-70.

35. Ibid., 270.

36. David F. Epstein, *The Political Theory of the Federalist* (Chicago: Univ. of Chicago Press, 1984), pp. 5, 9, 6.

37. Ibid., 51; 45 and 54; 4-5.

38. *Creation*, p. 492.

39. Cathy Matson and Peter Onuf, "Toward a Republican Empire: Interest and Ideology in Revolutionary America," *American Quarterly*, 1985, pp. 496, 520, and 523.

40. Peter S. Onuf, "Liberty, Development, and Union: Visions of the West in the 1780s," *William and Mary Quarterly*, 3d. ser., 33, (April 1986): 202, 203.

41. Epstein, *Political Theory of the Federalist*, p. 7.

2. The Political Objectives of Publius

1. Charles C. Tansill, ed., *Documents Illustrative of the Formation of the Union of the American States* (Washington, DC: Government Printing Office, 1927), p. 46.

2. Quoted in Linda Grant DePauw, *The Eleventh Pillar* (Ithaca, NY: Cornell Univ. Press, 1966), p. 32.

3. Ibid., pp. 172-76, 285-90.

4. Herbert J. Storing, ed., *The Anti-Federalist*, abr. Murray Dry (Chicago: Univ. of Chicago Press, 1985), pp. 24-25, 103.

5. "Letters of Caesar," in Paul Leister Ford, ed., *Essays on the Constitution of the United States* (Brooklyn: Historical Printing Club, 1892), pp. 284-85.

6. Jacob E. Cooke, "Alexander Hamilton's Authorship of the 'Caesar' Letters," *William and Mary Quarterly*, 3d ser., 17 (1960): 78-85.

7. Allan McLane Hamilton, *The Intimate Life of Alexander Hamilton* (New York: Charles Scribner's Sons, 1910), p. 82.

8. "Introduction," in Hamilton, Madison, and Jay, *The Federalist*, vol. 1 (New York: J. and A. M'Lean, 1788), p. iii.

9. Douglass Adair, "The Authorship of the Disputed *Federalist* Papers," *William and Mary Quarterly*, 3d ser., 1 (1944): 252, 253; Jacob E. Cooke, "Introduction," in Hamilton, Madison, and Jay, *Federalist*, pp. xix-xxx; Frederick Mosteller and David L. Wallace, *Inference and Disputed Authorship: The Federalist* (Reading, MA: Addison-Wesley, 1964).

10. Cooke, "Introduction," in Hamilton, Madison, and Jay, *Federalist*, p. xxviii.

11. Quoted in DePauw, *Eleventh Pillar*, p. 110.

12. Ibid., p. 185.

13. Alexander Hamilton to Gouverneur Morris, May 19, 1788, reprinted in *The Papers of Alexander Hamilton*, vol. 4, ed. Harold C. Syrett and Jacob E. Cooke (New York: Columbia Univ. Press, 1962), p. 651.

14. Quoted in Depauw, *Eleventh Pillar*, pp. 114-15.

15. Quoted in Mary-Jo Kline, ed., *Alexander Hamilton, A Biography in His Own Words* (New York: Harper and Row, 1973), p. 33.

16. Andrew A. Lipscomb, ed. *The Writings of Thomas Jefferson*, vol. 13 (Washington, DC, 1905), p. 4.

17. Syrett and Cooke, *Papers of Hamilton* 4:76.

18. Quoted in James Thomas Flexner, *The Young Hamilton* (Boston: Little, Brown, 1978), p. 62.

19. Tansill, *Documents*, pp. 98-99.

20. Quoted in Frank Monaghan, *John Jay* (New York: Bobbs- Merrill, 1935), pp. 65-66.

21. Quoted in George Pellew, *John Jay* (Boston: Houghton, Mifflin, 1897), p. 79.

22. Ibid., pp. 430, 421, 102, 192.

23. Ibid., pp. 175, 221, 168, 227-28, 107.

24. Morris, *Witnessess at the Creation,* 152.

25. Quoted in Monaghan, *John Jay,* p. 219.

26. Tansill, *Documents,* p. 105.

27. Brant, *The Virginia Revolutionist,* and idem, *Father of the Constitution,* passim. For a dissenting view, see Lance Banning, "James Madison and the Nationalists, 1780-1783" *William and Mary Quarterly,* 3d ser., 40 (1983): 227-55.

28. Quoted in Edward McNall Burns, *James Madison, Philosopher of the Constitution* (New York: Octagon Books, 1968), pp. 74, 31-32, 37.

29. Tansill, *Documents,* p. 105.

30. Brant, *The Virginia Revolutionist,* p. 79.

31. Irving Brant, *The Fourth President, A Life of James Madison* (New York: Bobbs-Merrill, 1970), p. 218.

32. Quoted in Brant, *The Virginia Revolutionist,* p. 33.

33. Tansill, *Documents,* p. 220.

34. Ibid., pp. 117; 390-91, 604-5, and 717.

35. Quoted in Monaghan, *John Jay,* p. 282.

36. John Jay to George Washington, January 7, 1787, reprinted in *The Correspondence and Public Papers of John Jay,* vol. 3, ed. Henry P. Johnston (New York: G.P. Putnam's Sons, 1891), p. 228.

37. Furtwangler, *Authority of Publius,* pp. 32-39.

38. Boyd, *Papers of Thomas Jefferson* 12:69.

39. Forrest McDonald, *E Pluribus Unum* (Indianapolis: Liberty Press, 1965), pp. 18-19.

40. "Centinel, Letter 1," reprinted in Storing, *Anti-Federalist,* p. 14.

41. Beard, *Economic Interpretation of the Constitution,* pp. 149, 176.

42. Robert E. Brown, *Charles Beard and the Constitution* (Princeton, NJ: Princeton Univ. Press, 1956), pp. 111, 89, 197.

43. Forrest McDonald, *We the People: The Economic Origins of the Constitution* (Chicago: Univ. of Chicago Press, 1958), p. 357; idem, *Novus Ordo Seclorum* (Lawrence: Univ. Press of Kansas, 1985), p. vii.

44. Beard, *Economic Interpretation of the Constitution,* pp. 176, 125.

45. McDonald, *E Pluribus Unum, op. cit.,* p. 19.

46. Adair, *Fame and the Founding Fathers,* pp. 11-12.

47. Plutarch, *The Lives of the Noble Grecians and Romans,* trans. John Dryden (New York: The Modern Library, [1932]), pp. 396, 900, 117-30.

48. Robert H. Weibe, *The Opening of American Society* (New York: Knopf, 1984), pp. 11-12.

49. Pellew, *John Jay,* p. 225.

50. Chilton Williamson, *American Suffrage from Property to Democracy* (Princeton, NJ: Princeton Univ. Press, 1960), p. 38.

51. Rakove, *Beginnings of National Politics,* pp. 333-59.

52. Syrett and Cooke, *Papers of Hamilton* 11: 470-71.

53. See note 41 above.

3. The idea of the Nation-State

1. Adair, *Fame and the Founding Fathers*, p. 13.

2. Plutarch, *Lives*, pp. 15; 34; 50.

3. Louis L. Snyder, *The Meaning of Nationalism* (New Brunswick, NJ: Rutgers Univ. Press, 1954), p. 61.

4. Elie Kedurie, *Nationalism*, 3d ed. (London: Hutchinson, 1966), p. 9.

5. Snyder, *Meaning of Nationalism*, pp. 40-54.

6. Charles C. Alexander, *Nationalism in American Thought 1930-1945* (Chicago: Rand McNally, 1973), passim.

7. Karl Marx and Friedrich Engels, *The Communist Manifesto*, in *The Portable Karl Marx*, ed. Eugene Kamenka (New York: Penguin Books, 1983), 206, 208-9; Snyder, *Meaning of Nationalism*, pp. 142-43.

8. There are numerous theorists of nationalism, whose formulations of the core doctrine of the creed vary appreciably. The statement of the present study owes most to the discussions in Hans Kohn, *The Idea of Nationalism* (New York: Macmillan, 1944), passim, esp. pp. 3-24; Friedrich Meinecke, *Cosmopolitanism and the National State*, trans. Robert B. Kimber (Princeton, NJ: Princeton Univ. Press, 1970), pp. 9-22; Mill, *Utilitarianism, Liberty, and Representative Government*, pp. 485-93; and Anthony D. Smith, *Theories of Nationalism* (London: Duckworth, 1971), passim. Other relevant sources are cited in the bibliography.

9. Rupert Emerson, *From Empire to Nation* (Cambridge, MA: Harvard Univ. Press, 1960), p. 43.

10. Smith, *Theories of Nationalism*, p. 158.

11. Ibid., p. 264.

12. Mill, *Utilitarianism, Liberty, and Representative Government*, p. 487.

13. Ramsay Muir, *National Self-Government: Its Growth and Principles* (New York: Henry Holt, 1918), p. 9.

14. Gerald Stourzh, *Alexander Hamilton and the Idea of Republican Government* (Stanford, CA: Stanford Univ. Press, 1970), p. 49.

15. For a complete discussion of this topic, see chapter 7 below.

16. Kohn, *Idea of Nationalism*, p. 5; Hugh Seton-Watson, *Nations and States* (London: Methuen, [1977]), p. 5.

17. Meinecke, *Cosmopolitanism*, p. 10.

18. Emerson, *From Empire to Nation*, pp. 18, 19, 44, 244, 245.

19. Seton-Watson, *Nations and States*, p. 9.

20. Thucydides, *The Peloponnesian War*, in *The Greek Historians*, vol. 1, ed. Francis Godolphin, (New York: Random House, 1942), pp. 647-53.

21. George H. Sabine, *A History of Political Theory*, 3d ed. (New York: Holt, Rinehart and Winston, 1961), p. 17.

22. Aristotle, *Politics*, trans. Benjamin Jowett (New York: Modern Library, 1943), pp. 138, 144; 144; 144; 287; 288; 288; 289.

23. Storing, *Anti-Federalist*, p. 113.

24. Kohn, *Idea of Nationalism*, pp. 580, 217, 207, 581.

25. Machiavelli, *The Prince,* in *The Chief Works and Others,* pp. 13-14; idem, *The Discourses,* in *The Chief Works and Others,* p. 329.

26. Thomas Hobbes, *Leviathan* (New York: E.P. Dutton, 1962), pp. 109; 88; 98; 96-97, 129.

27. John Locke, *Two Treatises of Government* (New York: New American Library, 1963), pp. 380, 407, 418, 419, 441, 358.

28. Kohn, *Idea of Nationalism,* p. 229; Smith, *Theories of Nationalism,* p. 5.

29. C.L. de Secondat de Montesquieu, *The Spirit of Laws,* vol. 1 (London: George Bell and Sons, 1899), pp. 293, 6, 2:91, 1: 120.

30. Ibid., 1: 37.

31. Ibid., 1: 126, 121.

32. Sabine, *History of Political Thought,* p. 594.

33. Morley, *Freedom and Federalism,* p. 44.

34. Sabine, *History of Political Thought,* p. 593.

35. Jean-Jacques Rousseau, *The Social Contract and Discourses,* trans. G.D.H. Cole (New York: E.P. Dutton, 1950), pp. 71, 65, 92, 57, 96, 97.

36. Jean-Jacques Rousseau, *The Government of Poland,* trans. Wilmoore Kendall (New York: Bobbs-Merrill, 1972), pp. 8, 11, 19, 20, 11.

37. Ibid., pp. 76, 43, 3, 37.

38. Wilmoore Kendall, "Introduction," in Rousseau, *Government of Poland,* pp. xxii-xxiii.

4. Jay Describes a Nation

1. Walter Hartwell Bennett, ed. *Letters from the Federal Farmer to the Republican* (University, AL: Univ. of Alabama Press, 1978), p. 9.

2. All citations to *The Federalist* are to the Cooke edition and are indicated by page references in the text.

3. Ford, *Essays on the Constitution,* p. 248.

4. Jackson Turner Main, *The Antifederalists* (Chapel Hill: Univ. of North Carolina Press, 1961), pp. 283-84; Merrill Jensen, *The New Nation* (New York: Knopf, 1967), p. xiv; Herbert J. Storing, *What the Anti-Federalists Were For* (Chicago: Univ. of Chicago Press, 1981), p. 24.

5. Syrett and Cooke, *Papers of Hamilton* 6: 651; Robert A. Rutland, ed., *The Papers of James Madison,* vol. 10 (Chicago: Univ. of Chicago Press, 1962), p. 312.

6. Storing, *Anti-Federalist,* p. 317.

7. Ibid., pp. 114-15.

8. Ford, *Essays on the Constitution,* pp. 255-56.

9. Syrett and Cooke, *Papers of Hamilton* 5: 276.

10. Tansill, *Documents,* p. 157.

11. Charles Edward Merriam, *A History of American Political Theories* (New York: Macmillan, 1903), p. 103.

12. Dietze, *Federalist,* p. 115.

13. Monaghan, *John Jay,* p. 93.

14. Tansill, *Documents,* p. 329.

15. The best recent summary of these issues is found in Richard B. Morris, *The Forging of the Union* (New York: Harper & Row, 1987), pp. 10-30.

16. Carlton Hayes, *The Historical Evolution of Modern Nationalism* (New York: Russell and Russell, 1968), p. 33.

17. Dietze, *Federalist,* p. 208; Rossiter, *Federalist,* pp. xvii, xix; Hans J. Morgenthau, *Politics Among Nations* (New York: Knopf, 1954), pp. 484-85.

18. L.H. Butterfield, ed., *Diary and Autobiography of John Adams,* vol. 2 (Cambridge, MA: Belknap Press, 1961), p. 156.

19. Lynn Montross, *The Reluctant Rebels* (New York: Harper and Brothers, 1950), pp. 426-31.

20. Ibid.

21. Wills, *Explaining America,* p. 249.

22. Wills, *Explaining America,* pp. 248-49.

5. Hamilton Aims To Centralize

1. Dietze, *Federalist,* pp. 285, 312.

2. Morris, *Witnesses at the Creation,* p. 40.

3. Ford, *Essays on the Constitution,* p. 256; Storing, *Anti-Federalist,* p. 113.

4. Ford, *Essays on the Constitution,* p. 257.

5. Epstein, *Political Theory of the Federalist,* p. 51.

6. Diamond, "Federalist's View of Federalism," pp. 22-23.

7. Horrocks, *Short History of Mercantilism,* pp. 205, 39.

8. Francisco de Miranda, *The New Democracy in America,* trans. Judson P. Wood, ed. John S. Ezell (Norman: Univ. of Oklahoma Press, 1963), p. xvi.

9. Thomas Jefferson, *Notes on the State of Virginia,* ed. William Peden (New York: W.W. Norton, 1972), p. 290.

10. Storing, *Anti-Federalist,* p. 144.

11. Ford, *Essays on the Constitution,* p. 258.

12. Epstein, *Political Theory of the Federalist,* pp. 54-55.

13. Ibid., p. 55.

14. Ford, *Essays on the Constitution,* p. 267.

15. Storing, *Anti-Federalist,* pp. 136-40, 142. Hamilton, Madison, and Jay, *Federalist,* pp. 199-203, covering all of the quotations from *Federalist* No. 32. Ibid., pp. 203-8, covering all of the quotations from *Federalist* No. 33.

16. Leonard W. Levy, ed., *Judicial Review and the Supreme Court* (New York: Harper and Row, 1967), p. 6.

6. Madison Argues for a National Regime

1. Alpheus T. Mason, *"The Federalist*—A Split Personality," *American Historical Review* 57, no. 3 (April 1952): 639.

2. Gaillard Hunt, ed., *The Writings of James Madison,* vol. 2 (New York: G.P. Putnam's Sons, 1900), pp. 361-69; Tansill, *Documents,* pp. 161-63; Epstein, *Political Theory of the Federalist,* pp. 103, 213, 214.

3. William O. Winter, *State and Local Government in a Decentralized Republic* (New York: Macmillan, 1981), p. 26.

4. Wills, *Explaining America,* esp. pp. 185-92; Epstein, *Political Theory of the Federalist,* esp. pp. 154-61.

5. Howard Zinn, *A People's History of the United States* (New York: Harper and Row, 1980), pp. 96-97.

6. Adair, *Fame and the Founding Fathers,* p. 98; David Hume, *Essays Moral,*

Political and Literary (New York: Oxford Univ. 1963), p. 515; Epstein, *Political Theory of the Federalist*, p. 101.

7. Epstein, *Political Theory of the Federalist*, pp. 102-3; see also Wills, *Explaining America*, pp. 204-5.

8. Epstein, *Political Theory of the Federalist*, p. 213.

9. Brant, *Virginia Revolutionist*, p. 68; François-Marie Arouet de Voltaire, "Short Studies on English Topics," in *The Works of Voltaire*, vol. 19 (New York: Dingwall-Rock, 1927), pp. 218-19.

10. Plutarch, *Lives*, p. 88.

11. Rousseau, *Social Contract*, p. 27.

12. Mason, "Split Personality," p. 635; Adair, *Fame and the Founding Fathers*, p. 101.

13. Stourzh, *Alexander Hamilton*, p. 49.

14. Diamond, "Federalist's View of Federalism," p. 56.

15. Storing, *Anti-Federalist*, p. 110.

16. Diamond, "Federalist's View of Federalism," p. 37.

17. Beer, "Liberalism and the National Idea," p. 153.

18. Tansill, *Documents*, pp. 290-94, 324-26, 345, 379-81, and elsewhere.

19. Ibid., p. 171-72.

20. Ibid., p. 625; Hunt, *Writings of Madison* 5: 283.

21. Tansill, *Documents*, pp. 413, 451.

22. Ibid., p. 117.

23. Syrett and Cooke, *Papers of Hamilton* 10: 302-4.

7. Madison Separates the Powers

1. Tansill, *Documents*, p. 121.

2. J.R. Pole, *Political Representation in England and the Origins of the American Republic* (London: Macmillan, 1966), pp. 92, 393.

3. Rousseau, *Social Contract*, p. 96.

4. Pole, *Political Representation*, p. xiii.

5. Polybius, *The Histories of Polybius*, vol. 1 (Bloomington: Indiana Univ. Press, 1962), p. 474.

6. Montesquieu, *Spirit of Laws* 1: 163.

7. Wills, *Explaining America*, pp. 109-11.

8. Montesquieu, *Spirit of Laws* 1: 168.

9. Morley, *Freedom and Federalism*, p. 32.

10. Epstein, *Political Theory of the Federalist*, pp. 54, 141.

11. Merrill D. Peterson, ed., *James Madison, A Biography in His Own Words* (New York: Newsweek Book Division, 1974), p. 168.

12. Storing, *Anti-Federalist*, p. 124.

13. Tansill, *Documents*, pp. 349, 694.

14. Ibid., p. 496.

15. Stourzh, *Alexander Hamilton*, p. 106.

16. Tansill, *Documents*, p. 172.

17. Ibid., p. 380.

18. Beard, *Economic Interpretation of the Constitution*, p. 160.

19. Tansill, *Documents*, p. 221.

8. Hamilton Provides Leadership

1. Syrett and Cooke, *Papers of Hamilton* 5: 3.
2. Corwin, *The Constitution,* p. 563.
3. Tansill, *Documents,* p. 224.
4. Ford, *Essays on the Constitution,* pp. 260-64.
5. Tansill, *Documents,* p. 223.
6. Alexander Pope, *Selected Works,* (New York: Modern Library, 1951), p. 124. The quote should read: "Whate'er is best administer'd is best."
7. DePauw, *Eleventh Pillar,* p. 21.
8. Tansill, *Documents,* pp. 221-22.
9. Tansill, *Documents,* p. 202.
10. Beard, *Economic Interpretation of the Constitution,* pp. 154-56.
11. Corwin, *Constitution,* p. 167.
12. Tansill, *Documents,* pp. 390-91.
13. Corwin, *Constitution,* p. 229.
14. Rutland, *Papers of Madison* 11: 293; Tansill, *Documents,* p. 625.
15. Storing, *Anti-Federalist,* pp. 119-22, 153-54; Bennett, *Federal Farmer,* pp. 11, 27-28, 35, 105-12.

9. Publius the Nationalist

1. Stourzh, *Alexander Hamilton,* pp. 106-9.
2. Rousseau, *Social Contract,* p. 96.
3. Morley, *Freedom and Federalism,* p. 10.
4. Balitzer, *Nation of Associations,* pp. 29-40, 60.
5. Dietze, *Federalist,* p. 341.
6. Beard, *Economic Interpretation of the Constitution,* pp. 160-62.
7. Epstein, *Political Theory of the Federalist,* pp. 60, 85-86, 108, 163, 214.
8. See chaps. 2 and 3 of the present study.

10. The Significance of *The Federalist*

1. Dietze, *Federalist,* pp. 10-11, 12-15.
2. Mill, *Representative Government,* p. 498. Also see chap. 1 of the present study.
3. Kwame Nkrumah, *Africa Must Unite* (New York: International Publishers, 1970), pp. 75, 82, 150, 155, 157, 219, 193.
4. Ibid., p. 206.
5. Ibid., p. 220, 173, 203, 218, 221.
6. Ibid., pp. 68-69.
7. Ibid., p. 74.
8. Richard Hofstadter, *The Idea of a Party System* (Berkeley: Univ. of California Press, 1969), p. xii.
9. Nkrumah, *Africa Must Unite,* p. 165.
10. Charles V. Hamilton, *American Government* (Glenview, IL: Scott, Foresman, 1982), pp. 3-4.
11. Peterson, *James Madison,* pp. 362-64.

12. Daniel Webster, *The Writings and Speeches of Daniel Webster,* vol. 4, National Ed. (Boston: Little, Brown, 1903), p. 75.

13. Quoted in J.D. Richardson, ed., *Compilation of the Messsages and Papers of the Presidents,* vol. 2 (Washington, DC, 1908), pp. 1203-19.

14. Roy P. Basler, ed., *The Collected Works of Abraham Lincoln,* vol. 4 (New Brunswick, NJ: Rutgers Univ. Press, 1953), p. 269.

15. Theodore Roosevelt, *The Works of Theodore Roosevelt,* Memorial Ed., vol. 9 (New York: Charles Scribner's Sons, 1925), pp. 362, 366.

16. Theodore Roosevelt, *The Works of Theodore Roosevelt,* National Ed., vol. 7 (New York: Charles Scribner's Sons, 1926), p. 459.

17. Roosevelt, *Memorial Edition* 9: 364.

18. Roosevelt, *National Edition* 12: 338.

19. Roosevelt, *Memorial Edition* 19: 83, 124, 125.

20. Roosevelt, *Memorial Edition* 9: 28, 19: 146.

21. Roosevelt, *National Edition* 16: 88, 89.

22. Ibid., p. 97.

23. Roosevelt, *Memorial Edition* 19: 139, 144.

24. Roosevelt, *National Edition* 16: 89, 95.

25. Ibid., p. 51.

26. Roosevelt, *Memorial Edition* 19: 73.

27. Irving Brant, *Storm Over the Constitution* (Indianapolis: Bobbs-Merrill, 1936), pp. 55, 57.

28. Brant, *Father of the Constitution,* pp. 181, 180.

29. Ibid., p. 175.

30. Brant, *Virginia Revolutionist,* p. 300.

31. Brant, *Storm Over the Constitution,* p. 37.

32. Arthur M. Schlesinger, Jr., *The Vital Center* (Boston: Houghton Mifflin, 1962), p. 16.

33. William E. Sinon, *A Time for Truth* (New York: Berkley Books, 1979), p. 24.

Bibliography

NOTE: The edition of *The Federalist* edited by Jacob E. Cooke, considered definitive by modern scholars, has served as the basis for this study, and is listed under the names of Hamilton, Madison, and Jay. Other editions of *The Federalist* are listed under the names of the editors.

Books

Adair, Douglas. *Fame and the Founding Fathers*. Edited by Trevor Colbourn. New York: W.W. Norton, 1974.

Alexander, Charles C. *Nationalism in American Thought, 1930-1945*. Chicago: Rand McNally, 1973.

Aristotle. *Politics*. Translated by Benjamin Jowett. New York: The Modern Library, 1943.

Bailyn, Bernard. *The Ideological Origins of the American Revolution*. Cambridge, MA: The Belknap Press, 1967.

Balitzer, Alfred. *A Nation of Associations*. Washington, DC: American Society of Association Executives and the American Medical Political Action Committee, 1981.

Bancroft, George. *History of the United States of America*, vols. 1-6. New York: D. Appleton, 1882-86.

Basler, Roy P., ed. *The Collected Works of Abraham Lincoln*. 8 vols. New Brunswick, NJ: Rutgers Univ. Press, 1953.

Beard, Charles A. *An Economic Interpretation of the Constitution of the United States*. New York: Macmillan, 1913.

———. *Economic Origins of Jeffersonian Democracy*. New York: Macmillan, 1927.

Bennett, Walter Hartwell, ed. *Letters from the Federal Farmer to the Republican*. University, AL: Univ. of Alabama Press, 1978.

Benson, George, ed. *Essays in Federalism*. Claremont, CA: Institute for Studies in Federalism, 1962.

Boyd, Julian P., ed. *The Papers of Thomas Jefferson*. Princeton, NJ: Princeton Univ. Press, 1950-1986.

Brant, Irving. *The Fourth President, A Life of James Madison*. New York: Bobbs-Merrill, 1970.

———. *James Madison: Father of the Constitution*. Indianapolis: Bobbs-Merrill, 1950.

———. *James Madison: The Virginia Revolutionist*. New York: Bobbs-Merrill, 1941.

———. *James Madison and American Nationalism*. Princeton, NJ: Van Nostrand, [1968].

————. *Storm Over the Constitution*. Indianapolis: Bobbs-Merrill, 1936.

Brown, Robert E. *Charles Beard and the Constitution*. Princeton, NJ: Princeton Univ. Press, 1956.

Burnett, Edmund Cody. *The Continental Congress*. New York: W.W. Norton, 1964.

Burns, Edward McNall. *James Madison, Philosopher of the Constitution*. New York: Octagon Books, 1968.

Burns, James MacGregor. *The Deadlock of Democracy*. Englewood Cliffs, NJ: Prentice-Hall, 1963.

Butterfield, L.H., ed. *Diary and Autobiography of John Adams*. 4 vols. Cambridge, MA: Belknap Press, 1961.

Cooke, Jacob Ernest. *Alexander Hamilton*. New York: Charles Scribner's Sons, 1982.

Corwin, Edward S. *The Constitution and What It Means Today*. 14th ed. Princeton, NJ: Princeton Univ. Press, 1978.

Crevecoeur, J. Hector St. John de. *Letters from an American Farmer*. New York: Penguin American Library, 1981.

Dawson, Henry B. *Current Fictions Tested by Uncurrent Facts, Number 1*. New York: J.M. Bradstreet and Sons, 1864.

DePauw, Linda Grant. *The Eleventh Pillar*. Ithaca, NY: Cornell Univ. Press, 1966.

Deutsch, Karl W. *Nationalism and Social Communication*. Cambridge, MA: MIT Press, 1962.

Deutsch, Karl W., and William J. Foltz, ed. *Nation-Building*. New York: Atherton Press, 1963.

Dietze, Gottfried. *The Federalist: A Classic on Federalism and Free Government*. Baltimore: Johns Hopkins Univ.. Press, 1960.

Emerson, Rupert. *From Empire to Nation*. Cambridge, MA: Harvard Univ. Press, 1960.

Epstein, David F. *The Political Theory of the Federalist*. Chicago: Univ. of Chicago Press, 1984.

Fairfield, Roy P., ed. *The Federalist Papers*. Baltimore: Johns Hopkins Univ. Press, 1981.

Flexner, James Thomas. *The Young Hamilton*. Boston: Little, Brown, 1978.

Ford, Paul Leister, ed. *Essays on the Constitution of the United States*. Brooklyn: Hisstorical Printing Club, 1892.

————. *The Writings of Thomas Jefferson*. 10 vols. New York: G.P. Putnam's Sons, 1898.

Furtwangler, Albert. *The Authority of Publius*. Ithaca, NY: Cornell Univ. Press, 1984.

Hamilton, Alexander, James Madison, and John Jay. *The Federalist*. Edited by Jacob E. Cooke. Middletown, CT: Wesleyan Univ. Press, 1961. (First hardcover edition published in 1788 by J. and A. M'Lean, New York.)

Hamilton, Allan Mclane. *The Intimate Life of Alexander Hamilton*. New York: Charles Scribner's Sons, 1910.

Hamilton, Charles V. *American Government*. Glenview, IL: Scott, Foresman, 1982.

Hayes, Carlton. *The Historical Evolution of Modern Nationalism*. New York: Russell and Russell, 1968.

Hobbes, Thomas. *Leviathan*. New York: E.P. Dutton, 1962.

Hofstadter, Richard. *The Idea of a Party System*. Berkeley: Univ. of California Press, 1969.

Horrocks, J.W. *A Short History of Mercantilism.* New York: Brentano's Publishers, [1925].

Hume, David. *Essays Moral, Political and Literary.* New York: Oxford Univ. Press, 1963.

Hunt, Gaillard, ed. *The Writings of James Madison.* 9 vols. New York: G.P. Putnam's Sons, 1900-10.

Hutchinson, William T., and M.E. Rachal, eds. *Papers of James Madison.* Chicago: Univ. of Chicago Press, 1962-

Jefferson, Thomas. *Notes on the State of Virginia.* Edited by William Peden. New York: W.W. Norton, 1972.

Jensen, Merrill. *The New Nation.* New York: Knopf, 1967.

Johnston, Henry P., ed. *The Correspondence and Public Papers of John Jay.* New York: G.P. Putnam's Sons, 1891.

Kamenka, Eugene, ed. *The Portable Karl Marx.* New York: Penguin Books, 1983.

Kedurie, Elie. *Nationalism.* 3d ed. London: Hutchison, 1966.

Kline, Mary-Jo, ed. *Alexander Hamilton: A Biography in His Own Words.* New York: Harper and Row, 1973.

Kohn, Hans. *The Idea of Nationalism.* New York: Macmillan, 1944.

Levy, Leonard W., ed. *Judicial Review and the Supreme Court.* New York: Harper and Row, 1967.

Lipscomb, Andrew A., ed. *The Writings of Thomas Jefferson.* 18 vols. Washington, DC, 1905.

Locke, John. *Two Treatises of Government.* Introduction and notes by Peter Laslett. New York: New American Library, 1963.

Machiavelli, Niccolò. *The Chief Works and Others.* Translated by Allan Gilbert. Durham, NC: Duke Univ. Press, 1965.

Main, Jackson Turner. *The Antifederalists: Critics of the Constitution.* Chapel Hill: Univ. of North Carolina Press, 1961.

McDonald, Forrest. *E Pluribus Unum: The Formation of the American Republic.* Indianapolis: Liberty Press, 1965.

McDonald, Forrest. *Novus Ordo Seclorum: The Intellectual Origins of the Constitution.* Lawrence: Univ. Press of Kansas, 1985.

————. *We the People: the Economic Origins of the Constitution.* Chicago: Univ. of Chicago Press, 1958.

Meinecke, Friedrich. *Cosmopolitanism and the National State.* Translated by Robert B. Kimber. Princeton, NJ: Princeton Univ. Press, 1970.

Merriam, Charles Edward. *A History of American Political Theories.* New York: Macmillan, 1903.

Mill, John Stuart. *Utilitarianism, Liberty, and Representative Government.* New York: E.P. Dutton, 1951.

Miranda, Francisco de. *The New Democracy in America.* Translated by Judson P. Wood; edited by John S. Ezell. Norman: Univ. of Oklahoma Press, 1963.

Monaghan, Frank. *John Jay.* New York: Bobbs-Merrill, 1935.

Montesquieu, C.L. de Secondat de. *The Spirit of Laws.* 2 vols. Translated by Thomas Nugent. London: George Bell and Sons, 1899.

Montross, Lynn. *The Reluctant Rebels: The Story of the Continental Congress.* New York: Harper and Brothers, 1950.

Morgenthau, Hans J. *Politics Among Nations.* New York: Knopf, 1954.

Morley, Felix. *Freedom and Federalism*. Indianapolis: Liberty Press, 1981.

Morris, Richard B. *The American Revolution Reconsidered*. New York: Harper and Row, 1967.

————. *The Emerging Nations and the American Revolution*. New York: Harper and Row, 1970.

————. *The Forging of the Union*. New York: Harper and Row, 1987.

————. *Witnesses at the Creation: Hamilton, Madison, Jay and the Constitution*. New York: Holt, Rinehart and Winston, 1985.

————. *John Jay: The Making of a Revolutionary 1745-1780*. New York: Harper and Row, 1975.

————. *John Jay: The Winning of the Peace*. New York: Harper and Row, 1980.

Mosteller, Frederick, and David L. Wallace. *Inference and Disputed Authorship: The Federalist*. Reading, MA: Addison-Wesley, 1964.

Muir, Ramsay. *National Self-Government: Its Growth and Principles*. New York: Henry Holt, 1918.

Nkruman, Kwame. *Africa Must Unite*. New York: International Publishers, 1970.

Pellew, George. *John Jay*. Boston: Houghton, Mifflin, 1897.

Peterson, Merrill D., ed. *James Madison, A Biography in His Own Words*. New York: Newsweek Book Division, 1974.

Plutarch. *Lives of the Noble Grecians and Romans*. Translated by John Dryden. New York: The Modern Library, [1932].

Pole, J.R. *Political Representation in England and the Origins of the American Republic*. London: Macmillan, 1966.

Polybius. *The Histories of Polybius*. vols. 1 and 2. Translated by Evelyn S. Shuckburgh. Bloomington: Indiana Univ. Press, 1962.

Pope, Alexander. *Selected Works*. New York: Modern Library, 1951.

Rakove, Jack N. *The Beginnings of National Politics*. Baltimore: Johns Hopkins Univ. Press, 1979.

Richardson, J.D. *Compilation of the Messages and Papers of the Presidents*. 20 vols. Washington, DC, 1908.

Roosevelt, Theodore. *The Works of Theodore Roosevelt*. Memorial Ed. New York: Charles Scribner's Sons, 1925.

————. *The Works of Theodore Roosevelt*. National Ed. New York: Charles Scribner's Sons, 1926.

Rossiter, Clinton, ed. *The Federalist*. New York: New American Library, 1961.

Rousseau, Jean-Jacques. *The Government of Poland*. Translated by Wilmoore Kendall. New York: Bobbs-Merrill, 1972.

————. *The Social Contract and Discourses*. Translated by G.D.H. Cole. New York: E.P. Dutton, 1950.

Rutland, Robert A., ed. *The Papers of James Madison*. Chicago: Univ. of Chicgo Press, 1962- .

Sabine, George H. *A History of Political Theory*. 3d ed. New York: Holt, Rinehart and Winston, 1961.

Schlesinger, Arthur M., Jr. *The Vital Center*. Boston: Houghton Mifflin, 1962.

Seton-Watson, Hugh. *Nations and States*. London: Methuen, [1977].

Simon, William E. *A Time for Truth*. New York: Berkley Books, 1979.

Smith, Anthony D. *Nationalism in the Twentieth Century*. New York: New York Univ. Press, 1979.

————. *Theories of Nationalism.* London: Duckworth, 1971.

Snyder, Louis L. *Global Mini-Nationalisms.* Westport, CT: Greenwood Press, 1982.

————. *The Meaning of Nationalism.* New Brunswick, NJ: Rutgers Univ. Press, 1954.

Storing, Herbert J. *What the Anti-Federalists Were For.* Chicago: Univ. of Chicago Press, 1981.

————. *The Anti-Federalist.* Abridged by Murray Dry. Chicago: Univ. of Chicago Press, 1985.

Stourzh, Gerald. *Alexander Hamilton and the Idea of Republican Government.* Stanford, CA: Stanford Univ. Press, 1970.

Syrett, Harold C., ed., and Jacob E. Cooke, assoc. ed. *The Papers of Alexander Hamilton.* New York: Columbia University Press, 1961-1975.

Tansill, Charles C., ed. *Documents Illustrative of the Formation of the Union of the American States.* Washington, DC: Government Printing Office, 1927.

Thucydides. *The Peloponnesian War.* In *The Greek Historians,* edited by Francis Godolphin, vol. 1. New York: Random House, 1942.

Tocqueville, Alexis de. *Democracy in America.* New York: Random House, Vintage Books, 1945.

Tugwell, Rexford G. *The Compromising of the Constitution.* Notre Dame, IN: Univ. of Notre Dame Press, [1976].

Voltaire, François-Marie Arouet de. *The Works of Voltaire.* 22 vols. New York: Dingwall-Rock, 1927.

Washington, George. *The Writings of George Washington.* Edited by J.C. Fitzpatrick. Washington, DC, 1939.

Webster, Daniel. *The Writings and Speeches of Daniel Webster.* 18 vols. National Ed. Boston: Little, Brown, 1903.

Wiebe, Robert H. *The Opening of American Society.* New York: Knopf, 1984.

Williamson, Chilton. *American Suffrage from Property to Democracy.* Princeton, NJ: Princeton Univ. Press, 1960.

Wills, Garry. *Explaining America.* Garden City, NY: Doubleday, 1981.

————. ed. *The Federalist Papers by Alexander Hamilton, James Madison, and John Jay.* New York: Bantam Books, 1982.

Winter, William O. *State and Local Government in a Decentralized Republic.* New York: Macmillan, 1981.

Wood, Gordon. *The Creation of the American Republic.* Chapel Hill: North Carolina Press, 1969.

Zinn, Howard. *A People's History of the United States.* New York: Harper and Row, 1980.

Articles

Adair, Douglass. "The Authorship of the Disputed *Federalist Papers.*" *William and Mary Quarterly,* 3d ser., 1 (1944): 97-122.

Banning, Lance. "James Madison and the Nationalists, 1780-1783." *William and Mary Quarterly* 40 (1983): 227-55.

Beer, Samuel H. "Federalism, Nationalism, and Democracy in America." *The American Political Science Review* 72, no. 1 (March 1978): 9-21.

Beer, Samuel H. "The Idea of the Nation." *The New Republic* 3522 (July 19 and 26, 1982).

Beer, Samuel H. "Liberalism and the National Idea." *Left, Right and Center: Essays on Liberalism and Conservatism in the United States,* ed. Robert A. Goldwin (Chicago: Rand McNally, 1965), 142-69.

Cooke, Jacob E. "Alexander Hamilton's Authorship of the 'Caesar' Letters." *William and Mary Quarterly,* 3d ser., 17 (1960): 78-85.

Diamond, Martin. "The Federalist's View of Federalism." In *Essays In Federalism,* edited by George Benson. Claremont, CA: Institute for Studies in Federalism, 1962.

Mason, Alpheus T. *"The Federalist—A* Split Personality." *American Historical Review* 57, no. 3 (April 1952): 625-43.

Matson, Cathy, and Peter Onuf. "Toward a Republican Empire: Interest and Ideology in Revolutionary America." *American Quarterly,* 1985, 496-531.

Morris, Richard B. "Explaining America: The Federalist. By Garry Wills." *Columbia Law Review* 82, no. 2 (March 1982): 406-09.

Onuf, Peter S. "Liberty, Development, and Union: Visions of the West in the 1780s." *William and Mary Quarterly,* 3d ser., (April 1986): 179-213.

Other Sources

Cohens v. Virginia, 6 Wheat., 418-419 (1821).

Text of the Address by the President to the National Conference of State Legislatures, Atlanta, Georgia. Washington, DC: The White House, Office of the Press Secretary, July 30, 1981.

Index